Penny Tassoni's
Continued Success with the EYFS

presenting
Penny's EYFS
Makeover
DVD

www.pearsonschoolsandfe.co.uk

✓ Free online support
✓ Useful weblinks
✓ 24 hour online ordering

0845 313 4444

Heinemann

Part of Pearson

Heinemann is an imprint of Pearson Education Limited, Edinburgh Gate, Harlow, Essex, CM20 2JE.

www.heinemann.co.uk

Heinemann is a registered trademark of Pearson Education Limited

Text © Penny Tassoni 2010
Edited by Katherine Carr
Original design by Hicks Design, developed for this book by Pearson Education Ltd/ Sophie O'Leary-Smith
Typeset by Phoenix Photosetting, Chatham, Kent
Original illustrations © Pearson Education Ltd 2010
Illustrated by KJ-A Artists.com
Picture research by Sally Cole
Front cover illustrations © Vectorgirl (wellingtons), Chewystock (paintbrush), Joingate (button). Back cover photograph © Roddy Paine.

First published 2010

14 13 12 11 10
10 9 8 7 6 5 4 3 2 1

British Library Cataloguing in Publication Data
A catalogue record for this book is available from the British Library

ISBN 978 0 435 03259 3

Printed in the UK by Scotprint

Pearson Education Limited is not responsible for the content of any external internet sites. It is essential for tutors to preview each website before using it in class so as to ensure that the URL is still accurate, relevant and appropriate. We suggest that tutors bookmark useful websites and consider enabling students to access them through the school/college intranet.

Even outstanding settings can benefit from an occasional makeover. Over the years I've worked alongside some fantastic practitioners to do just that. Now for the first time we've captured some of this magic on film – take a look at the DVD in the back of this book, and watch our EYFS Makeover Stories unfold in three very different settings:

- Stepping Stones Preschool

- Lorna and Richard Owen, Childminders

- Funshine Nursery

You'll be amazed at how small changes can make big differences.

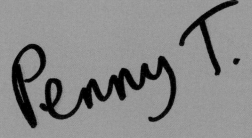

Acknowledgements

This book is in many ways quite a special one for me. Not only is it my 30th project as a writer but it is the first time I have been filmed. My continued thanks go to the team at Heinemann, with particular thanks to Virginia Carter and Lindsay Lewis, Rachael Hemsley and Katherine Carr. I would also like to thank my mother, Jennifer Enderby, for her expert proof reading once more. I am especially grateful to Patrick Rowe and Tahira Patwa from Lightshop Films for their fantastic work on the DVD and Ariel Sultan who was responsible for composing the music. I also need to thank the three settings for their patience, support and enthusiasm: Lorna and Richard Owen, Sandra and her team at Stepping Stones Preschool, and Petra and her team at Funshine Nursery. My thanks also go to Fergus Garrett at Great Dixter for his expert gardening advice.

I would also like to thank all those practitioners that I meet both internationally and at home who, through their comments and suggestions, have shaped this book. Particular thanks in this respect go to Kirsten Due (Denmark) and my dear friends Leman Cetin and Regina Kruse-Özçelik (Istanbul).

Finally, I must thank once more the Tassoni Team: my two daughters who acted as my wardrobe consultants during the filming, and my husband, Jean-Michel, without whom any writing would not be possible.

Credits

The author and publisher would like to thank the following individuals and organisations for permission to reproduce photographs:

(Key: b – bottom; c – centre; l – left; r – right; t – top)
Alamy Images: Alaska Stock LLC 126, Golden Pixels LLC 92t; Corbis: Laurence Mouton / PhotoAlto 174; Patrick Rowe: Patrick Rowe 100-101, 109t; Pearson Education Ltd: Creatas 166t, Jules Selmes 14b, 42b, 61, 114cl, 140t, 172t, 192t, Lindsay Lewis 66br, 81bl, 97tr, Lord and Leverett 98cr, Penny Tassoni 109br, 115tl, Studio 8 2br, 5c, 9br, 12, 26cr, 32b, 40, 47b, 58, 64-65, 73, 76br, 88tl, 95, 132, 134t, 136t, 138t, 142t, 144t, 146t, 148t, 150t, 152t, 154t, 156t, 158t, 160t, 162t, 164t, 168t, 170t, 176t, 178t, 180t, 184t, 186t, 190t, 130-131; Pearson Education Ltd: Jules Selmes 8b, 18cl, 23cr, 28-29, 37t, 102b, Lindsay Lewis 83t, Tudor Photography 71bl; Photolibrary.com: Caroline Schiff 21br, Lucianne Pashley 10br, mauritius images , Richard Clark 188t, Scott Barrow 121; Shutterstock.com: Pkruger 182t. All other images © Pearson Education.

We would also like to thank the following organisations for permission to reproduce materials: p.70 Description of two-year-old children from Carolyn Meggitt's, *Child Development: An Illustrated Guide*, 2nd edn, Heinemann, 2006 ISBN 9780435420482. Reproduced with kind permission of Carolyn Meggitt. p.71 the 'Language for Thinking' basic and expanded statements from nationalstrategies.standards.dcsf.gov.uk/node/84490. Reproduced under the terms of the Click-Use licence.

Every effort has been made to contact copyright holders of material reproduced in this book. Any omissions will be rectified in subsequent printings if notice is given to the publishers.

Contents

Introduction

Welcome to this book and DVD, which I hope you will find interesting and useful. As with all books, there is a whole team of people that work behind the scenes; with this one, most of the credit goes to Virginia Carter as not only is she the publisher for this project, but it was her idea to create a book alongside a DVD. Earlier in the year I had mentioned that I enjoyed going into settings and working with staff to solve problems or to provide inspiration and she turned this comment into the cornerstone of the project – so if you enjoy watching what my family call 'Penny Tassoni meets Supernanny and Changing Rooms', it is Virginia and Lightshop Films that you need to thank.

The content of the book and what I wanted to show on film was quickly decided. Through my training and work with practitioners, I had spotted some recurring issues which are common to most settings: outdoor play, observation and planning, and creative development. We also decided to include some further activities for you to use with the children you look after, as feedback from my first EYFS book suggested that the activity section was particularly popular.

Once the project had been drawn up, Virginia and her colleague Lindsay Lewis began looking for a production company that would be in tune with our ideas and were immediately impressed by the enthusiasm and professionalism of Tahira Patwa and Patrick Rowe of Lightshop Films.

Dates were set and we began to look for three different types of settings: a pre-school, a childminder and a nursery. The main factor when choosing the settings was that they would already be showing either good or outstanding practice. Other practical considerations such as location, space and their availability to work with our tight schedules narrowed it down to the three wonderful settings where we eventually filmed: Stepping Stones in North Hinksey, Oxford; Lorna and Richard Owen, childminders in Fleet; and Funshine Nursery in Beckenham, Kent.

Filming was tiring, but turned out to be quite fun, even though I quickly realised that despite watching plenty of television, I knew nothing about being a presenter! I have to say at this point that whilst having a microphone woven through your clothes and a camera staring you in the face is pretty stressful, not only did Sandra, Lorna and Petra do brilliantly, but they turned out to be born stars. The staff and the children in the settings were fantastic too and just carried on being themselves.

The final part of the project was to write the book, which is divided into five main sections. The middle three sections relate closely to the DVD and can be read before or after watching the film. (The DVD itself lasts for just over 30 minutes, and is split into three distinct 'Makeover stories', of about 10 minutes each – so you can watch in short chunks, or watch the whole DVD straight through if you have the time.) In the sections of the book corresponding to the three 'Makeover stories' you will see that I have added in further information about each of the topics shown on the DVD, as well as providing detailed explanations of the film clips.

Structure of Penny's EYFS Makeover DVD

Creative development

In this section I work with Stepping Stones Preschool to develop ideas for encouraging creativity. Look out for the fabulous painting wall!

Observation and planning

In this section, I visit childminders Lorna and Richard Owen and we discuss ways of making observation and planning easier. Lorna and I are fans of using modern technology.

Outdoor play

In this section, I work with Funshine Nursery to create a more stimulating and natural outdoor area in their small, but busy garden. See what you can do with a few bamboos!

Structure of the book

Issues and challenges

This section looks at some of the common issues and challenges that face many early years providers.

Creative development

This section looks at how you might audit your provision and provide activities and resources that will encourage children's creativity. This section links with **Makeover Story 1** on the DVD.

Observation and planning

This section looks at the process of observation and planning. It also looks in some detail at how you might incorporate digital methods of recording children's progress as well as specific ideas for what you might observe. This section links with **Makeover Story 2** on the DVD.

Outdoor play

This section looks at how an outdoor area can be developed on a low budget to enhance children's play and creativity. This section links with **Makeover Story 3** on the DVD.

Activities

This section is full of lots of inventive activities to engage and develop children of different ages. It is broken down into three sections:
- Activities for children aged 6–18 months
- Activities for children aged 18 months to 3 years
- Activities for children aged 3–5 years

Issues and challenges

On my travels and during my training, I have noticed that several issues and challenges seem to keep cropping up. As you might expect, some are sector-specific, whilst others are more generic. In this chapter, therefore, I will be covering the following:

- Settling children in
- Key people
- Getting children ready for school
- Child-initiated and adult-led activity
- Continuous provision
- Snack time
- Providing for babies
- Providing play for toddlers
- Boys

Settling children in

Children are not parcels that can be dropped off at a depot and then retrieved later. From very early on in their lives, children know who should be looking after them and will react badly when there are changes. Unhappy children cannot learn and so thinking about how best to help children settle in has to be a priority for all of us. One of the best things about the EYFS is that for the first time all settings have had to establish a key person system. The idea behind the key person system is quite simple. One adult will get to know a child and their family so that when the time comes for the child to be separated, the child does not become distressed. The child's key person is effectively taking over from the parent and will be the child's safe base whilst the parent is absent.

Beginning the process

Settling children in is a process which, unless there is a crisis and care is needed at short notice, needs to be done gradually. The first step is to help parents gain trust and confidence in you. Parents need to feel that you will be able to take good care of their child. One way of doing this is to provide parents with some information about you. Whilst professional information such as how many years you have worked with children is fine, parents often respond better to the more personal approach. The box below outlines one way in which you might do this.

Finding out about the child's needs

It's a good idea for you to learn as much about the child as possible beforehand. This information might help you to work out whether the child will need a more intensive settling in period. This information needs to be gained before the settling in process begins and so you might invite parents in to talk through their child's needs. If this is not possible, you might be able to do this over the phone.

In addition to the usual questions that we might ask parents, for example, about health and dietary issues, there are some additional points that I feel are useful to cover:

Experience of separation

It is worth finding out whether children have had experience of being cared for by someone other than their parents. We also need to find out how well that turned out for the child. If the child and parents were happy, this bodes well as both have learnt that

Kirsten's suitcase

A few years ago, I met a Danish educator called Kirsten Due. She and her team use a small toy suitcase to help children and their parents get to know the team. The idea is amazingly simple, but very effective and so I urge you to try it out! Once parents feel that they 'know' us, they can find it much easier to trust us and also to talk more openly.

Put seven or eight items that represent bits of your life into a small suitcase or bag. Share these with parents and their child by saying something such as, 'As I will be your child's key person, I thought you might like to know a little bit more about me. (Picking up a photo) This is a photo of my dog Charlie. I put it in because I spend a lot of my free time walking him in the park.'

Ideas for items:

O a photograph of your own children if you are a parent and/or children that you have worked with in the past

O a photograph or item associated with your pets

O a postcard or souvenir from a holiday

O a book or toy that you often use when you are with children.

Taking your personal items out of a suitcase is a great way of attracting children's interest.

separation can be positive. On the other hand, if the separation was not so successful and the child was upset, both parent and child would have had a negative experience, which may make them more fearful.

Personality

Some children are more extrovert than others. This can mean that they find meeting new people or adapting to new environments a little easier. It can be worth asking parents how their child reacts when they go somewhere new. Is their child keen to try out new things or do they need more time?

Parental anxiety

It is helpful to try to find out the level of parental anxiety. When parents feel anxious about their child, there is a good chance that this will be conveyed to their child even in the most subtle of ways. Approaching this with parents does require sensitivity, but you could say something such as, 'Many parents can feel a little anxious about leaving their child. This is quite normal. How are you feeling?'

When parents report that they feel very anxious, it is worth reassuring them that you will do everything in your power to make sure that when the time comes, they will feel better about it.

Family circumstances

There are some family circumstances that might make it harder for children and their parents to separate. Finding out as much about the child and their family as possible requires skilful listening and sensitive questions. Some parents find it easier to talk about things when there is a form to go through whilst others can find this daunting.

You will need to judge which is the best approach. Hopefully, by having already talked about yourself and shown parents just how keen you are to help the child to settle well, parents may be ready to talk. In my experience, the following factors can be significant.

Changes to family structure

Any recent change to the family structure such as birth of a sibling, parental separation or the loss of someone close to the child, including an au pair, can be unsettling for the child.

Changes to family routine

Children are not as adaptable as adults think they are. Listen out for any changes to the usual routine for the child, such as having a parent who has started working nights or a recent change of address.

Developmental issues

It is worth finding out about the child's developmental progress to date. Listen out for comments about a child being premature or that they were slow to walk. These may signal that the child will need additional support and in some cases that parents have learnt to be a little more protective.

Sleep

It can be worth finding out how much the child sleeps and whether they frequently wake up in the night. Children who are tired are more likely to find separation harder to cope with as lack of sleep interferes with emotional regulation.

Settling children in without tears

I believe, and have seen, that if we are careful about settling children in, it is possible to do so without tears. This requires that the key person develop a relationship with the child before any separation takes place. This approach is very popular with parents as hearing your child cry when you cannot help them is pretty traumatic. For this approach to be successful, parents need to know exactly what will happen and their role at each one of the stages outlined on p.5. You can brief them by phone or put a document together for them to read. I quite like creating a tickchart so that parents can see the progress that their child is making.

For children who have already had good experiences of separation, I would expect them to whizz through the stages quite quickly – maybe even in a single visit. For children who are likely to have strong levels of separation anxiety, it may take ten short sessions of around an hour to complete the process. The key is to go at the speed of the child.

Stage 1
Getting to know the key person

Stage 2
Beginning to withdraw

Stage 3
In and out of sight

Stage 4
Goodbye and back again

Stage 5
Separation for a short time

Stages of settling children in.

Stage 1 – Getting to know the key person

Stage 1 is for the child to begin the process of getting to know their key person. For this to happen, parents need to know that whilst they should stay near their child, they should take a bit of a back seat and let the key person play with and talk to the child. I find a puppet usually works for this. As you can see on the DVD when I am at Lorna's house, children are fascinated by my mouse puppet and quickly overcome their initial shyness. If you are settling children in during the summer months, consider making these first introductions outdoors so that it feels less intense for the child.

Stage 2 – Beginning to withdraw

Once children begin to smile at you and are a little more comfortable with you, the next step is for parents to begin to withdraw. This means the parent physically sitting or standing a little way back from the child. Parents need to be briefed not to make eye contact with their child or to do anything to gain their attention. A selection of magazines or some other

parents to talk to can be useful to help parents with this. Most children will go over to their parents or check that they are still there, but if the parents are not entertaining them, children will, after a while, prefer to play with their key person.

Stage 3 – In and out of sight

Once the child can cope with their parent being at a slight distance, the next step is for parents to move in and out of sight. The aim is that parents just pop out of sight for about three seconds and then resume their position. Expect that at first children will stop what they are doing with you to be near their parents, but if what you are doing is fascinating, they will after several attempts decide that they are better off being with you. This little exercise helps children to learn that their parents do go, but that they come back. Once children no longer seem to react and are happy to be with you, then you can move to stage 4.

Stage 4 – Goodbye and back again

In this stage, parents will practise saying goodbye and popping out for a couple of minutes before returning. This is important as this reinforces the lesson learnt in Stage 3 that their parent does go away, but they always return. Once a child is happily playing with you, the parent needs to come over and say that they are just popping to the toilet/car or to get a book but that they are coming back. They must then go straightaway – no dithering – but then return within a couple of minutes. Expect that the child might protest and even go to the door, but as the parent returns quickly, the child does not have time to get upset. Once the child is settled with you once more, the parent repeats the exercise. Some children will get the hang of this within two or three turns, but others may need longer. Once parents and children can 'crack' this, they are just about ready for a proper separation.

Stage 5 – Separation for a short time

This is the final stage and is one where the children will be separated for half a session or a couple of hours. Make sure that you have interesting things planned for the children. Begin by repeating the stage 4 exercise a couple of times. Once the child is settled, indicate to the parent that it is time to separate for a little longer. Tell the parent that if the child becomes upset, a call will be made immediately and it is important that they return swiftly. (If the child has coped well with Stage 4, this is quite unlikely.)

These children are happy and relaxed in the presence of their key person.

Your questions answered

○ *How many visits will be needed?*

This will depend on how quickly the child moves through the stages. Some children who are older, confident and have had experience of being separated will sail through the stages within an hour. Others may need to have several visits of a maximum of an hour at a time. When a child is making a return visit, make sure that you start at the last stage at which the child was comfortable.

○ *How long can parents stay for?*

Parents should stay for as long as they want, but the reason why many parents are reluctant to leave is that they are not sure their child can cope alone. By using this staged approach, most parents can see their child is ready to 'fly solo' and so are happy to leave.

○ *Should parents play with their child when they first arrive at the setting?*

I am not much of a fan of this approach as some children come to the conclusion that the setting is a place where they play with their parent rather than with the staff. It can be worth parents and the key person playing together with the child to start off with as this signals to the child that their parent trusts the key person.

○ *What should we do if a child becomes upset after separation?*

It is not good for children to be left crying and so I would always reunite a child with their parent quickly. If the staged approach is used, this situation is less likely as the child should have developed a bond with their key person first.

○ *We have a child who cries for a couple of minutes, but then is happy – what should we do?*

Some children are sad when they leave their parents. This is a natural emotion and it is worth acknowledging

it. For children who get into a habit of crying, it is worth taking a photograph of them when they are happy in the setting and asking parents to show it to them before they come in the morning. This seems to help children 'remember' that they like being in the setting. You can also ask children at the end of the session to put some toys into a bag so that when they arrive the next day, the bag will be waiting for them. This can work well, especially if you involve the parents as they can remind their child about the bag on the way to the setting.

○ *What should happen if the child's key person is going on holiday or is off sick?*

Once children have settled in, it is important that they become familiar and comfortable with at least one other adult. I see this person as being their 'Plan B'. Whilst children should feel happy with all the adults in the setting, a 'Plan B' needs to be a surrogate key person. In baby and toddler rooms, I suggest that the key person does three-quarters of the care activities, such as feeding and nappy changing, but that 'Plan B' does the remaining quarter. This means that the child becomes used to them.

○ *Should we do home visits?*

Home visits are wonderful and should be done wherever possible. They allow parents to feel more relaxed and the child often remembers the key person's visit. If you do not have the time or opportunity to visit every single child, you may do some prioritisation and so visit just those families that you feel will need extra support. When you carry out a home visit try to take a photograph of you and the child together so that you can remind the child of your visit.

Transitions

Some settings are very good at settling children in initially, but then do not consider the effects of transition on children, for example, moving from one room to another or from one class to another. For children,

changing 'person' is a significant event and time needs to be taken to help the child get used to the new person who will be looking after them. Think about whether the new person can drop in and play from time to time or whether the key person can take the child to visit them.

Key people

Whilst we have looked at the settling in process, key people need to keep on spending time with their key children afterwards. These relationships need to be seen as continuous and so thought should be given as to how each child will spend some time with their key person. For childminders, this can be easier as often they will be the only adult, but in group care, children may go between different adults.

Meal times

Some settings organise their routines so that the key children and key person sit together in small groups.

Story times

Story times can be held in key person groups. For this to work well children need to be at a similar language level.

Activities

Many settings will make sure that children's key people carry out the adult-directed activities with 'their' children.

Physical care

For babies and toddlers, physical care should be carried out by the key person plus their 'Plan B'. Feeding, nappy changing and wiping down are also moments when children might get one-to-one interaction and so it is helpful if they are carried out by the key person.

Greetings

Some settings will begin their sessions by putting children into their key person groups for a few minutes. This can work well as the key person can talk to the children about what toys and resources are on offer and also hear their news. This only works well if it is for a few minutes and if it feels more like a chat rather than a structured session.

Getting children ready for school

Moving to a reception class can be quite daunting for children and so it is no wonder that many parents and practitioners work hard to get children ready for school. Having spoken to many reception teachers, however, it is clear that there can be a mismatch between what settings feel they need to do and what is actually required. So it's very important that you have good communication with reception teachers.

It may seem obvious but the starting point is to have some contact with the reception teachers where the children will be going. Whilst I know that many settings have very good relationships with reception classes, this is not a universally shared experience. Barriers include reluctance by some schools to engage, whilst some settings have children that may go on to five or six different schools. It is important though to find ways of communicating, even if this is through an exchange of emails. The ideal would be to have a meeting and to see the reception class 'in action'. I would suggest that wherever possible you try and find out about the following:

Staffing levels in the reception class

This is important as children may be going from a ratio in your setting of 1:8 to a class where, at times, the ratio may be closer to 1:30. If staffing levels are relatively low, it will be important to ensure that you are working in ways that encourage children to be self-reliant and independent (see later sections).

Organisation of teaching

It is worth finding out how children are taught. Many reception classes will work with small groups whilst the other children are playing. Whole group activity might be limited to short sessions.

Letters and sounds/reading

Many reception classes begin by working on children's phonemic awareness, for example rhymes or hearing sounds, before starting on the phonic programme. Children will also be looking at books with no words and 'talking' their own story. By talking to reception teachers, you can together work out how best to prepare children for this.

Handwriting policy

Some reception classes begin with cursive (joined up) handwriting immediately. If this is the case, it may not be helpful for children to have learnt by heart how to print their name. Instead, you might need to work with children to practise 'bouncing' movements and flicks which will produce something like this

Break and lunchtimes

Find out what happens at break and lunchtimes. Are children playing in a large area alongside older children? Find out what children have to do at lunchtime. In some schools children are expected to carry a tray and to manage their own food. If this is the case, you might like to create cafeteria-style snack or lunch times and also encourage parents to help their child to practise carrying a tray with food on it.

Learning about expectations

As well as finding out about what children will be doing in the reception class, it is worth knowing what the reception teacher really needs the children to be able to do in the first few weeks. This is a useful conversation to have with the teacher as it can genuinely help us prepare children and their parents for the transition. Below are some of the points that I hear reception teachers make in answer to this question.

Make sure that children can dress themselves

Many children come into reception classes unable to be competent or speedy when it comes to putting on and removing their coats or getting ready for PE. As most reception classes now have an outdoor area, getting dressed is a frequent activity. This means in the run up to starting school, you could play games with children that involve dressing, for example, pick up a card, turn it over and then put on or take off the item of clothing shown on the card – hat, gloves, coat, shoes.

Make sure that children can use the toilet independently

Many children in a reception class have to take themselves off to the toilet without adult support. They need to be trusted not to hang around for too long or flood the washbasins. If staff in your setting usually accompany children to the toilet, try to find ways of reducing the amount of support so that they get used to going alone.

Make sure children can dress themselves before they go to a reception class.

Make sure that children can play independently

Many parents are surprised and in some cases disappointed at just how much play there is in most reception classes. Teachers and teaching assistants usually intensively work with small groups whilst the rest of the class are meant to be playing or, in teacher speak, 'Getting On'. Children therefore need to be able to play for periods of time without squabbling or becoming restless. This requires good social skills and concentration. Start to look at the children you work with and notice which children can play independently of an adult and can keep themselves occupied. It is also worth making sure that children practise playing in this way at home. This may mean suggesting turning off the television for periods of time for children who use this as their main way of entertaining themselves.

Encourage fluent, confident speech

Children who have fluent, confident speech are more likely to cope with the demands of the reception class. Fluent speakers find it easier to listen and process what is being said to them. This means that they can benefit from whole-group time or listening activities. They are often much quicker to pick up reading.

In the weeks and months before children move to the reception class, audit their level of language. Think about how fluent children are and whether they are likely to reach fluency and confidence by the time they are due to start. If you identify this, you can give certain children a boost, either in pairs or by small-group adult-led activities. Children who have English as an additional, or indeed emerging, language may also need increased opportunities to work with adults. Making sure that as many children as possible have fluent speech must be a priority as the adult to child ratio in many reception classes makes it virtually impossible for teachers to do the one-to-one interaction that the children will need. (See pp.84–85 for observing and planning for language development.)

Work on rhymes and auditory discrimination work

As well as being able to speak confidently and fluently, children need plenty of opportunities for rhymes and auditory discrimination work. This is the foundation for learning letter-to-sound representations. Working on auditory discrimination should therefore be a focus of small group work with children who are about to start school. You can use the Letters and Sounds pack which at the time of writing is available online (you can get to it from publications.education.gov.uk) but also consider doing plenty of games such as I Spy or packing teddy's bag with objects that begin with a specific letter sound. You should also try and work on children's nursery rhyme knowledge. Look out for the traditional nursery rhymes as they have strong sounds. If you are keen, you could plan according to the sounds in them; for example, *Five Little Peas in a Pea Pod Pressed* is pretty good for 'p's!

There is little point doing 'sound of the week' type of work in a formal way because children in the reception class are likely to be starting from scratch with sound work.

Make sure that children can handle and are interested in books

During the reception year, children really begin the journey towards reading. Children who are interested in books have a huge head start. Think about whether your children have had sufficient experience with

Children who are interested in books have a head start.

books, for example, holding a book, turning pages and making comments about what they can see in the pictures. Sharing stories with children is an important adult-led activity. This work needs to be done with individual children or with pairs as children need to see how text runs from left to right and be close enough to pictures and free enough to talk openly about what is happening. Try to encourage parents in the weeks leading to school to read bedtime stories or to borrow books from the library.

Make sure that children enjoy ' having a go' in their mark-making

Too much emphasis is often given to children writing their name, sometimes at the expense of their confidence in mark-making. Many reception teachers find that children say things such as, 'I can't write'.

Watch out for children who will attempt only their name rather than have a go at other 'play writing'. Children who are confident to 'have a go' will make faster progress in their writing once they have started school because as they attempt to write new words, they spend time thinking about the sounds and letters required. Children who are only happy to write their name or copy what an adult has written are not doing this. If you identify children who are worried about writing, try and look for activities where they can mark-make with sensory materials or in role play situations.

Check that children have developed the tripod grasp

Whilst it is possible to write with a variety of grasps, the most effective is the tripod grasp (where children are holding a pencil between finger and thumb with the middle finger acting as a support). As a consequence of children being introduced to writing relatively early in this country, they often develop 'dodgy' pencil grips. It is worth identifying which children in your setting have not conquered the tripod grasp. Once identified, encourage these children to make freer larger marks with implements other than pens, for example, paint brushes or sticks. It can be worth giving these children a total break from using pens so that the habit can be broken. If this is not possible, look out for felt pens that put children's hands in a palmar grasp (like a fist) as this is a neutral position.

Make sure that children can play a simple game

Board games and simple card games help children to learn many skills including counting, matching and

logical thinking. They also help children to take turns and to learn to cope when they do not win. Games such as Snap or Picture Lotto are still being played in some families, but not all. Try and give the children who are moving to school the experience of playing these types of games. These are wonderful adult-led activities. Once children have mastered them, they often choose to play them as a child-initiated activity.

Meaningful counting

Counting is linked to children's cognitive development, but also to their direct experiences of counting. Whilst many children can count aloud, it takes more skill to count individual objects. Try therefore to provide as many meaningful opportunities as possible for this to take place with individual or pairs of children. Whole group counting tends not to be that effective as children often 'drone' rather than point directly to and focus on the objects that are being counted.

This child is developing a nice tripod grasp.

Passing on records

Most local authorities have produced profiles for settings to complete and pass onto schools. It is worth noting that parents should be asked for their permission before you pass information across to a school. Whilst early years profiles are usually quite detailed, I would suggest also putting together a simple A4 cribsheet for each child. This can be drawn up with parents' help. The idea is to give reception teachers a quick guide that will help them care for the child in the first few days and weeks, for example, it might say that a child is not good at asking for the toilet. Below are some things that you might like to include on the cribsheet, although do check that nothing is already in place as the last thing this sector needs is more paperwork!

Photograph of the child

Reception teachers are often trying to absorb information about many children at once. Putting a nice photograph of the child on the sheet can be helpful.

Health needs

Whilst food allergies and other medical needs will be recorded in other places, it can be worth including this here.

Friendships

Some children have a strong friendship with another child and are likely to cope only if they are with this child.

Play interests

It can be helpful to know what keeps the child happy in terms of play interests. This means that appropriate resources can be put out or the child directed towards them.

Essential things to know about this child

Put down four or five points that would help someone new to work effectively with the child, for example, 'tends to be cheeky when nervous', 'gets tearful when father is working away from home'.

Supporting transition

Moving to school can be a big step for children so it is important that we find ways to make it as smooth as possible. See if you can visit the reception class and take photographs of the room when it is empty and also the outdoor space. These can then be turned into a book that children can look at and talk to you about. If permission is given, it can also be worth obtaining some photographs that show the usual routine in the school. Toilets and lunchtime are often fears for children and so photographs showing these can be useful. If the school is in walking distance, it can also be worth walking the children up to it at lunchtime so that they can hear and see children happily playing. If you are a childminder, you may also have the advantage that you pick up from the school and so can familiarise a child during these times.

Child-initiated and adult-led activity

All settings are meant to be providing a balance of child-initiated and adult-directed activities for children. No definition of what constitutes this 'balance' is given although I would suspect that it tips in favour of more child-initiated play than adult-directed activity.

Child-initiated activity is about the child having the freedom to play with materials that they have chosen and in the way that they wish. In reality, the level of freedom does depend on the range of resources available for them and how relaxed the staff can be.

Adult-led activity can be said to be anything that the adult has planned and prepared – in other words anything that an adult is in charge of. Adult-led activities are extremely important and, if well chosen, can give children knowledge and skills that they cannot otherwise gain, for example, learning to play a board game or carrying out a cooking activity.

Working out your balance

It is worth working out what in reality you offer in terms of balance. I often ask settings to calculate how many minutes children are in their setting and for how much of this time children can choose what they want to do. Many settings forget that story times, registration and getting ready for lunch are actually adult-led activities. Once this is taken on board, some settings are quite shocked at how little time children have for child-initiated activity.

Providing for child-initiated activity

For children to benefit from child-initiated activity, they have to find things to do that feel satisfying for them as well as enjoyable. Satisfying might mean that a challenge is involved or that the materials themselves are pleasurable to use.

Through child-initiated play, this child is developing his imagination and plenty of other skills.

Child-initiated activity might not always be play

Whilst most child-initiated activity is play, some children will want to do something else such as cook or hear an adult read a story. Provided that it is the child who wants to do this and it is therefore genuinely self-chosen and provided there are plenty of other options in your environment, then it is a child-initiated activity. The key for adults during this time is to follow the child's lead. For example, a child may say that they want you to read one book, but then halfway through asks you to read another.

Time

One of the big changes that I notice about children from 3 years old onwards is that their play can be more complex and intricate. I love watching the way in which they start to look around for ways of enriching their play by incorporating other elements into it, for example, bringing over some sand to act as food. I also note how, when children are very engaged, they need a lot of time to adjust and work on their play. In some ways the better the environment that settings provide for child-initiated activity, the more time children need so that their play can become complex. This is why 20 minute bursts are not sufficient and also why children need opportunities to return to their play.

Range of resources

What is available for children will have an effect on how much they can gain from child-initiated activity because it affects their concentration and therefore how much they can learn. A good measure of the quality of the environment that you have created is children's length and level of concentration. (We look at a method of measuring this on p.77) If a group of 3-year-olds only have a couple of jigsaws, a sand tray with little sand in it, a tired set of LEGO® and a meagre role play area, it is unlikely that the quality of child-initiated activity will be high. The consequence of poor resources is usually seen in terms of children's behaviour as some children will inevitably try and find unacceptable ways of creating stimulation. Below are some practical tips that I find helpful when advising settings on resourcing for child-initiated activity.

Recognising play needs

Children's interests and their play needs change as they develop. The way 2-year-olds play is very different from 3-year-olds, yet sometimes pre-schools and nurseries that combine these age groups do not focus sufficiently on this. (See p.23–25 for providing play for toddlers.) It is therefore important to observe children carefully when you can see that they are challenged and interested in their play as this will help you to think about what is holding their interest and why.

Sensory materials

When I ask practitioners about materials and resources that seem to hold children's attention and engage them, many will mention a sensory material. Water, sand or dough, as well as many other sensory materials, seem to be a 'must' when it comes to providing for child-initiated activity. As well as putting out sensory materials, it is worth thinking about whether the quantity is sufficient and varied. I like seeing two mounds of dough on a table as the two colours open up more possibilities for children. It is also worth thinking about how and where you present these materials. Water in a bucket can make a good change from water always in a water tray.

Auditing toys and resources

Some toys and games do help children to engage and concentrate. Most settings know which items are popular with children and allow for complex play. As storage is usually an issue in most settings, consider carrying out a 'toy audit' to check that the toys taking up cupboard space are ones that children do find engaging. It is also worth looking out for resources that you have in abundance. Think about what they do. Where there is unnecessary duplication, think about 'losing' some so that there is more space for a wider and more interesting range of resources.

Freshness

Children love novelty and engage well with things that they have not seen before. This is one way in which the brain can be easily stimulated. I believe that all settings should think about how long children spend in their care. A morning of three hours may not seem such a long time – but three hours, four times a week over two years will be close to 1,500 hours. If the same things are available for child-initiated activity throughout this time, there is a real likelihood of them becoming stale. Settings often tell me that some children in the last few months seem to 'outgrow' the setting. I think that it is not so much that they have outgrown the setting, but that they have become over-familiar with what is on offer. It is therefore worth thinking about rotating some toys and resources, bringing in more everyday items and also not laying things out in the same place each time.

Role of the adult during child-initiated activity

There is a danger that some people think that their role during child-initiated play is to stand back and supervise. Whilst leaving children to organise and focus on their play can sometimes be the right thing to do, adults also have other options during child-initiated play. Below are some ideas of how you could support their play.

Being a play partner

Some children benefit when adults join in their play. The key to doing this is not to take ownership of the play, but to act as an interested play partner. This role requires some skill, but is appreciated by children if you are able to do it. There are particular groups of children who will benefit from us playing in this way, including babies, toddlers and children who have language needs. These children need more adult interaction in order to boost their language. Leaving such children to play alone for long periods will not give them the language that they need.

In addition, some children need an adult to act as a play partner because their social skills are not sufficiently developed for them to play with other children. Modelling how to play can therefore be of benefit to them.

Observing children's activity

It is worth taking time to observe children's self-chosen activity. This can help you to assess their overall development as well as giving you ideas for future planning. As we will see in Chapter 3 Observation and planning, this does not necessarily mean hanging around with a clipboard!

How is this adult supporting this child's self-chosen play?

Facilitating play

In some ways, I see this role as being that of a discreet butler. You are there to serve children and their interests. This may mean discreetly putting out a few more corks for a toddler who is totally engaged in dropping corks into a bottle but is about to run out of them, or doing a little bit of surreptitious tidying so that a piece of a jigsaw puzzle that has been knocked off a table is quietly returned without bothering the children. It may also mean replenishing the water outdoors when the children have been using it to water the plants.

As well as this discreet type of facilitation, adults can ask children if they would like more resources. They can also offer their help if they see that children have set out to do something, but that they do not quite have the expertise or materials to accomplish it. This more overt role is still a sensitive one as we do not want to divert children from following their own ideas.

Recognising children who need more direction

Children are very different, not just developmentally but also temperamentally. I notice that some children do seem to need a little direction before they can get going during child-initiated activity. It may be that they are new to the setting or that they are not confident in engaging with the materials. It is important therefore to spot the 'wanderers' and consider whether a subtle intervention is required. It may be that the child likes to see what is on offer before making a decision or stands back first before engaging with other children and so no direction is needed.

Providing play cues

Many settings will put out materials in such a manner that children are likely to play with them in a certain way, for example, putting farm animals amongst shredded paper. For some children, this is exactly what is needed as it gives them a starting point for their play. It means that when they go over to an area, there is an immediate attraction. If you decide to work in this way (and there are many good reasons for doing so), it is important that there are other possibilities for children to bring something of their own to the play. This might mean putting out other resources so that children can incorporate them into the play or use them instead of the items you originally put out. Where settings insist that the children should only play with the items in the way that the adult intended,

the activity is no longer child initiated because the 'freedom' and choice element has disappeared.

Evaluating provision for child-initiated activity

How do you know that children are learning from their child-initiated activity and that it is challenging whilst being enjoyable for them? This is a key question that you should ask frequently in your setting. One indication that children are gaining from child-initiated activity is the level of concentration that they show and the complexity of their play. We may also look at the duration of their play as well as the skills that they are showing. It is important to regularly do some sort of evaluation so you will know when to bring out new resources, change the layout or enrich particular areas.

Child-initiated play for babies

Non-mobile babies rely heavily on adults to give them stimulation and opportunities for play. Child-initiated activity is often about providing treasure baskets and learning to take your cue from the child. Babies will show that they are not interested by turning their heads away and so, from this, you know that it's time to find something else of interest. Once babies are mobile, there should be a range of accessible materials so they can choose independently. They will, however, benefit from an adult engaging with them as language development is critical in these months. It is also worth remembering that, like older children and adults, babies can get bored too! This means that a single treasure basket is not likely to be stimulating for a baby who may spend 200 hours a month in a setting.

Adult-led activities

Adult-led activities have the potential to enhance children's knowledge and skills and this in turn can enrich child-initiated activity. Sadly, some adult-led activities that I have seen are either intrinsically boring or carried out in such a way that children cannot gain from them. Happily, I have also seen some wonderful adult-led activities that children are clearly enjoying and benefiting from. So what makes a good adult-led activity? These are my thoughts:

Participative

Excellent activities tend to have a high level of participation from the children – we know that children are active learners and so practitioners who plan good activities always choose activities that keep children engaged. Poor adult-led activities are ones where children are expected to be passive recipients of what is being said or shown.

Appropriate level of challenge

Adult-led activities need to be based on children's developmental stage. When activities are too difficult for children the adult is likely to take over or become very authoritarian in style. Knowing whether a child can use scissors, for example, will be key to whether a child can do some dead-heading in the garden.

Fun or fascination

Children need to enjoy the activity and so this means that there must either be a fun element to it or an element of fascination. I have seen a child totally fascinated by using a magnifying sheet to look at a bee pollinating a flower. Sometimes fascination comes from seeing or doing something that is totally new for the child and out of their experience. Children soon learn whether or not adult-led activities are likely to be interesting. If they are, children will often come to adults readily and may even ask what has been planned. Equally, if the track record in the setting is for adult-led activities to be mainly dull, children are pretty reluctant to take part.

Interaction of adult

Children can learn some language from each other, but mainly language is acquired by being with a warm, sensitive adult. One of the many things that distinguishes a quality adult-led activity is the way in which the adult engages with the children. Ideally, adults should use detailed language when showing or describing things to children and accurately name or put language to something that a child has seen or is doing. With young babies, the adult needs to provide a fairly continuous dialogue, but as children develop language, adults need to think about developing a chatty two-way style of interaction.

Activities have genuine value

Good adult-led activities do have genuine value for children. The adult may be giving children opportunities that they cannot otherwise access independently, for example, using a grater, programming the microwave. I see time that adults spend with children as being extremely valuable – and cannot understand why it would be wasted doing something that is either mundane or something that the children can do easily by themselves. When

thinking about activities, you should therefore be aware of the skills, knowledge or development that it will enhance. The next step is to ask whether the children could develop these independently of the adult, for example, children can learn to listen to other children by simply playing alongside them.

Group size

In broad terms, I would argue that the larger the group, the less learning can be gained by the individual child – and the greater the stress on the adult! This means that adult-led activities are often more effective when carried out with very small groups of children, and if necessary repeated, rather than with large groups. As there is a requirement (see the EYFS statutory framework, p.37) that activities should be tailored to meet the individual needs of the children, I cannot see how doing adult-led activities with large groups fits in. Where I have encouraged settings to split their story times into small groups, sometimes run concurrently, they always report that children seem more attentive and that the time is not wasted in asking children to be still or not to fidget.

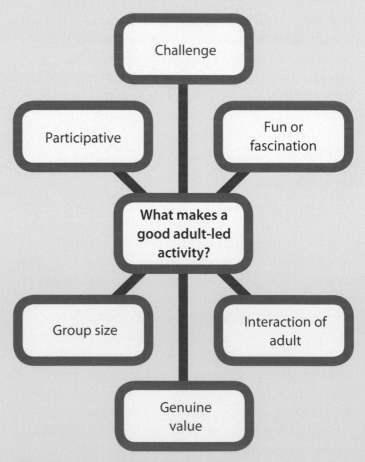

What makes a good adult-led activity?

Evaluating adult-led activities

The best adult-led activities are ones that children seem to remember in some way and often want to repeat. Even a baby will clap their hands to indicate that they would like to do pat-a-cake again with you. I worry about adult-led activities that have taken a lot of time out of the child's session, and where they have no memory of what has been said to them. Circle time for me is a case in point. Unless games are played, few children in the traditional circle time model seem to remember what another child has said. As the supposed aim of this is to support children's listening and social skills, one might come to the conclusion that it is not working. Contrast this with adult-led activities that work well, for example, going on an outing or playing a board game. When these are done well, children are keen to talk about them or repeat them.

Continuous provision

Many settings that get 'outstanding' in their Ofsted report have moved towards a continuous provision model of working. (Where children have access to outdoors, the term 'free flow' might be used either instead of or alongside continuous provision.) This model of working brings together adult-led and child-initiated activity so that they are provided alongside each other. It means that throughout a session, there are always some children engaged in a self-chosen activity whilst other children are benefiting from adult-led activity. This model works well across the age bands and in many different settings.

Benefits of continuous provision

Continuous provision is a useful model as it allows children to play for longer periods of time and avoids stop-start interruptions, for example, all going to get on coats. It is a more fluid model and means that, provided it is carefully planned, children can get more quality interactions and focused time with adults. It also prevents unwanted behaviour as children in this model do not have to spend time waiting. I am a great fan of continuous provision, especially where children can go in and out of doors freely, and I often observe that children's child-initiated activity then lasts longer and becomes more complex.

Moving towards continuous provision

If you currently work in a setting which follows a structured routine (for example, registration, free play,

whole group story), it is important to move towards continuous provision so that children can have more time for child-initiated activity and also have more focused adult time. Over a number of years, I have found that changing a well-established and, in some cases traditional, routine can take time. Sometimes staff also have to be persuaded that it is the right thing to do. Below are some suggestions as to how you might get the ball rolling in your setting:

Abandon registration

Registration can take up a lot of time. Time gained here often allows for 20 more minutes of play. In this time, key people can talk to each of their children and sign them in.

Split whole group activities

If a setting is used to doing whole group story time or whole group snack time, it is a big step to go towards a more fluid approach. The first step might be to split the group into two, three or four groups: one group carries on playing, while another goes outdoors and the final group has a story. It does not matter how exactly it is done, the key is to get away from doing everything *en masse*.

Carry out more key group activities

Where settings are in a habit of whole group working, another starting point might be that key people carry out small activities, for example snack time, story time or going outdoors, with their key groups. This helps staff to see how much more rewarding it is to work in small groups.

Evaluating effects of routine

Sometimes I have helped staff to understand the effects on their current way of working by tracking the activity, language and concentration levels of individual children. In very structured settings, children tend to be more passive, their language use is reduced and they often have long periods of disengagement. Interestingly, they may also not get any meaningful one-to one interaction with staff members. Once changes are made, we are then able to track the same children again and see whether the changes have made any difference.

Keeping the play going

If continuous provision is to work well, children do need to have enough opportunities for child-initiated play that feel challenging. This means that sufficient materials and resources should be available and the way that they are presented should not be too limiting. A small amount of dough at a table with a couple of cutters and a rolling pin is unlikely to engage children for half an hour! As I have already mentioned, it also means thinking about rotating resources and you need to be quick on your feet to enrich play opportunities that are working well. For me, a good test of any play provision is whether children are so engaged that staff, in theory, could just stand back. (They're not meant to, of course!) When your provision is at this point, then you can add in the adult-led activities and do some wonderful individual and small group work with children.

Continuous provision only works well when children are properly engaged in child-initiated play.

Things to watch out for

Whilst continuous provision works very nicely, there are a couple of things to watch out for in group care. Firstly, you should check that children are engaged during child-initiated play and are not floating around aimlessly (see p.15). Secondly, it is important to watch out for younger children or those who are new to the setting. Make sure that they have sufficient adult attention and are helped to play. It is easy for some children to go under the radar in terms of interaction and activity. One way to avoid this is to create a grid which shows children's names and the number of times that they have been involved in a meaningful conversation with an adult or have fully participated in an activity. Whilst this might seem quite mechanical, it at least can help you recognise whether any children are slipping under the radar. It can also flag up how often children are spending time with their key person.

Snack time

If you work in group care, you are likely to provide children with snacks. There are many different approaches to snack time – some better than others. To begin with, it is worth thinking through the following questions.

- Why are snacks important for children?
- What type of snack should be served?
- Does it matter if a child does not want a snack?
- Does it matter at what time the snack is served?
- Does snack time have to be a social occasion?

For me, the answers go something like this. Snack time is nutritionally important and so foods that are served should be healthy. Children who are not hungry or thirsty should not forced to eat as this sets up unhealthy attitudes towards food. Ideally, snacks should be served at least an hour before a meal so that children are hungry for a main meal. A fairly relaxed attitude towards timings should be taken in the mornings to accommodate those children who have not had any breakfast. I would argue that snack time should be a social time for children, but not necessarily an 'occasion' as such. Just being in the company for a short time of one other child or adult will do. Being forced to sit next to someone that you do not like, or waiting for 20 others to finish is not in my opinion necessary for young children.

Possible approaches to snack time

Whole group snack time

Unless you work with small numbers of children, five or fewer, I would avoid a whole group snack time. The amount of time spent consuming the snack in comparison to the amount of time spent waiting to have hands washed or waiting for others is often quite short. Whole group snack time also assumes that all the children are hungry for a snack. It often disrupts children's play and in some ways is a bit institutional.

When I have seen whole group snack time, I often see that staff are quite stressed and are spending time managing behaviour rather than sitting down and enjoying being with the children.

Small group snack time

This is a halfway house and can be a good stepping stone if you wish to move towards a more fluid approach to snack time. The idea is that an adult, preferably the children's key person, asks the children to join them at the snack table. Four or five children at a time will therefore sit and eat together with an adult. By having one small group after another, you avoid all the children washing their hands at the same time. I particularly favour this model if you know that children at home do not sit and eat as a family.

Snack bar or rolling snack time

Many settings have moved away from an official snack time and now offer children a chance to help themselves to a snack when they are ready. This can work well, especially with children over 3 years old, as they are usually quite independent and enjoy having the choice and responsibility. This approach also stops children from being pulled away whilst they are otherwise happily engaged. If you adopt this approach, you will need to have a system to record which children have eaten. You will also need to think about how to support children who may have allergies.

Making snack time an activity

Some settings use snack time as an adult-directed activity. The children prepare and, in some cases, go shopping for the snacks. The children mark-make menus, wash and chop up fruit and set the table as a small group. A variation of this is to set up a role play area in which the adults play the part of the waiter and the children 'order' their snack. Children sit in small groups and talk to each other as they would in a restaurant.

Varying snack time

If children spend a lot of time in your setting, it is worth finding ways of varying snack time so as to keep it an interesting and stimulating experience.

Create a weekly menu

Creating and displaying a weekly menu of snacks can help children know what day of the week it is and so make each day feel slightly different.

Picnic

It is now easier than ever to clean children's hands with gel or wipes and so a picnic outdoors or on the floor in the home corner can be organised easily.

Combining snack time with a story

If you organise your snack times in small groups, children can listen to a story whilst eating – this is very pleasurable for children.

Changing the location

As well as picnics, it can be worth doing a little furniture moving so that children have snacks in different places – this is important as some children spend hundreds of hours each year in the same room.

Providing for babies

Whole books are written about how to work well with babies, but here I would like to give some tips about how to support play and interaction in baby rooms. (If you are a childminder, you might like to skip to Activities to support children's learning and development that shows some of the daily activities that support bonding and interaction.) In my experience, there is a bit of a taboo when it comes to working with babies. On my courses, I often ask people the direct question as to whether they get bored working with babies or find that their shift seems long. The answer is usually yes. I am not surprised by this as, if staff are not in stimulating environments, there is a real danger that their ability to maintain energy and enthusiasm dwindles. This is not about staff being lazy. It is more about thinking how we can create a 'busy' environment which works well for both staff and, of course, the babies.

Stimulating environments

Whilst Tony Blair famously said 'education, education, education', the key to babies getting a good start in life is interaction, interaction, interaction. The trouble is that when adults are bored, it is difficult for them to find anything meaningful to talk about. Traditionally, babies have learnt language by hearing an adult (usually their mother) giving a running commentary while engaged in adult tasks such as cooking, washing and cleaning. They were out and about as parents took them shopping, met up with other parents and hung the washing outdoors. Babies also experienced interaction with older siblings and would often spend time watching them play. In this context language occurred quite naturally as adults had plenty to talk about and babies had plenty of things to take their attention. Contrast this with babies and staff who may spend 8 out of 10 hours in the same room, day after day and week after week. (I suspect that I might even be generous in assuming that two hours a day are spent outdoors or in other rooms) I have therefore come to the conclusion that in order to do a good job with the babies, it is important to create an environment and routines that keep both the practitioner and the baby stimulated.

Using the ratios effectively

Babies were not designed to be in large groups. They need plenty of one-to-one interaction with the same person if they are to feel genuinely settled and attached. This is why in England the required staff–baby ratio in day care is 1:3. Occasionally, I hear practitioners say things such as, 'but we have 15 babies,' and I have to remind them that unless they have sufficient staff for a 1:3 ratio, they are breaking the law. (Note that the ratio of 1:3 needs to be maintained even if a staff member is on a break elsewhere in the building.) Sadly, though, some settings do operate as if there were 15 children, with staff saying that they cannot go outdoors unless all the babies are awake. The danger of all staff keeping an eye out for all the babies is that close bonds are not formed and the amount of individual attention and interaction that a child receives can be very limited. If you currently work with the large-group approach, I would urge you to observe how much interaction individual babies receive over a day.

Mother ducking!

I would therefore suggest that for most of the day, each member of staff is allocated three babies to spend their time with. I often refer to this as 'mother ducking'! The aim is that staff should have their key children as a priority. On days when a staff member has five of their key children in, the staff member in the room that does not have their quota will look after the additional two.

By working with just three babies and by planning activities and organising the day around them, these babies will get more interaction. It means that when one baby is asleep, the staff member will be able to focus on the other two.

Bringing in siblings and older children to play

It seems sad that some babies develop stronger bonds with children who, after a few years, they will never see again, rather than with their siblings. I feel that if siblings are in the same setting, we should try and create opportunities for them to play together. Many settings put siblings together for meal times which is already a good starting point. Having a sibling with babies does change the language level in the baby room and straightaway provides a new focus. Of course, this can only happen if ratios permit and if the older child is gentle, but by and large it is worth considering. You may find that the older child enjoys playing with the baby toys and ignores their younger sibling, but this does not matter – the main thing is that they are spending some time together.

Creating different 'rooms' within the baby room

Few babies cared for in home environments spend hours at a time in a single room. Babies will often spend time in a kitchen, bedroom and lounge. Every time the baby goes into a different room, they are likely to see different lighting and colours on the wall and feel different textures on the ground. If you work in a baby room, you might like to sub-divide the space and think about ways of creating a similar effect even if is on a small scale. Try and think about putting down more than one surface so that crawling babies have a different sensation, for example, a rug or a piece of lino. If you are re-flooring a baby area, bear in mind this need for different textures. Once you have physically created different 'rooms', think next about putting different toys and experiences in them. One room or area could be for treasure basket play, another could be where you carry out sensory activities. Once you have created the different rooms, try moving between them with the babies that you are responsible for that day; for example, spend half an hour with three babies in the sensory area, whilst a colleague is spending half an hour in the room which has treasure basket play.

Planning outings for different days of the week

I often ask practitioners what makes a Tuesday different to a Thursday for the babies in their care. If there are not clear differences, there is a danger that there is not sufficient stimulation. A simple way of stimulating both children and adults is to go for different walks and outings. The regulations concerning the staff–child ratios in respect of outings is fair and provided that a risk assessment has been carried out, there is no automatic need to increase the adult–child ratio. This means that a member of staff with appropriate qualifications could go for a 'round-the-block' walk with three children in a buggy. Just being out in the fresh air and popping to the local shop can provide opportunities for speech and stimulation. Ideally, I would aim to have a series of regular outings to local areas such as the park, library, supermarket and shop.

Daily activities for babies

Many practitioners struggle with planning activities for babies. The irony is that the EYFS demands very little in terms of actual activities, but does require practitioners to work in quite traditional ways with babies. To support practitioners, I have created a list of activities that are important for interaction and bonding. They do not take up very much time or organisation, but if carried out with each baby each day, will promote this interaction and bonding. The daily activities also have a benefit for practitioners as they provide a focus and often keep practitioners moving – staff tell me that the day working with babies goes so much faster when they use the activities.

High play

Babies love being swung up above an adult's head. I dub this 'high play'. It is beneficial for the babies because they can see the environment from a different point of view. They also make strong eye contact with the adult.

Share a story

Babies need to be introduced to books early on. Make sure that each day, each of your babies has shared a book with you.

Play that incorporates ICT

Look out for toys that incorporate ICT, for example, a pop-up toy that lights up or a musical mobile. Look out also for books that make sounds.

Finger rhymes

There are different types of rhymes. Rhymes help babies to listen to sounds and also encourage them to vocalise. Finger rhymes include *Two Little Dicky Birds* and *Pat-a-Cake*.

Action songs

Action songs with babies require whole body movements, for example, *Humpty Dumpty* or *Row, Row, Row the Boat*.

Rocking

Babies love being rocked. Try rocking them in your arms or in a buggy, pram or seat.

Swinging

Being swung is a different type of action to being rocked. Prioritise putting up a baby swing indoors and another one outdoors. Make sure that the swing is high enough so that a mobile baby cannot be hit by it. Consider putting up two swings side by side so that babies can enjoy this experience together.

Peepo play

Each day make sure that babies can enjoy this type of play. Partially cover the baby and then 'find' them. You can do this with a blanket, hat or soft sheet. Once babies understand the game, be ready for them to hide you!

Children love the element of surprise of Peepo.

Knock down play

Babies love watching things being knocked down. As soon as they can, they will want to join in. Look out for stacking beakers and other containers, such as small cardboard boxes.

Being carried

Babies benefit from being carried – on the hip, close to the chest or on the back. They enjoy the human contact as well as seeing the world from different heights. Use this as an opportunity to show babies things out of the window or walk them around different parts of your setting.

Treasure basket play

Babies benefit from good quality treasure basket play. Collect together as many items as possible made from natural materials, for example, metal spoons and wooden pegs. Make sure that you have several different treasure baskets so that the baby is always exploring different combinations.

Links to the EYFS

Table 1 below shows how suggested activities link to the areas and aspects of learning if all of these activities are done in a session as well as an outing. Many people who look at the table

Table 1: How suggested activities link to the areas and aspects of learning

Area of learning	Aspects of learning	
Personal, Social and Emotional Development	Dispositions and Attitudes	✔
	Self-confidence and Self-esteem	✔
	Making relationships	✔
	Behaviour and Self-control	✔
	Self-care	
	Sense of Community	
Communication, Language and Literacy	Language for Communication	✔
	Language for Thinking	✔
	Linking Sounds and Letters	✔
	Reading	✔
	Writing	
	Handwriting	
Problem Solving, Reasoning and Numeracy	Numbers as Labels and for Counting	✔
	Calculating	✔
	Shape, Space and Measures	✔
Knowledge and Understanding of the World	Exploration and Investigation	✔
	Designing and Making	✔
	ICT	✔
	Time	
	Place	✔
	Communities	
Physical Development	Movement and Space	✔
	Health and Bodily Awareness	✔
	Using Equipment and Materials	✔
Creative Development	Being Creative – Responding to Experiences, Expressing and Communicating Ideas	✔
	Exploring Media and Materials	✔
	Creating Music and Dance	✔
	Developing Imagination and Imaginative Play	✔

will automatically feel reassured. They are likely to be doing some or all of these activities with babies. Of course I am hoping that each activity is done every day so that we can be sure that every baby is getting interaction and close contact with their adult.

Sensory activities

In addition to the small games and interactions with their key person, babies need some sensory experiences. When choosing sensory activities, look for ones where the baby can do most of the activity independently, for example, smearing yoghurt. Foot painting, on the other hand, is heavily adult led and so I would argue is of less benefit as the baby cannot repeat it alone or go at their own speed.

Providing play for toddlers

On my travels, I see that planning play and activities for this age group seems to present quite a challenge. Practitioners often comment that the children do not seem to stay at anything for any length of time and that if they are mixed in with children aged 3 and over, they tend to sabotage the older children's play.

Understanding their stage of development

A good starting point is to check that your expectations of 2-year-olds are realistic. I find that many practitioners overestimate the social skills of 2-year-olds whilst underestimating their emotional needs. This tends to lead to a deficient model when some practitioners talk about them, saying for example, 'they can't sit still' or 'they can't share'.

Below are some key points that I tend to raise when working with practitioners:

Proximity

Usually, 2-year-olds like to be in sight of or with their adult. I often see children break off from an activity to go and find their key person if, when they look up, the adult is no longer in sight.

Independence

It may seem a contradiction, in view of what I have written about proximity, but many 2-year-olds want and need opportunities to be independent. This means that whilst they want an adult to be standing near, they may want to put on their shoes by themselves or struggle to drag a chair over to a table on their own.

Language needs

Between the ages of 2 and 3, children should make huge leaps forward with their language and communication skills. This can only take place if the layout and organisation of the setting creates opportunities for adults to spend time interacting with children. When children are doing well with their language, they tend to steam ahead with their social skills and seem also to develop more sophisticated play.

Active not passive

Many parents and practitioners underestimate just how active 2-year-olds need to be. Most toddlers are pretty busy people and very exploratory in nature. In terms of planning, this means that passive activities, such as a group story, are unlikely to be successful.

Onlooking and parallel play

Whilst 2-year-olds are very interested in others, they do not always find it easy to engage in cooperative play. It takes a high level of skills to read the signals that another person is giving you and to adapt your actions to it. You are therefore likely to find that children tend to play next to each other or copy each other's actions after observing for a while.

Although children might not play co-operatively at this age, they do enjoy playing near others.

Repetitive play

It can come as a surprise that many young children will want to repeat an action over and over again. They may take fill up a jar with sand and immediately find another jar to fill up. This is normal behaviour and a key way in which toddlers behave. This means that you need to allow time and sufficient resources for toddlers to play in this way; for example, providing sufficient shells for them to drop into a bottle one by one.

Behaviour

As language and social skills are still developing, children at this age will find it hard to share, wait to take turns or cope when they see something that they want. It is important for everyone to accept this as being normal behaviour.

Attention

It is normal for children under 3 years old to need a lot of adult attention. They may also show jealousy towards other children who are getting attention. This means that attention-seeking behaviours are fairly normal. The trick is to ignore these behaviours wherever possible, but to recognise that more positive attention needs to be given.

Planning for play – Toddlers

Once we have taken on board the limitations and the picture that most 2-year-olds present, the next job is to plan for their play needs. In my experience, the traditional layout of activities into areas such as construction, role play, mark-making, dough etc works very well with children from about 3 years old, but does not necessarily work with younger ones. For this age group, I suggest making sure that they have opportunities based on play patterns or, if you prefer, play schemas. If you are not familiar with play schema theory do consider researching it further as it can be very helpful as a way of understanding children's play. Below are some common play patterns that I see young children use. It is not a complete list, but may be helpful in kick-starting your setting's journey.

Posting

You will see this when children push items through a wire fence or enjoy putting things down the back of a radiator. In many settings, I see children taking the washing up bowl out of the play kitchen and posting anything that they can find down the plug hole!

Providing for this: Think about tubes and drain pipes and objects that can be safely popped down them.

Dropping

Some children will stand at a table and pick up objects one by one and then watch them fall out of their hand.

Providing for this: Look for items that children can drop into a water bucket safely, for example, rubber ducks and balls.

Open and closed

Children are often fascinated with opening and closing things. This might be standing by a cupboard door and just opening and closing it. Some children will also put things in and take them out of the cupboard.

Providing for this: Look out for a cupboard that is safe for children to use for this play. Think also about cutting a 'door' in a rigid cardboard box. Some settings may also be able to put up a curtain on a pole that will allow the children to swish it open and closed.

Moving things around

Many children have an absolute yen for moving things from one place to another. You may spot a child going around a room picking up as many bits and pieces as possible and putting them into a pushchair before taking them on a joy ride!

Providing for this: You will need pushchairs, brick trolleys, 'sit and rides' or anything that has wheels which can be loaded up. It can be worth providing small containers of odds and ends to avoid toddlers taking things away from other children. It is important to have sufficient pushchairs etc. because children tend to copy each other and will want to have the same as another child.

From one container to another

As well as large-scale removal, you may also notice that many children want to put objects and sensory materials from one container to another. Sand for example may be transferred by way of a scoop or hand into an adjacent bucket.

Providing for this: Try putting out more than one container when you are setting out toys and other items. Think also about scoops, spoons and ladles that will allow children to transfer items.

In and out

Many children love putting things in containers or boxes and then shutting them. This leads to an 'in and out' type of play. You may see a child put something in a saucepan, put the lid on it and then after a moment take it back out again.

Providing for this: Provide plenty of boxes and containers that can have lids and also items, such as stacking beakers or Russian dolls. Look out for some small items that children can put inside the boxes or containers, such as wooden clothes pegs.

Small spaces

Many young children like somewhere small and cosy that they can disappear into. This may be about feeling secure or just an extension of Peepo play that we see in babies.

Providing for this: Put up makeshift tents or dens by draping sheets around furniture or across fences outdoors. Children will often want to help you to make these spaces. Make sure that they are really small so that only children can fit inside them!

Throwing

Many 2-year-olds will pick up items and just throw them for apparently no reason and often without aim. Avoid seeing this as a behavioural issue, but instead look to create legitimate opportunities.

Providing for this: Look out for beanbags and other items that are satisfying to throw. To avoid incidents, consider doing this as an adult-directed activity, for example, throwing potatoes into a paddling pool. Note that very light plastic balls do not seem to be sufficiently satisfying for most children so look for heavier items.

Climbing

Most children enjoy climbing. Active 2-year-olds need opportunities to climb and if they are not provided they will use tables and chairs or anything else they can find.

Providing for this: Think about what you have available to help children climb – in the DVD and on pp.108–110, you will see how tree trunks can provide an ideal challenge. Think about providing for climbing indoors by using solid stage blocks or low benches.

Water

Whilst toddlers enjoy many sensory activities, water seems to be especially interesting to them and it is wonderful to watch how many different ways they will explore it.

Providing for this: I have moved away from water trays for this age range as they are often too high. Consider putting out two or more buckets with containers nearby. Many children will drop things into the buckets, but also spend time moving the water out into the other container.

Planning further opportunities

The play patterns that I have outlined are not a definitive list, but might act as starting points for your basic provision if you are working with this age group. It is also worth watching to see what other things the children you work with want to do. A good tip is to make a note of anything that you have to put a stop to, for reasons of health and safety, and focus on the action that probably drove the child's interest, for example, a child who stands over a table of items and makes a swishing movement from side to side may enjoy mark-making with large felt-tip pens.

Boys

Some of the things that I have read and heard about boys' development give me serious concerns. Firstly, most of it is negative and secondly, it ignores the premise that all children need to be seen as individuals. It is true that the Early Years Profile data shows that, taken as a homogenous group, boys are performing less well than girls. But before panic sets in, I would suggest that we look at this very carefully. Most boys are doing well. The profile results (2009) show that the majority of boys are meeting the levels that are thought to be required for successful progression into Year One, that is, 6 or more points. Secondly, when we look further into the profile we will see that it is specific groups of boys that are more at risk. This would suggest to me that additional support may need to be given to these children.

Development is a complex affair

There are many simplistic statements made about boys. They are said to be active, boisterous, lacking in concentration and unable to sit still. Such statements are not helpful as they ignore the complex and individual nature of development. When you begin to dig down a little deeper, you will find often find that boys really do come in all sorts of shapes, sizes and with different interests. Parents who have several boys will tell you that their boys are all very different. Expectations, experiences, birth order and of course a dose of nature all shape children, as does the socio-economic group of their families. I would argue that development is so complex that we cannot make assumptions about half of all children – especially when gender itself is part of a continuum.

Active enough?

I often hear that boys are active and enjoy running around. This is frequently seen as a problem. I am not so sure that it is, unless what they are doing is genuinely unsafe. The current recommendations published by NICE (National Institute for Health and Clinical Excellence) are that children should be engaged in moderate to vigorous physical activity for at least an hour during the course of a day. You might like to observe whether all of the children in your setting are meeting this recommendation. As many children are transported in cars or pushchairs, it may be that some settings need to increase the opportunities for physical activity and that may mean that some girls might need to do a little more!

Levels of interaction

We know that good language development is a key to success in terms of managing behaviour, learning to read and problem solving. One thing that settings can do is to audit the level of interaction that each boy receives, focusing particularly on the group of boys that are perceived as being more challenging. This is a useful exercise as sometimes settings realise that little interaction between staff and children is taking place. This is important because if children are to make progress they need opportunities for shared, sustained conversation.

Play interests need to be catered for

I would argue that girls' and boys' play and developmental needs are not dissimilar. Both need plenty of interaction, stimulation and opportunities for child-initiated play. What can be different though, is their play interests. These tend to be driven by the exploration of gender concept and we can see this emerging from around 3 years old onwards. Children from 3 years old are influenced by the other children around them as they are also exploring friendship. I suspect that this is why in some settings there seem to be cults of superheroes and gaggles of princesses. By 4 years old, some children are so gendered in their approach that they would go thirsty rather than drink from the 'wrong' coloured cup.

As with all aspects of child development, I suspect that children explore gender concepts at different levels tand whilst some children are only choosing opportunities that they feel to be sufficiently gendered, others are not so bothered. This goes for both boys and girls. Hence, we may see a boy perfectly content to dress up in a pink skirt while, in the same provision, another boy will only come to the writing table if he perceives it to be a pirate's office. It is important to observe just how interested individual children are in 'gender' as we may spot that their choices of play could be reducing their opportunities for learning. This goes for both girls and boys as some girls are not choosing to use construction materials that could support later problem solving and spatial awareness development.

Allow boys and girls to engage in whatever play takes their fancy.

Meeting developmental and learning needs

Settings that have a good track record working with boys tend to be good at using children's play interests as a means to an end when it comes to providing for their developmental and learning needs. A tin of toys that need fixing works wonderfully for those boys who see themselves as builders but delivers opportunities for sustained shared thinking with the adult. In the same way, putting briefcases, ties and jackets in combination with mark-making can prompt some boys to try out mark-making as the props help them to imagine they are in an office. A favourite challenge of mine is also to drop a small wooden ladybird down between two flagstones and ask children to 'rescue' it.

Sufficient challenge

Some boys are very good at giving us feedback as to whether or not our setting or the activities we are providing are sufficiently challenging. Unfortunately, without the diplomatic skills to tell us, they are likely to show it through their actions. This means that when you see unwanted behaviour, a good starting point is to analyse objectively just how challenging the resources and activities are for the children. I have seen a group of boys who one minute were pushing each other over, then a few minutes later were helping an adult to rake up leaves. They were calm, serious and busily chatting. The adult had provided a new focus and challenge for them.

If you are wondering why boys tend to show more unwanted behaviour when they are bored, you might be interested in looking at research around parents' and adults' attitudes towards managing behaviour and gender. It would seem that from the word go, adults have higher expectations and are more controlling of girls' behaviour. If this is true, it would account for the way that girls who may be equally bored do not necessarily show it in their actions.

Role models for literacy activities

Boys and girls are influenced by other children, but also adult role models. For some time, it has been thought that boys benefit from having male role models, particularly in terms of literacy activities. Anecdotally, practitioners have told me that when there is a male staff member, the boys seem to be more engaged and interested in mark-making activities and reading. Unfortunately, not every early years setting has a male member of staff. If you are on a school site, try and set up a working arrangement so that older boys regularly come down with their books and work at a table indoors. This can have an amazing effect with younger boys asking if they can sit with them. If this is not possible, think about inviting fathers, grandparents and students on work experience in to the setting. Obviously visitors to the setting have to be supervised and, where necessary, security checked. If this is still not possible, collect and display photographs of 'real men' who are reading or writing.

Creative development

Creative development is one area that some settings struggle with. To deliver it well requires a level of confidence from members of staff and also some practical strategies and activities that we can use with the children. We chose Stepping Stones Pre-school as, like many pre-schools, they were working in a single large room that had little storage. The building was also shared by the after-school club which threw up its own set of complications as sharing a building is not always easy. When I arrived, Sandra and her team already had a strong idea of what they wanted to achieve as they had attended some training which had given them some thoughts. My visits were intended to give them the impetus to get going and, as creative development is a large area, we focused on just a few aspects. For the purposes of this book, however, I thought it would be useful to widen the net and discuss creativity in more general terms.

In this chapter I will be covering the following:

- What is creativity?
- 'Anything can happen here' area
- Junk modelling and collage
- Creating a painting wall
- Using small trays for painting
- Combining mark-making and painting with music
- Small world play
- Role play
- Sensory materials
- Button tins
- Music and dance

What is creativity?

It is important for us to think about the nature of creativity in order for us to provide an environment in which creativity can be developed in children. In many ways creativity is about exploring ideas and making new connections as well as about self-expression through traditional routes such as music, painting and drama. Interestingly, there is also an element of non-conformism about creativity. Just repeating exactly what everyone else has done is not creative and so you may find that some of your more creative children are also the ones who try and do things 'their' way. Whilst anything that endangers the health and well-being of the child or others cannot be allowed, for a setting to be a creative one the adults within it have to be flexible in their approaches with children. This flexibility was a key strength at Stepping Stones. There is a wonderful moment in the DVD where we see children doing everything imaginable to the vegetables that were put out in the role play area on my second visit, and the staff were good at allowing this exploration whilst keeping a careful eye on the children.

Developing a creative setting

Creativity is about exploring new ideas and having permission to do so. Ideally, we should be striving to create an environment that allows children to develop their own ideas and to use and combine materials and toys in any way that suits them. The reality is that there are issues about health and safety, keeping the environment attractive and maintaining some law and order when there are many children in one place. Having said that, I believe that there are many ways in which we can encourage children's natural curiosity and sense of creativity both indoors and outdoors.

Passing ownership to children

Settings that provide a genuinely creative environment are good at setting up opportunities, equipment and resources for children and then almost standing back a little. They allow children to explore and take ownership of what they are doing. It was good to see this at Stepping Stones when, for example, children at the painting wall were able to mix colours and put paint onto the wall where and how they wished (see more on how to set up a painting wall on p.36).

A key question when planning an activity is therefore, 'Whose activity will it be?' Twenty pre-cut butterflies all painted with orange and yellow spots is more about the creativity of the adult who organised the activity than the children who acted as little more than factory hands. This means that you do not have to be good at art, music or drama in order to provide a creative environment. Instead, you just have to be good at providing time, equipment and resources and a positive attitude.

Equipment and resources

Some equipment and resources are very open ended, meaning that they provide infinite possibilities for play, for example sand, or LEGO®. Interestingly, it is these materials that tend to be very popular with children. You might like to do an audit of your equipment and resources and think about whether they provide children with opportunities for them to put their own stamp on their play or whether they are very directive. It will be impossible to create an environment that contains exclusively totally open-ended resources, because games such as picture lotto or jigsaw puzzles are very important for children. The point, however, is to ensure that there is a balance in favour of open-ended materials and that you are aware of this when planning the environment for children.

Attitudes of adults

The starting point is perhaps our own and other adults' attitudes when it comes to letting children be creative. Many truly creative moments for children will not involve an end product and so an adult hoping that a child will create a collage may be disappointed to find that the children are more interested in examining the items that have been put out for sticking. In the same way, an adult hoping to make 'nice' cards for children to take home may find that children want to use the resources in a very different way from the one intended. Adults therefore may have to learn not to impose their own ideas on children in such situations. I sometimes feel it can be useful to ask two questions when children are doing something that adults have not intended: 'Does it matter?' and 'Can it be tidied up?'

On the DVD, you may see that staff at Stepping Stones were well on their way to allowing children to explore freely – you may spot, for example, the clip of the child having a lovely time at the collage/mark-making table. By the end of our filming, she had gone on to produce a 'book' with some wonderful patterns and designs in it.

Confidence

Bound up with the attitudes of adults is also their level of confidence. It can take time for adults to gain the confidence they need to allow children to play or explore in ways that the adult is not expecting. Adults also need confidence to *ad lib* when it comes to storytelling or to try out new things with children. For some people, this may mean that they will need to take small steps over a period of a few weeks in order to make the changes that will enable their setting to become a creative one for children.

Time

Children need sufficient time if they are to engage with materials creatively and if they are to explore and develop ideas. One of the strengths of Stepping Stones was that children did have good blocks of time in which to play and engage in activities. If your setting has frequent stops and starts, you may need to review your routine. A snack table that is open at certain times rather than a whole group snack, for example, can immediately create a longer block of time for children to engage in activities.

Auditing the creativity of your setting

- Are children often told what they cannot do?
- Do adults engage with children positively when they are involved in a creative activity?
- Do children see staff being creative?
- Are staff focused on end products in art, design, craft (including painting and collaging), music and movement?
- Are there any areas within creativity where children have fewer opportunities?
- Are there any areas within creativity in which you could benefit from further knowledge or training?
- Do you work in ways that allow children to have choices and ownership of activities and opportunities?

'Anything can happen here' area

At Stepping Stones, I dropped in the idea of creating an 'anything can happen here' area. Although Sandra and her team did not have time to introduce this, they liked the idea. The basis of 'anything can happen here' is to create a small area where children can follow their own thoughts and play quite freely. You may remember doing this as a child – putting various toys and bits together to play with or making some muddy mixture in a bucket outdoors. Today, we often sterilise children's play by separating materials and toys into certain areas. I can understand why we do this, as with many children in a room it may otherwise feel quite chaotic and many adults simply cannot cope with this way of working. Creating an 'anything can happen here' area is therefore useful as it puts this type of play in a designated area and so keeps everyone fairly happy.

Benefits

An 'anything can happen here' area should give children opportunities to explore materials and resources that are not normally grouped together. This allows them to make new connections and play in different ways. In some cases, children will make new products, but this is not necessarily the aim. A practical benefit of having a designated area for what adults might see as 'chaos' is that it can give them an insight into what children can do and help them understand the way that children need to play. It is therefore quite a safe way of helping a setting to become more creative in their approach.

Creating an 'anything can happen here' area – indoors

Begin by looking out for a corner or area that can be coned off or where furniture can be moved around to create a perimeter. This helps children to realise that this is a special area for them. Ideally, you should look for an area which is not carpeted and is preferably close to water. Once you have identified the area for your provision, put in a table and then many small quantities of different materials and toys. The more the merrier. One way of doing this is to take small amounts of what you already have from each of the different areas, for example, some items from the role play area, some items from construction play as well as a little bit of dough, sand and water.

Think about visiting your local scrap store so that children have access to unusual items and to large quantities of paper and card. Below is a list of some groups of materials and toys that when combined together can prove inspirational for children. Note that you will need to group materials that are safe for the age/stage of the children with whom you work:

- sensory materials – sand, water, paint, dough, shredded paper

- tools – scissors, rolling pin, stapler, spoons of different sizes, brushes

- small world items – farm animals, play people, cars

- junk modelling – cardboard tubes, boxes

- haberdashery – buttons, laces, elastic, feathers

- paper (use scraps) – gummed and sugar paper, thin card

- adhesives – glue, masking tape, sticky tape, double-sided tape, string

- containers – buckets, cake tins, ice cube trays

- fabrics – chiffon, scarves, tinsel, Lycra®

- items from the scrap store – anything that takes your fancy!

Creating an 'anything can happen here' area – outdoors

The same process applies outdoors, but you should be able to do things on a larger scale. Consider also putting out a table as children may require a surface to work on. I would hope that children are able to have far more choice of materials and that they can experiment more with sensory materials than is possible indoors. Think about having buckets, spoons, sticks and a selection of sensory materials such as sand, water, bark chippings and paint.

Terms and conditions!

Whilst the aim is to give children a chance to be creative and to try out new ideas with a wide range of materials, it is important that children also know that 'terms and conditions' apply. These are my suggestions.

Children love having a range of materials available for them to get creative with.

Usual standards of behaviour apply

We want children to enjoy themselves and play without the usual boundaries, but this does not mean that they have a licence to behave badly. Interestingly, some settings find that the threat of being removed from this area is pretty powerful as children do not want to miss out.

Nothing can be brought into the area unless an adult has given permission

One of the reasons why it is important to create a specific area is to signal to children that it is a special area and they may not be able to play in this way elsewhere. It is therefore important at the start to make it clear to children that if they wish to find something else to bring into the area, it must be agreed first by an adult.

At the end of the session, everyone must clean up and tidy up

Cleaning and tidying up is part of life and so I feel that children must be involved at the end of the session in putting the area back to some semblance of order. Settings that have tried an 'anything can happen here' area have been pleasantly surprised by just how purposeful children's play is and also how much they have enjoyed the tidying-up process. This might mean washing up the brushes or removing paint out of Barbie's hair!

Role of the adult

It is important that adults understand what the purpose of this area is in order that they can supervise and intervene appropriately. Adults must understand that unless the children are doing something dangerous or are behaving in anti-social ways, it does not matter what they choose to do. This means that if a child feels like drowning the farm animals after wrapping them in paper the adult should not worry.

However, it is important that adults do supervise and this will be a major strategy when it comes to the risk assessment of this activity.

Observing children

Watching children play with a range of materials in a very free way may give you insights into individual children's needs and interests. Keep an eye out for children who seem to be very angry or destructive in the way that they play and think about whether they may have some underlying emotional needs. You may also notice some children who have very clear ideas about what they would like to do and this may be a starting point for planned activities for them later.

Creating an 'anything can happen here' area for babies

In some ways this concept links nicely to treasure basket and heuristic play and if you are not already providing these types of play, this would be a good starting point (see pp. 21–22). If you do already provide them, you might like to add 'anything can happen here' areas as well. These areas may be enclosed and contain a variety of objects both natural and man-made for babies to explore. As babies are likely to be mouthing, items will have to be risk assessed and a good level of supervision will be required. Think about putting lights and soft music in this area so that babies will have a very sensory experience.

What to observe

Watching children as they play in these areas can be quite fascinating. Children are sometimes very creative and thoughtful about what they do. Consider the following:

- How engaged is the child in the activity?
- What materials seem to engage the child?
- How much language does the child seem to use?
- Does the child work or play alongside other children?
- How does the child use the materials?
- Can you identify what the child is trying to achieve?
- How can this play be developed further?

Links to the EYFS

Personal, Social and Emotional Development	'Anything can happen' areas can give children a great sense of freedom and so there are links to Self-confidence and Self-esteem. Children are also trying out new ideas and persevering and so there are links to Dispositions and Attitudes. If clearing away is part of the activity, children will also be working towards Self-care.
Communication, Language and Literacy	This is the type of area in which children tend to use language quite spontaneously. They are likely to communicate with others and also want to show adults what they have done. There is also scope for adults to support children with their Language for Thinking by asking questions such as, 'I wonder why that doesn't stick'. As children are busy with their hands, they are also developing the fine motor skills that will be necessary for Handwriting.
Problem Solving, Reasoning and Numeracy	There is a natural link between being creative and problem solving. Children are also likely to be making or designing things and so will be exploring Shape, Space and Measures. With adult interaction, children can also have their attention drawn to numbers, linking to Numbers as Labels and for Counting.
Knowledge and Understanding of the World	To maximise Knowledge and Understanding of the World outcomes, I would regularly take photographs or video clips of children engaged in this area and encourage them to view them. This would mean that there will be a link to ICT and also Time. Children are also investigating and exploring and may also be involved in Designing and Making.
Physical Development	This type of activity/area will link nicely to Using Equipment and Materials. Depending on how large a space you create and the size of containers and other materials that you put out, there may also be a link to Movement and Space.
Creative Development	As you might expect, an 'anything can happen here area' is likely to link to the aspect Developing Imagination and Imaginative Play. It also links nicely to Exploring Media and Materials and, if children share and notice the ideas of others, there should be good links to Being Creative – Responding to Experiences, Expressing and Communicating Ideas.

Junk modelling and collage

Children love sticking things and exploring new textures and materials. At Stepping Stones, the staff knew that they wanted to create a workshop area and whilst this was still work in progress, you can see that we created a table which had many items on it for children to use for collage. Our first visitor was a girl who spent all afternoon painstakingly sticking lentils and other small items into a small book. I would suggest that ideally, over time, this be extended to create a junk modelling/collage area so that children can really create interesting pictures and products.

Benefits of junk modelling and collage

Junk modelling and collage tend to give children enormous satisfaction as they can create their own products and follow their own ideas. Children also learn about the properties of materials and about shape. This admittedly means that sometimes things fall apart or are pulled off pieces of paper, but this is all part of the learning process for children. I am always impressed by how children really follow their ideas and are sometimes quite ambitious in their projects. Whilst young children will often just handle items and gain pleasure from feeling the glue or rubbing a feather against their face, older children often work cooperatively together and can, if adults give them the time, take on intricate projects.

Resources

A wide range of resources is needed for a good junk modelling and collage area. There are no rights or wrongs, except in risk assessment terms, but the key is to find things that children like or are very unusual. A visit to your local scrap store as well printer or copy shop may yield some interesting finds. Below are some of the essentials when it comes to resources.

Haberdashery

Items of haberdashery can be wonderfully exciting for children. Think about buttons, sequins, ribbons, string and pieces of elastic. Effectively anything that sparkles or is unusual in texture will do!

Boxes, tubes, plastic bottles and tins

For junk modelling, children need some basic shapes to start them off. Whilst the usual focus is on cardboard items such as boxes, try and widen your net so that children can have plastic bottles, tins and interesting bits and pieces such as a plastic tube or a short length of hosepipe.

Paper and card

It should be possible to provide children with a wide range of paper and card. Think about cellophane, tissue paper and foil as well as the traditional sugar papers and thin card. It can be worth putting together a scrap box so that children can find interesting shapes of different sizes. You could also buy some rolls of paper, for example, brown paper and lining paper, so that children can have the option of creating a large piece of work.

Stationery items

Have a look around a stationery shop for inspiration for your collage/junk modelling table. Doilies, confetti and card-making accessories as well as crayons, paints and stamps can be exciting materials for children. Ask parents to collect old greeting cards, stamps and envelopes to bring into the setting too.

Bits and bobs

It is worth putting together a 'bits and bobs' box which may include household items, such as corks and string as well as items that we know children find fascinating, such as keys or clips. Bits and bobs can enrich children's sculptures and collages. Look out for shells, lids, small plastic bottles and fridge magnets.

Adhesives and staplers

Children need a good selection of different types of adhesives in order to stick and join items together.

Look out for staplers as well as different types of tape, such as masking tape, double-sided tape and sticky tape. Think also about glue sticks and pens as well as the traditional PVA and spatulas.

Mark-making items, scissors and string

It is worth putting out plenty of items that children can use to mark-make, such as felt tips, gel pens and other types of pens. Children will also need scissors, a hole punch and string or wool.

Presenting items

Presentation can be key to children's engagement. I am a great fan of creating a 'treasure tin' by putting many of the small items together, for example, ribbons, pom-poms sequins and tinsel. This means that children never quite know what they will find and they automatically do a little sorting. (Backstage, so to speak, it is worth keeping items in separate pots so that you can find what you are looking for easily.) At Stepping Stones, Sandra liked this idea and we found a square metal tin to put in a good selection of collage materials.

Role of the adult

A good starting point is to understand that many children will enjoy exploring what is available and younger children may not be interested in actually gluing anything at all. This is fine as the exploration in itself is creative. Once children are interested in making things, the role of the adult is that of an interested facilitator. As an adult, you have more experience of how to join things and so showing children or holding things for them is part of your role. It is also worth accepting the way that some children can be very flexible in their thinking – one minute they are making a space rocket, but then after seeing something else that takes their fancy, they decide that the rocket has become a treasure box. This is all to be expected, as are children who have definite ideas that will not be derailed on any account.

A key factor in the quality of what children produce is often time. Expect that children who are really benefiting from this opportunity will want to carry on for quite a while and that some projects may span a few sessions. It is therefore important to clear a shelf where ongoing projects can be kept.

Links to the EYFS

Personal, Social and Emotional Development	Children gain confidence and also the desire to learn and concentrate from this type of activity. This links nicely to Dispositions and Attitudes and also Self-confidence and Self-esteem. As this type of activity is linked to developing skills there are also links to Self-care.
Communication, Language and Literacy	Children are likely to talk about what they see and touch as well as what they are hoping to make. This means that there are good links to Language for Communication and Language for Thinking. The hand–eye co-ordination also supports Handwriting. Children may also wish to mark-make or write as part of this work and so there are possible links to Writing.
Problem Solving, Reasoning and Numeracy	There are easy and wonderful links to Problem Solving, Reasoning and Numeracy as children have to consider Shape, Space and Measures in order to construct or to collage. Children also count materials and often will group small items together e.g. picking out the sequins or pompoms and so there are links to 'Calculating'.
Knowledge and Understanding of the World	A rich collage/junk modelling area can set up many opportunities for Knowledge and Understanding of the World. Children are involved in Exploration and Investigation and Designing and Making. You can also include ICT by putting out materials that have microchips inside, such as greeting cards that 'sing' when opened. Children can also take photographs of their models and collage and so can look back at them and this will help with Time.
Physical Development	Children will be Using Equipment and Materials and so this aspect is covered well. If there are health and safety issues that you point out to children, you may also be looking at Health and Bodily Awareness.
Creative Development	As you might imagine, a rich collage/junk modelling table will cover many aspects of this area of development: Responding to Experiences, Expressing and Communicating Ideas; Exploring Media and Material; and Developing Imagination and Imaginative Play. The only aspect that is not really covered is Creating Music and Dance – unless, of course, children make musical instruments.

What to observe

It is worth looking at how children tackle projects and how persistent they are.

- What materials does the child choose to use?
- What does the child intend to make?
- How easily does the child manipulate the materials?
- How much language does the child use?
- How much support does the child seek from the adult?
- How persistent is the child?

Creating a painting wall

One of the ways in which you can provide children with a wonderful creative experience is by creating a painting wall in your setting. Since I first saw one being used in a French nursery, I have been a real fan of them. At Stepping Stones, the staff had already identified an area which they wished to turn into a workshop. Like many settings they relied on a painting easel, but of course this meant that only two children could paint at a time and also children could not see each other as they painted. Creating a painting wall was quite simple, although did require a little bit of furniture moving. It was wonderful to watch the children enjoy the freedom that having a large space to paint in gives them.

Painting walls are a great way to provide children with a wonderful creative experience.

Benefits of using a painting wall

There are many advantages of creating a painting wall for children. Firstly, children are able to paint on a much larger scale and they can also paint at different heights, for example, from the floor up until just above their heads. This gives children a great sense of freedom. It also prevents situations arising where children stop painting because they have run out of paper. Children are also likely to benefit because they can use large arm movements, so putting up a painting wall works well in toddler rooms. There are social benefits too. Children can watch and be inspired by each other. They can also collaborate on paintings – I have seen many friends work together whilst having a lot of fun. The wall can also be used to teach children specific handwriting movements (see p.78).

There are practical benefits too. The wall can be very versatile. Children can paint side by side in their allocated space or paint as part of a group. By using a wall, you are also not cluttering up precious floor space with an easel. Best of all, there are not lots of finished paintings hanging around waiting to dry.

How to create a painting wall

Creating a painting wall is quick and easy and once organised should provide a permanent place where children can paint and mark.

Identifying a suitable space

The first job is to identify a suitable space. This might mean rearranging furniture as we did at Stepping Stones or being ready to ditch a display area. If you cannot find anywhere within your room, think about whether you can create a painting wall in a corridor or hallway. If you still cannot find anywhere, think next about patio doors or cupboard doors. If you are still struggling, you may need to identify a space outdoors, although it is more likely to be used on a day-to-day basis if you keep it indoors.

Protecting the wall

The next job is to protect the wall. At Stepping Stones, I brought with me a large piece of polythene sheeting. You can buy this off the roll at hardware shops, garden centres and some DIY outlets. You might also like to ask your local furniture shop if they have spare polythene as quite often sofas for the showroom are wrapped in thick plastic sheeting. You could also use 'plasticky' shower curtains which are available in the discount shops. To keep the polythene in place, I used a wide roll of masking tape. This is worth buying fresh as old tape tends to break apart and fairly long lengths are needed for this. Tape all the way around the polythene sheeting.

Creating a boundary

A concern that is often raised is that children will think that it is fine to paint on walls (possibly even at home!). To allay this fear, I suggest that you clearly signal to children that it is a special wall by putting a trim all the way around the painting area. This could be tinsel or those corrugated strips used for display boards. The idea is that the children can clearly see that there is a physical boundary. It also makes the wall more attractive as a feature when it is not being used.

Putting up the paper

Next you need to put up the paper. I would suggest using either large sheets of paper or a roll of paper. On the DVD we used cheap lining paper. Lining paper is quick to put up and also gives children more space to paint. If you wish to create separate children's painting areas, you can just draw vertical lines at regular intervals so that each child can see how much room they have.

A flat surface nearby

As well as the painting wall, you will need to make available some sort of a flat surface near the children. This will allow them to collect paint and tools for the painting wall. In Stepping Stones, we used a table alongside the wall, but you could consider an old-fashioned tea trolley or something similar if you are tight on space.

Covering the floor

Sometimes the best places for a painting wall are in a carpeted area. It would be great to say that this does not matter, but of course it does. One solution is to put down a strip of carpet protector. This has the advantage of being non-slip and it does not ride up. I have also known settings that have put down a large piece of lino and taped it in place.

Items for children to paint and mark with

One of the wonderful things about working with young children is that we are often giving them their first experiences of doing things. Once you have your painting wall in place, you might like to try putting out a range of different articles for children to work with. The eventual idea is that children will come to know what marks are made with different tools so that they can choose what they would like to do. Below are some materials that work well.

Sponges

Look out for natural and man-made sponges of different sizes and shapes. Avoid the ones that give pre-determined shapes such as cars and butterflies as these can be quite limiting for children. Model ways in which you might use sponges alongside children, for example, dabbing movements, swirling movements or using the edges only.

Brushes

I am a fan of having large adult paintbrushes available for children. These give children a great sense of freedom and encourage large movements. (We used these at Stepping Stones.) In addition, children will need other sizes of brushes going from small fine brushes to thick brushes.

Items for printing

It is worth collecting a range of items that can be used for printing. Put these in a specific box so that children understand that they have this particular use. The spider diagram on p.39 shows some of the items that I have found to be quite popular.

Markers

The painting wall can also be used for marking. A range of large markers and felt tips can be put out. Aim to put out only ones that work and if necessary ration the number available.

Building up a picture

One of the great things about a painting wall is that children can keep returning to it and adding on layers. At Stepping Stones, you can see that children were happily sticking collage materials onto the painting. The painting had been done earlier and, once it was dry, the children were adding to it. This is important as children often 'paint and go' and therefore do not learn about the way in which painting can be just the starting point.

Role of the adult

Young children benefit from watching adults paint or mark alongside them. This is particularly true of children under 3 years old. Children often watch our movements and try to copy them, but they also pick up positive attitudes about mark-making and painting. It is therefore important that adults are comfortable using markers and paints alongside children. Some adults feel that they have to be good at drawing or painting, but this is not true. The key is for children to see that adults are ready to concentrate and persevere. It is very important for adults not to make negative comments about their own work as this can make children feel that painting and drawing is something that has to be 'right'. When I work with adults who are not comfortable, I usually suggest that they just enjoy taking the pen or brush 'for a walk' rather than to attempt a full-scale masterpiece. Surprisingly, most adults find that when they focus on the sensation of painting rather than worry about the 'product' they actually find it enjoyable.

Bringing out children's language

As well as enjoying the painting and mark-making experience, we need to think about encouraging children's language use. Talking to children about what they are enjoying is therefore important as is drawing their attention to colours, shades and shapes that they have made. This needs to be done in a chatty style rather than a questioning one, for example, 'That's a lovely shade of red. I think that they call it crimson. It reminds me of a jumper that I had as a child.'

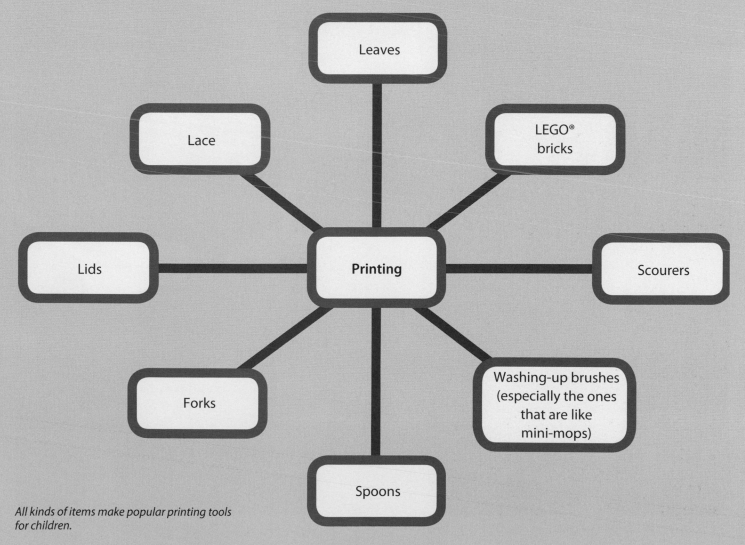

All kinds of items make popular printing tools for children.

Encouraging children to stick collage materials on the painting helps them to see that painting can sometimes be the starting point.

Links to the EYFS

If children are using a painting wall either to draw or to paint, there are likely to be strong links to the EYFS.

Personal, Social and Emotional Development	There is something very powerful about making a large mark on a sheet of paper. Painting or mark-making in this way can therefore link to Dispositions and Attitudes and also Self-confidence and Self-esteem. If children are involved in washing up and clearing away, they will also be covering Self-care.
Communication, Language and Literacy	Large-scale painting and marking link nicely to Writing and Handwriting. It is worth noting that these are two different aspects. Handwriting is about encouraging fine motor development, whilst Writing is about children learning to represent their sounds and words as marks. If adults are working alongside children, there should also be opportunities for Language for Communication and Language for Thinking.
Problem Solving, Reasoning and Numeracy	Painting on a large scale has links to Shape, Space and Measures as children are likely to make marks of different shapes and sizes. For children to benefit, adults need to draw children's attention to this.
Knowledge and Understanding of the World	If children try out new tools and materials, there are clear links to Exploration and Investigation. Where children are representing experiences that they have had, there might also be a link to Time.
Physical Development	If children often use a range of brushes and other tools, Using Equipment and Materials should be nicely covered.
Creative Development	As you would expect, a painting wall will deliver three of the four aspects of creative development. The first aspect is Being Creative - Responding to Experiences, Expressing and Communicating Ideas. There will be clear links to this if children have the opportunity to use a range of materials and are able to talk to each other and adults about what they are doing. Children will also be Exploring Media and Materials and Developing Imagination and Imaginative Play.

What to observe

Mark-making and painting on a painting wall can give us quite a bit of information about the child. Consider these points:

○ How confident is the child in making a mark?

○ Which hand does the child use to make a mark?

○ Does the child notice what other children are doing?

○ Does the child co-operate with other children?

○ What does the child say about the marks that have been made?

○ How engaged is the child in the activity?

Using small trays for painting

For children to learn about colour, it is important that they experience mixing colours and also see a range of different shades. Whilst adult-led activities can specifically look at this with children, I believe that we should incorporate it into children's painting experiences. We did this at Stepping Stones by using small trays and putting very small quantities of paint onto them. You might see the children holding them as they are busy painting. I would expect most children to be able to cope with this by 3 years old.

Benefits of using small trays

Children can mix colours on the tray or on the paper and see how colours combine to create different shades. This helps children later on to notice colour and also gives them the skills to know how to create a particular colour. In some ways, giving children trays is the equivalent to giving them an artist's palette.

This is in contrast to paint that is provided in pots which inhibits children from mixing colour. In addition, painting in this way also helps strengthen children's hand preference as each hand is used for a different purpose: one hand is acting as a stabiliser by holding the tray whilst the other hand is active. (In terms of hand preference, the active hand is likely to become more dominant over time.)

Trays also have some other practical advantages. Firstly, children are not likely to overload their brushes with paint and so have better control of their marks. For practitioners, this means fewer paintings that are dripping wet. It also means that children can be responsible afterwards for washing up their own trays and means less paint is wasted. In my experience, paint in pots tends to turn to a grey-purple hue after a few hours as children usually put the wrong brush into a pot.

Small quantities are key when preparing painting trays.

Combining mark-making and painting with music

Music can change the way that children respond when painting or drawing. It can give children new ideas or help them to express their feelings.

Benefits of combining with music

It is helpful if children learn to enjoy making marks and painting in response to music. Children can learn to focus on certain sounds, for example a loud bang, and to make a mark to symbolise this. Painting or working to music can also mean that children can be exposed to music that is unfamiliar to them. Think about providing classical music and also world music.

What to observe

If you put music on or sing songs as children mark-make or paint, you might like to look out for the following:

O Which children seem to make marks in time with the beat?

O Does the children's painting change according to what they are hearing?

O Do any children make marks in response to specific sounds?

O Do children join in with the music as they are busy?

O Does the music make a difference to their level of concentration?

Links to the EYFS

By simply putting on some music near a painting or mark-making area, there will be links to different aspects of the EYFS.

Personal, Social and Emotional Development	Putting on music can give children a different painting experience and so this links nicely to Dispositions and Attitudes. Children also may gain Self-confidence and Self-esteem as, through a range of music, they can express themselves quite differently. If children sometimes listen to music from different cultures and communities, there will be links to Sense of Community.
Communication, Language and Literacy	Mark-making and painting to music may encourage children to make marks that have meaning for them. This links to Writing. The act of mark-making or painting will, as we have already seen, link to Handwriting. If adults are working alongside children, there may also be opportunities to comment about the mood of the music and so there is a link here to Language for Communication.
Problem Solving, Reasoning and Numeracy	Some types of music may create responses in children which will encourage them to make large or small movements. If these are noticed by the adults, there is a link to Shape, Space and Measures.
Knowledge and Understanding of the World	If children are involved in putting on the CD and using a remote control, there is a nice link to ICT. Using world music and also children's favourite music will also be an opportunity for considering Communities.
Physical Development	As with all painting and mark-making activities, children will be Using Equipment and Materials.
Creative Development	As you might expect, there is a strong link to all of the aspects of Creative Development. Children will be involved in moving to music, linking to Creating Music and Dance and will be Exploring Media and Materials. In addition, some children will find that the music stimulates their imagination, linking to Developing Imagination and Imaginative Play.

Small world play

The term 'small world play' is used to describe imaginative play that involves small-scale figures, animals, cars etc that link to the real world. Imaginative play, especially small world play, really starts to get going from around 3 years old, although younger children may be interested. It would seem to me that there is often a link between children's language development and their interest in small world play and so a child who is 2½ with good language may well be interested. Sandra and her team at Stepping Stones had a good range of small world materials and so all that was required was to add some extras.

Benefits of small world play

Small world play is creative as children use their imagination to literally create a 'small world'. As part of this play, children usually talk to the figures, and so organise their thoughts. Small world play can engage children by themselves, but often children come together and organise their play by talking first. You might hear comments such as, 'you put your train there, and then mine will come along'.

The spider diagram below shows the types of toys that children enjoy using for small world play.

Examples of the small world toys you should have available.

Providing for small world play

Small world play often works best on the floor or on a low table. The table height on which the farm animals were put at Stepping Stones was wonderful. It allowed children to kneel, crouch and stand over the table. I also notice that when a low table is available, children seem more fulfilled in their play. They often take some characters or items below the table, as if they were characters temporarily leaving the stage. When small world play is put out on the floor, children play in a similar way, but often hide items behind cushions or furniture!

Adding in the extras

In order to make small world play more imaginative and potentially more fulfilling for children, it is worth thinking about adding in some extra materials and items for children. At Stepping Stones, I put a small quantity of hay onto the table with the farm animals. I also put out some rubber matting as this had an interesting texture. Earlier in the filming, I had put out a hamster house, which is the ball-shaped straw object with holes that you might just catch sight of. Together these items gave the small world play an additional boost. Children pretend to feed the animals, but also explore the hay. (Note that you would need to check that the hay did not provoke any allergic reactions.) Below is a list of extras that might be worth considering.

Shredded paper

This goes well with animals, including farm animals and dinosaurs. Think about putting out strips of tissue paper so that further texture is added.

Turf

Many garden centres will give you a small piece of turf that you can put in a builder's tray or a gravel tray. Turf can be used with animals and with cars and other types of transport.

Leaves

Autumn leaves and green leaves can work well to create a background for play. If you have a garden area, children may also enjoy collecting the leaves. (Do check that they are not poisonous.)

Ice cubes and blocks of ice

Putting out ice cubes and blocks of ice works well alongside play people, cars and animals. Some settings freeze items inside the blocks of ice – think about putting grass or small leaves inside as well as figures.

Sand, gravel and bark chippings

A small quantity of dry sand, gravel and bark chippings put on to a builder's tray can give children a 'ground' for their play. Providing 'ground' in this way is particularly important for children when they are playing with cars and lorries as well as farm animals. It helps children get more from their play and they are likely to concentrate for longer.

Cardboard boxes, tubes and small tins

The types of items that are normally associated with junk modelling can work well with small world play. It is often better to put these out rather than buy the accessories that come with small world play. Children seem to adapt these and incorporate them into their play in a way that fosters their imagination.

Enclosures

Many children enjoy taking small world toys with them into a small space. This means that a child might enjoy playing with farm animals in a tent or between a gap in the furniture. I often wonder if this allows children to feel that they really are in a world of their own. To support this play, think about creating dens or putting fabric over furniture indoors so that children can play 'privately'.

Bringing in mark-making

Small world play can lend itself to mark-making. If you put out pads and pens, Post-it® Notes or stickers alongside the play, children may often 'write'. Older children sometimes write down the 'rules' for their small world characters, whilst others write their characters' names using letters. Where cars and trains are being used, timetables or signs can be written. Sometimes adults will need to prompt this by making a suggestion or asking if they can write something down. Once children have seen this role modelling, it can give them the impetus to incorporate it into their play.

These children are pretending that this box is a cave.

Links to the EYFS

Small world play can link to many aspects of the EYFS, especially if additional resources, such as writing materials, are provided for children to use alongside it.

Personal, Social and Emotional Development	Children are likely to be concentrating and also enjoying their play and so there is a clear link to Dispositions and Attitudes. Small world play also helps children feel in control and so there are links to Self-confidence and Self-esteem. Assuming that children are also engaged in tidying away at the end of the activity, they will also be doing some Self-care.
Communication, Language and Literacy	Small world play usually prompts children to talk. If they are playing with other children they will be developing Language for Communication, whilst also developing Language for Thinking as they use their language for developing ideas. Small world play also involves intricate hand movements and so there is a link to Handwriting. If paper, pens and other mark-making is part of the play, children may also be Writing.
Problem Solving, Reasoning and Numeracy	There is an opportunity for children to be using Numbers as Labels and for Counting if several characters are put out and adults take time to draw children's attention to the quantity. Children may also sort out characters and items, and if they group them in any way, there is a nice link to Calculating. Finally, if children are playing with boxes, containers and other items that help them to explore size and shape, there is a link to Space, Shape and Measures.
Knowledge and Understanding of the World	There are plenty of links here, providing that small world play is put out with interesting resources for children to explore and use. If this is the case, there are links to Exploration and Investigation and to Designing and Making. In addition, there are potential links to ICT, if you can find resources that complement play which have a gadget aspect to them, such as items that light up or make a sound.
Physical Development	The main link to physical development is Using Equipment and Materials and so it is important that good resources are put out for children.
Creative Development	Small world play links nicely to Being Creative – Responding to Experiences, Expressing and Communicating Ideas. It also has a strong link to Developing Imagination and Imaginative Play. If interesting and unusual resources are provided, children will also be Exploring Media and Materials.

What to observe

Children can find small world play fulfilling in many different ways. Things to observe are:

- How engaged is the child in the activity?
- Does the child play alongside others, on their own or cooperatively?
- How much language does the child use?
- How do they use language, for example, to talk aloud or to communicate with others?
- What does the child use to support their small world play?
- How much does the chid move?
- Which resources seem particularly popular?
- How can you enrich the play further?

Role play

Whilst I tend to use the term 'role play', others may use 'pretend play', 'dressing up' or 'home corner'. Whatever term you use, I suspect that we all know what we mean as we watch children who are pretending to be someone else or who have transported themselves into another world which might be that of a princess, superhero or chef. As with small world play, role play tends to get going once children have some language although even young toddlers will pretend to put a teddy to bed or cuddle a dolly. At Stepping Stones, the children were avid role players. I will never forget their passion for 'cooking' and their desire to make cakes using play dough to sell in the shop. If you are working with children from around 2½ years old, it is worth investing time and a little money in collecting resources and preparing a layout for role play.

Benefits of role play

Role play seems to support children's overall development, but has particular benefits in terms of their social and emotional development and their language development. It is also interesting to see how long children can be engaged in role play and how complicated the plots and stories of older children are.

Providing for role play

By 3 years old, role play is one of the key ways in which children are playing and also learning. This means that role-play opportunities should be created in and out of doors and that equal thought should be given to their provision. Whilst there are no rights and wrongs when it comes to providing role play, over the years I have spotted some things that are worth considering if you wish to improve your role play provision.

More than one role-play area

It is helpful if you create more than one role-play area at a time, for example, a home and a shop. This means that children can move from one area to another and so are able to have more fulfilling play. It also stops overcrowding as children tend to play well in pairs or very small groups. The same is needed outdoors, for example, home and petrol station or home and garden centre.

Creating specific areas for home corner play

To help children play effectively in the home corner, it is worth creating specific rooms, for example, a kitchen/diner, bedroom and lounge. It might be that one day the children have the lounge complete with remote control, screen and cushions or better still a sofa! On another day they may have the nursery complete with baby dolls, changing mat and a cot. By creating different rooms, it means that children who spend a lot of time engaged in home corner play can develop different play patterns and vocabulary. It also means that children who have English as an additional or emerging language are able to see and hear accurate names for items, for example, duvet cover or nappy.

Providing the right props for the right situation

When I am setting up role play, I try to think about what children will need in order to have a satisfying play experience. This means providing as many 'real' props as possible – a metal saucepan with a lid rather than a plastic one, food to cook with or real money to go in the cash till (use larger coins to avoid a choking hazard). When providing props, it is also helpful to focus on the usual sequence of actions associated with any scene. Below is a suggested sequence along with the props required for shopping at a general store.

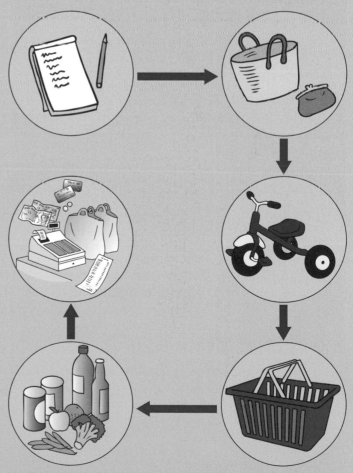

Thinking through the sequence of events will enable you to provide the right props.

49

When settings do not provide key props for children, I have noticed that children are quite good at improvising, for example, when cooking, children will take scoops of sand or buckets of water into the 'kitchen'. Unfortunately for the children, their ingenuity is not always appreciated by staff.

The table below shows some common role play areas and what I would see as essential items to support children's play in areas of home corner play.

Table 2: Role-play areas and essential props.

Role play area	Items
Kitchen/diner	Metal saucepans × 2, wooden spoon, sieve, dried pasta, play dough, baking sheet, silicone fairy-cake cases, rolling pin, mixing bowl, storage tins, table, cardboard boxes to act as a cooker/microwave/etc, plates × 4, cups × 4, knives, forks and spoons, table and chairs, salt and pepper pots (put fine sand inside) and, if possible, washing up bowl with water, drainer and tea towel
Child's bedroom	Basket of toys, lilo or airbed, sheet, duvet cover, pillow, books, cuddly toys
Nursery	Nappy-changing mat, nappies, dolls, cot, baby bottle – with water provided for it, rattle, car seat, high chair, baby's bowl, baby gym, baby blanket and, if possible, baby bath with water.
Lounge	Television and DVD player (can both be made out of boxes), DVDs with cases, remote control, telephone, book case, somewhere to sit e.g. cushions or a sofa, dolls or cuddly toys

Dressing up

Dressing up for some children is an important part of engaging in role play. To this end, children will need some props that support the type of role play being provided, for example, a chef's hat, a fluorescent jacket or a stripy overall. My approach to dressing-up clothes is about giving children a hint of the role rather than fully cladding them. Baskets of props can therefore be a useful way of storing items for children and wherever possible, consider looking for clothing and props that can be used for a variety of roles. I personally find the princess type of ready-made costumes a distraction as many children fight to get them and once they are wearing them do not necessarily use them to be in 'role'. At Stepping Stones, for example, you might spot a lovely girl wearing a princess dress, but who is not actually being a princess, whilst on the other hand, you may equally notice that when the boys were pretending to be cooks, they did not need any clothes. Below is a list of my favourite essential items for a dressing up basket:

- fluorescent jackets
- fabric skirts with elasticated waists
- tinsel
- selection of belts
- selection of ties (sew the knot or use elasticated ones)
- selection of different types of shoes, for example, Wellington boots, trainers, heeled, walking boots
- selection of hats – builders' helmets, disposable forage hats (used in kitchens and factories), hair nets
- selection of scarves
- selection of fabrics – different textures and colours but suitable for children to make into capes or skirts
- adult handbags
- shopping bags
- briefcases
- selection of aprons or overalls, including plastic disposable ones used when nappy changing.

Less is more

I have a 'less is more' philosophy when it comes to equipping role-play areas. Too much stuff crammed into a small area tends to lead to an overall mess and children are not able to play effectively with it. It also means that setting up and tidying away become large operations. I would consider carefully how many of any particular item are required to support children's play, for example, how many cups are needed in a 'kitchen' or how many coins are needed in a cash till? If you are lucky enough to have plenty of props for role play, remember that children love variety and so rotating them rather than having them all out at the same time will often produce better play.

Involving children in the construction of role-play areas

There are times when role-play areas should be created in response to children's interests. These moments are precious and often result in wonderful play and learning with children. If you build on children's ideas, think about how they can retain ownership of their play by making resources, constructing the physical area etc. When children are genuinely involved in the construction of role play, the links across the EYFS will be stronger.

Basing role-play areas around children's knowledge

Successful role play is often linked to the experiences that children have had either directly or indirectly. This means that setting up a role-play area without thinking about children's knowledge base can make it less effective. I remember once seeing a group of children who were meant to be in a space rocket – instead of taking on the role of astronauts they were simply making tea. They were in effect using the rocket as a home corner!

Auditing your role play area

- Do children engage in role play in the designated areas? If not, where do they prefer to play?
- What props and dressing up clothes are used?
- Are these used to support role play?
- Which materials are rarely used or are picked up and quickly discarded?
- Which children rarely engage in role play?
- Do children's language and play vary in role-play areas from week to week?
- How do staff engage with children?
- How often are role play areas extended, created or changed?
- How does role play build on children's experiences?

Changing your role-play area

For me the ideal is always to maintain a home corner and alongside it have at least one other role-play area. There are hundreds of other role-play areas that you can create but the best ones, as we have already seen, reinforce and build on children's knowledge. Below are some examples of role-play areas that I have seen in action on my travels.

Party time

Many children have good memories of parties and so it can be a good role-play opportunity. Party clothes, invitations, food and games all have to be made and organised and so it can be wonderful in terms of learning across all areas of the EYFS.

Animal rescue centre

Most children like animals and an animal hospital or rescue centre can make a lovely role-play area. Consider inviting in staff from the RSPCA, Blue Cross or another local group to talk about their work. Use cuddly toys and encourage children to bring in cat baskets, hamster cages etc.

Corner shop/supermarket

Most children have been inside a local shop or supermarket and so have some knowledge about buying food items. Try to borrow real wire baskets and use real food stuffs to 'line the shelves'.

Shoe shop

Having new shoes is a major event for children. Creating a shoe shop is fairly easy although you may need to borrow a couple of measures for their feet.

In a few days' time the practitioner will create a 'garden centre' role play area to follow up this activity.

Garden centre

A starting point for this is a visit to a local garden centre or finding out which children have been to one. You can also use photographs and film clips of adults working in a garden centre, for example, potting plants, choosing plants or at the till.

Toy shop

Most children enjoy being in a toy shop. Look out for some boxes in which to display items and encourage children to choose the toys that they would like to put in the shop. Consider also visiting a local toyshop to see whether they might provide catalogues, posters or price tags.

Petrol station

Many children have seen their parents fill up with petrol and so creating a petrol station as part of the outdoor play can work wonderfully. Think about using small sections of hosepipe and attaching them to cardboard boxes to create the 'pump'. Look out for car accessories that can be put in the 'shop' area, for example, tools and fluorescent jackets.

Role of the adult

Supporting role play requires sensitivity and great thought. It is important for adults to see role play as a learning opportunity to broaden children's language and knowledge of the world, but at the same time, children do like their privacy in this type of play.

Enriching play

Sometimes the role of the adult is to observe children as they play and to work out ways to enrich their play. This might be done at the time by quickly getting out some additional resources or materials or over a period of time. At Stepping Stones, for example, it would have been great to have found a few white aprons for our budding chefs or a small chalk board so that they could have written up their 'specials'.

Observing development

Sometimes we need to watch children's role play in order to learn more about their individual development. I would always be interested to see how well children use their speech and also what roles they take when playing with other children. It is also interesting to note whether children who are new to English can hold their own with other children or whether they are relegated to having the bit parts –

being the baby, for example. From our observations, we might also plan adult-directed activities, for example, at Stepping Stones, the children's interest in cooking could have translated into making soup.

Joining in and leading play

There are times when adults need to be part of the play or to lead it. The adult may take on the part of a shopkeeper or the driver of a bus. You may have briefly seen in the DVD, that I played the part of a customer in a restaurant at one point. Taking on a role can help shape children's play and is particularly important with young children or those who need additional support. It can also mean that children learn the 'scripts' or vocabulary associated with particular situations.

Giving children experiences

Most children enjoy playing 'home' scenes. This is because they are familiar with them. Whilst this play is fine and needs to be maintained, children will benefit more if they can play out other roles and situations as well. This requires that children have experience of them and so one of the roles of the adult is to plan activities that will give children varied experiences. This might mean taking children on outings, inviting visitors in, reading books or showing children film clips and photographs.

Creating resources with children

Some role play can prompt us to work with the children on related adult-directed activities. A shop, for example, might need cans and boxes to have prices on them or a restaurant may require a menu or a sign. Working with children to help them create resources means that children are developing other skills in addition to those required for role play.

Bringing in mark-making

It is possible to engage children in mark-making alongside role play by simply providing some resources that will act as prompts, for example, a receipt book or till roll in a shop or blank 'parking tickets'. Many settings also find that clipboards seem to appeal to children in role play that involves anything that might require inspection and so is used for building sites. To kick start mark-making, it can be worth the adults in the setting modelling this as they play alongside children.

Links to the EYFS

Providing that role play is carefully supported by adults and that a range of resources and opportunities are available, there are many potential links to the six areas of learning.

Personal, Social and Emotional Development	There are strong links to several aspects of Personal, Social and Emotional Development. Children concentrate on and enjoy this type of play and so there are links to Dispositions and Attitudes. In addition, children take turns and socialise well with children and so there are links to Behaviour and Self-control. Children also gain in confidence when this is part of child-initiated play and so there are links to Self-confidence and Self-esteem. As children often use skills such as dressing and organising their play, there are also links to Self-care. Finally, there are opportunities to incorporate knowledge about other cultures and ways of life and so there are links to Sense of Community.
Communication, Language and Literacy	This is one type of play that has communication at its heart. This means that children use Language for Thinking and Language for Communication. If opportunities for mark-making are also included, there may also be links to Writing. There are also links to Handwriting if children engage with tools and activities involved in fine motor co-ordination.
Problem Solving, Reasoning and Numeracy	Some role-play situations will prompt children to use Numbers as Labels and for Counting and Calculating. Where children are dressing up, using equipment and moving around, there are also links to Shape, Space and Measures.
Knowledge and Understanding of the World	Role play can be linked to Designing and Making if children are creating resources for their role-play area or creating a structure for it. If gadgets, for example a cash register, are included, children will also be using some ICT. It can be useful to take photographs as the role-play area is being created so that children can talk about what they have done – if this is done, there are links to Time. It is also worth building on children's experiences outside the setting when creating role-play areas and so there are possible links to Place and even Communities.
Physical Development	The main link here is with Using Equipment and Materials. If children are engaged in large movements as part of their play, for example role play outdoors, there is also a link to Movement and Space.
Creative Development	The obvious link is Developing Imagination and Imaginative Play, but if children have imaginatively used and created resources, there are also links to Being Creative – Responding to Experiences, Expressing and Communicating Ideas and to Exploring Media and Materials.

Sensory materials

For many young children, the sensory experiences that we provide will allow them to explore materials and media and so be an outlet for their creativity. Even babies enjoy sensory materials. Having a good range of sensory materials is part of providing an enabling and creative environment for children.

Benefits of sensory materials

Sensory materials such as sand, water, or malleable materials as well as things such as gloop (cornflour and water), shaving foam and dried pasta work well because they provide open-ended play. This is why they have been popular with generations of children. Children can scoop, sculpt or simply enjoy the sensation on their hands.

Types of sensory materials

There is no excuse for settings to stick to a diet of sand and water. There are plenty of materials available that will give children different experiences.

For babies and very young toddlers

For this age, you have to choose materials that are safe to be mouthed or swallowed. Consider natural yoghurt, mashed potato, jelly and cold cooked spaghetti. Many settings also use gloop with babies as well. It is worth giving sensory materials after children have eaten so that they are not hungry, and dyeing them with natural blue and green food colouring. These are colours that babies and toddlers do not associate with food.

For older toddlers and children

Once children are no longer mouthing (from around 18 months), the world is your oyster in terms of sensory materials. The list below shows some of the unusual materials that I have seen used in settings:

- Coffee grinds
- Tea leaves
- Shredded paper
- Turf
- Hay and straw
- Fish gravel
- Fresh herbs
- Cat litter
- Gravel
- Shaving foam
- Whisked soap flakes
- Sugar cubes
- Bark chippings
- Sawdust
- Salt
- Cold couscous
- Coloured dry rice
- Cold cooked rice
- Cold cooked spaghetti
- Gloop (cornflour and water)
- Cold baked beans
- Pot pourri.

Providing for sensory materials

Sensory materials can be provided both in and out of doors. (See pp.112–116 for provision of sand and water outdoors.) It is important to have a range of materials – some of which need adult supervision but others that older children can access independently.

Safety issues

The starting point has to be safety. Think about the consequences of a material being on the skin or swallowed and whether it may trigger an allergic reaction in a child. It is therefore worth checking with parents whether children have known reactions to items such as shaving foam or to wheat-based products such as dough. Thought also has to be given to how accidental contact with a child's eye will be managed, for example if sand gets in it. For wet materials such as gloop, shaving foam and water, it is important to provide cloths to stop the floor from becoming slippery.

Containers

Whilst some settings do have the standard sand and water trays, I would argue that they are not essential. Trays of sand on tables can work well as you might spot in the DVD at Stepping Stones. For young toddlers, it is also worth putting an additional container nearby as children of this age love transporting materials. This means that undoubtedly the damp sand will be moved to another bucket or the gloop will be carried on a spoon to a jug.

Below are some popular ways of putting out sensory materials:

Sand and water trays

Commercially produced trays are fine, but they can be very heavy and cumbersome. Avoid moving them when they are full and do not rely only on them as children do need to experience materials in a variety of depths.

Builder's trays

These are large, fairly flat trays with a rim and are available at DIY stores. They can be put onto surfaces or on the ground. They are great for allowing children to climb into.

Cat litter and gravel trays

These are perfect for small scale provision of sensory materials and useful for children who would prefer to play individually.

Mop buckets

Mop buckets or other types of containers work nicely indoors for sand, water and other materials such as dry rice. Children can experience 'depth' although do expect some spills!

What you might provide alongside

As we will see, small world play and sensory materials work well, but children will also need to explore what they can make the materials do. The spider diagram below shows examples of objects that you could provide.

Spoons, scoops and trowels

These can be anything that allows children to dig down or to transfer materials.

Buckets, jugs, beakers and other containers

Look out for anything interesting and preferably non-plastic for children to put materials into – think about metal cream jugs.

Brushes, sticks and combs

Think about items that allow children to prod, poke and make marks.

Treasures

Treasures can include all sorts of items for children to find or put into other materials, for example, fake jewellery, coins and keys.

Small world items

These include toy cars, play people, farm animals and toy dinosaurs.

Tubes

These can be all sizes and lengths and made out of as many materials as possible, for example, plastic guttering, hose pipes and cardboard.

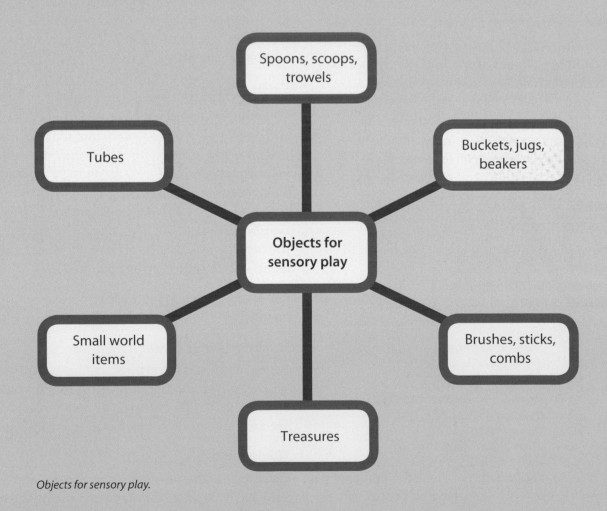

Objects for sensory play.

Links to the EYFS

Personal, Social and Emotional Development	Sensory materials encourage children to play independently and allow them to concentrate and so there are good links to Dispositions and Attitudes. Children also practise many skills which are linked to Self-care, such as pouring and spooning. It is interesting to see how children can often manage to play alongside each other or even cooperatively so there are links to Behaviour and Self-control.
Communication, Language and Literacy	Some children will talk as they play and will 'organise' what they are doing. This means there are links to Language for Thinking. The physical skills that children often gain mean that their hands are being developed ready for Handwriting.
Problem Solving, Reasoning and Numeracy	There are plenty of links to all aspects of Problem Solving, Reasoning and Numeracy, especially Shape, Space and Measures. The objects that are put out with sensory materials can help children to count and they may also group them, so there are links to Calculating. Sensitive interactions with adults can strengthen these links.
Knowledge and Understanding of the World	There are lovely links to Exploration and Investigation as well as to Designing and Making if children have ideas of what they wish to achieve, for example, a sandcastle or landscape for farm animals. It is possible to slip in ICT if you take photographs of children at play and afterwards involve them in bringing the photographs up on screen.
Physical Development	The strongest link for this area of development is Using Tools and Materials as children are likely to be making plenty of fine motor movements and using hand–eye coordination. If you talk to children about why they are washing their hands after using materials, you can link Health and Bodily Awareness in as well. Movement and Space can be linked as long as children are accessing large quantities of materials, for example in a walk-in sand pit or digging outdoors.
Creative Development	As you might expect there are some strong links here particularly Exploring Media and Materials and Being Creative – Responding to Experiences, Expressing and Communicating Ideas. Children are also likely to be Developing Imagination and Imaginative Play if they are using small world toys alongside sensory materials or if there are 'home items' such as pipes, funnels or jugs.

What to observe

- How engaged is the child?
- How long does the child spend using the materials?
- What other materials, objects and tools does the child use?
- Does the child play with others?
- What seems to fascinate the child?
- How could this play be developed?

Button tins

It is useful to provide as many different materials and media for children to explore. On my first visit to Stepping Stones, I took along my button tin as it is an easy activity to provide and, best of all, children love it. Button tins have been a source of fascination for children over a number of years, although in our modern age where clothes are usually bought rather than made, button tins are no longer a household item. This means that many young children today have not experienced the joy of opening up a tin and rummaging inside it to find some treasures. As creative development is about exploring materials and media and giving children new experiences, I would urge settings to put one together.

The joy of rummaging in a tin to find treasures!

Benefits of a button tin

Button tins work well with children as there should be plenty of different colours, textures and unusual items in them for children to explore. The tins often contain odds and ends which children like to pick out and talk about. The buttons themselves can be used for collage or to represent food in role-play areas or treated as magic coins. Items from other cultures, such as the blue glass 'evil eye' that I included in my button tin, can also prompt questions from children and provide an easy way to talk about different cultures. Button tins can also be used to support children's Problem Solving, Reasoning and Numeracy. Watch out on the DVD for how children pick out the red wooden ladybirds and so are almost instinctively grouping and sorting objects.

Putting together a button tin – health and safety

Begin by considering the developmental needs of the children. I always observe children carefully beforehand to determine whether any children are still inclined to mouth. Normally, mouthing disappears at around 18 months, but some children continue regularly to put items in their mouths. If you identify that you have children like this, you will need to choose items that cannot be swallowed. Interestingly, once children are past the mouthing stage, I usually find that if the activity is sufficiently sensory and visually attractive, children do not automatically put things in their mouths. I always put out a large quantity of items as, if there are very few, the sensory impact may not be sufficient and children may out of boredom put a button in their mouth – in the same way they might put a wax crayon in their ear.

What to put in the tin

Look out for as many real buttons as you can. The aim is to provide as many different colours, sizes and shapes as possible. Metal buttons and buttons from baby clothes with pictures on them are particularly valued by children. Try also to put in matching buttons so that when children sort them, they can find ones that are the same. My button tin has been put together from donations from friends, charity shops and also from a request on my local Freecycle forum. **Freecycle** groups match people who have things they want to get rid of with people who can use them, so keeping usable items out of landfills (see www.uk.freecycle.org.) In addition to the buttons, you will need to put in some interesting 'odds and ends'. Below are some of the items that I have found to be popular with children.

Magnets

Try to get as many different types of magnets as possible, for example, fridge magnets or magnets from kitchen doors. Look out for hematites. These are powerful magnetic rocks. They were very fashionable as a play item a couple of years ago when they were known as 'twizzlers'. You may find these in shops selling rocks and fossils.

Wooden animals

The wooden ladybirds that you can see on the DVD were bought in a hobby shop that sells items for making greeting cards. There were ten in a pack. I have a few green wooden turtles as well.

Coins and stamps

Foreign or old coins can grab children's attention and imagination. They can be useful in drawing children's attention to other cultures. I have some Japanese coins that have a hole in the middle. Stamps from other countries can also be a hit – look out for ones which have unusual photographs or pictures.

Raffle tickets

Odd as it may seem, some children are very interested in seeing raffle tickets, particularly if they are folded up. They enjoy looking at the number and often ask what it is for.

Shells

Small shells and large shells are often picked out by children. Look out for ones that are colourful or rough.

Paste jewellery

Any type of item that glitters and looks as if it could be valuable is popular with children. It makes them feel as if they have found treasure.

Varying the contents of the tin

Whatever you decide to put into your button tin, the trick is to pop in new items every time it appears. This means that children's imagination can be sparked anew. You can also put in items that link to a child's existing interest, for example, put in a small dinosaur for a group of children who you have seen playing with dinosaurs.

Presentation

As with many activities, presentation is important. Children enjoy 'opening' up the treasure and so think about finding an attractive box or tin for your collection of buttons. It is worth putting out a metal tray so that children can tip the contents of the tin into it. Consider using roasting tins as they have sufficiently high sides to prevent items from spilling onto the floor. Children also seem to enjoy the swishing sounds that the buttons make on the metal surface. In addition to the buttons, you could put out some small boxes or containers so that children can squirrel away their treasures to show you. It is always interesting to see what children pick out and sometimes their favourites may be a good starting point for other activities.

Role of the adult

I think that this activity needs an adult to be alongside the children for health and safety reasons, but also for children to have someone to share their 'finds' with. I would hope that adults join in with this activity, in the way that Sandra does on the DVD, but also that they encourage children to think about where the items might have come from and what they might like to do with them. This activity can encourage children to do some storytelling alongside the adult.

Links to the EYFS

As well as giving children a chance to explore unfamiliar materials, the button tin links well to the other EYFS areas.

Personal, Social and Emotional Development	Putting a tin on a table and letting children explore it helps them to feel positive about learning and so there is a good link to Dispositions and Attitudes. Children are also exploring the buttons and items by themselves and so there is a link to Self-confidence and Self-esteem. If you include items from other cultures, there is also a link to Sense of Community.
Communication, Language and Literacy	As you can see from the clip at Stepping Stones, children quickly have something to say and so there are good links to Language for Communication and Language for Thinking. In addition, children are likely to be developing fine motor skills and so there is also a link to Handwriting.
Problem Solving, Reasoning and Numeracy	The button tin can be organised in such as way that children will be doing Numbers as Labels and for Counting, Calculating and Shape, Space and Measures. For children to experience these, adults will need to count items, for example, the number of ladybirds, or comment about the way that children have grouped items. Putting out small boxes or tins for children to collect their treasures will also help children with Space, Shape and Measures, especially if you put some items in the button tin that are too large to go in their boxes.
Knowledge and Understanding of the World	As you can see in the DVD clip, there is a nice link to Exploration and Investigation and, if cultural items are included, to Communities. It can be useful to put in old items so that children can notice them and so are covering Time. (I have an old bakelite light switch which children seem to enjoy looking at.)
Physical Development	Children will be Using Equipment and Materials as they move items and have a good rummage around. It is worth noting how easily children pick out and handle items in terms of their co-ordination.
Creative Development	Providing that adults allow children to get on and explore, there are strong links to Being Creative – Responding to Experiences, Expressing and Communicating Ideas as well as Developing Imagination and Imaginative Play. Children will, of course, be Exploring Media and Materials.

What to observe

A good button tin can act as a starting point for further activities. Some children have a clear idea of what they would like to do with items from the button tin. You might like to observe the following:

O How engaged is the child?

O What does the child do when the tin is first presented?

O What does the child notice and pick out?

O What does the child say about the item or items?

O What does the child want to do with the item?

O Does the child try to find similar items?

O What other items are of interest to the child?

O What other items could be put into the tin in future?

Music and dance

This aspect of Creative Development is one that many settings worry about. The good news though is that it is not that difficult to provide for. The aim is not to turn out accomplished Grade 8 musicians or children who are ready to take up ballet. Instead, the aim of this aspect is to give children opportunities to hear, make and appreciate music as well as chances to move and respond to it.

Benefits of music and dance

For many years, links have been made between music and mathematics. This is because music has rhythmical patterns within it and patterns are an important part of understanding number. There are of course plenty of other benefits as well, such as self-expression and often an opportunity for children to hear and respond to music that is different from that which they encounter in their home environment.

Choosing instruments

Children need to explore a variety of different sounds. This means that you should try, over time, to build up a collection of different types of instruments – home-made and bought. Avoid instruments that are delicate or expensive and so are likely to cause adult anxiety if children are using them roughly or drop them! It is also worth having several that are the same so that squabbles do not break out over a favourite. When choosing an instrument, listen to the sound it makes and think about how skilful the child will need to be to create a sound. Try also to have a selection of tuned and untuned instruments.

Making instruments

Some settings feel that unless they have 'proper' instruments they cannot deliver this aspect. Whilst a selection of instruments can be useful, they are not essential because home-made instruments can still give children wonderful sounds to explore. If you make a range of instruments with children you will also be covering many other EYFS areas of development.

Singing

It is essential that children hear adults sing. This needs to begin as soon as possible and so babies should be sung to. Whilst you may worry about the sound of your voice, the good news is that children don't. Anything goes and so, if necessary, begin by singing along to

Have a range of instruments available so children can explore sounds.

taped music before venturing out on your own. Action rhymes as well as nursery rhymes with props can also help to take the focus off you! Once children have developed a repertoire, you may find that they start to change words or sing when they are involved in other activities, e.g. whilst painting.

Dance

Providing opportunities for dance needs to be thought about in the context of 'moving to music'. This means finding music to interest children – look out for music with strong beats and rhythms. Props such as scarves, fabrics and even masks can also help children to move to music. To be honest, there is an element of trial and error, but once you have found music that children enjoy, you can build on this. If you work with babies, providing for dance is about picking up the baby whilst you dance to the music. Babies tend to love this and quickly develop favourite songs!

Role of the adult

This is one area where adults may need to show a little direction. Try modelling actions yourself so that children can copy you, for example, for music – model loud and soft, for dance – model fast and slow. Having said this, you may find that some children will want to do their own thing and provided that their actions are safe, do not worry – the key is that they enjoy musical experiences. Try also to work in very small groups or pairs with children so that you do not spend your time doing crowd control. It is also important to introduce children to a range of music so look out for jazz, reggae and classical music as well as music from different cultures and countries. In record shops, this is often categorised as 'world music.'

Links to the EYFS

Personal, Social and Emotional Development	Music and dance is part of self-expression and so there are links to Self-confidence and Self-esteem. Providing that opportunities for music and dance are enjoyable, there are also links to Dispositions and Attitudes.
Communication, Language and Literacy	Children's speech and language can be promoted through nursery rhymes and songs. This means that there are links to Language for Communication. Music and dance also help children to notice individual sounds and so can support Linking Sounds and Letters.
Problem Solving, Reasoning and Numeracy	It is thought that music has close ties with mathematics. Nursery rhymes that deal with counting will link to using Numbers as Labels and for Counting. Through dance, children will also experience Shape, Space and Measures.
Knowledge and Understanding of the World	Music and dance can be linked to ICT if children are involved in recording the music that they make or use the CD player. If you use world music and also take the time to talk about their favourite music, there are good links to Communities.
Physical Development	Dance links nicely to Movement and Space whilst, if children are also using instruments, there are links to Using Equipment and Materials. With older children you can also draw in aspects of Health and Bodily Awareness.
Creative Development	Music and dance link, of course, to the Creating Music and Dance aspect as well as Responding to Experiences, Expressing and Communicating Ideas. If you put out props and materials for children to touch and use alongside music, they will also be Exploring Media and Materials.

What to observe

It is interesting to watch children as they are involved in music and dance.

○ Can the child move or react to the beat?

○ Does the child sing along or try to vocalise when you sing?

○ How does the child move to music?

○ Does the child enjoy using props to help them move to music?

○ Does the child have a favourite instrument/shaker?

○ Does the chid have favourite songs and music?

Your questions answered

○ *We are not allowed to use sand in our setting as it might scratch the floor. What can we do?*

I am aware that some settings that use rented premises do have restrictions placed upon them. Firstly, think about whether you can provide sand outdoors, even if you put it out in small quantities in trays. For indoors, consider a range of other sensory materials that will still give children the opportunity to explore textures (see pp.112–116).

○ *How should we respond to parents who are not happy unless their child brings a painting home each day?*

For some parents, a painting is proof that their child has had a good day and that the child has 'done' something. Unfortunately, not all children will play in ways that will produce an end product and so we may need to show parents film clips and photographs of their child engaged in activity. It can also be worth letting parents know that children may be working on some paintings or models over a series of days, for example, painting then mark-making before collaging.

○ *What if a supervisor likes everything to be tidy in the setting?*

Satisfying play for children that will allow them to be creative is not usually associated with tidiness! Having said that, it is important that areas remain attractive and safe and so there needs to be a balance. For me, one of the roles of the adults is to discreetly pick up things that have been discarded in the midst of play and also to quietly rearrange things so that they remain attractive. (You may spot me doing a little of that at Stepping Stones when the children were having a great time and were engaged in role-play.) Stopping children who are purposefully engaged in play to ask them to tidy up is likely to interrupt their train of thought. On the other hand, once children's activity has come to an end, it is important that they help clear up and if necessary clean up.

○ *Should we use ready mixed paint or powder paint?*

I have to confess to being a fan of ready mixed paint, provided that children have it on trays. Powdered paint (unless thickened) can be watery and whilst it is cheaper it is not always that satisfying. If ready mixed paint is put out in small quantities rather than in pots, it can go a long way and it is possible just to order the primary colours plus white and maybe black. Powdered paint can have its uses, for example for wax resist pictures, and so ideally settings should also have small quantities of it in stock.

○ *Should we get specialists in to do music and dance with the children?*

There is no particular requirement to get specialists in to do music and dance with children provided that you are creating opportunities for these activities. In the EYFS, most people with a little confidence do have the skills to deliver music and dance. If you decide to use a specialist, make sure that they understand the developmental needs of the children and also remember that children will benefit more from spending time in small groups with the specialist.

○ *Can we use CDs of rhymes and songs?*

Like many areas of our work with children, the key is 'moderation'. Children are better having a 'live performance' but CDs can be a good starting point if you do not know the words of rhymes or tunes. They can also be useful if you want children to move to the beat or accompany a tune with musical instruments. Buy good quality CDs that have rich sounds so that children can distinguish between the tracks (some sound all the same) and avoid relying on them all the time. Children do need the 'real thing'!

Observation and planning

One of the key topics that comes up time and time again is observation and planning. Along with assessment, observation and planning are requirements of the current EYFS that seem to keep giving people headaches. This is why I chose to focus on it for this book and accompanying DVD. For the DVD, we chose a childminder to work with as childminders have the same level of observations to carry out, but often have to find ways that are quick and easy. Lorna, who runs a successful childminding business with Richard, her co-minder (and husband), was an ideal candidate as she is interested in, and already using, digital methods to enhance her work. As you will see on the DVD, she was also great at sharing her ideas with me. Observation and planning is a huge area and whilst the DVD looks at digital ways of working, this chapter will look at ways in which you might create an observation system that links to planning. The following areas are covered in this chapter:

- Reviewing your observation and planning system
- Basic principles of observation
- How to create an observation process
- Traditional methods of observing children
- Using digital technology
- Types of digital technology that you can use
- Bringing it all together
- Suggestions for focused observations

Reviewing your observation and planning system

It is easy to read this kind of book and have a panic. Many settings are already doing a good job in terms of observation and planning for their children. Whilst this chapter will give you some ideas and suggestions for structuring your observation and planning process, it is worth first of all reviewing your own system. You may like to think about the following questions:

- How often are children observed in the setting?

- How much time is taken up with observation?

- Are you using technology to reduce the amount of work?

- Do observations cover all areas and aspects of development?

- Are you using a range of methods?

- Are observations evaluated regularly?

- Are the observations used to inform short- and medium-term planning?

- Would it be clear to others, for example, an Ofsted inspector or potential parent, how your observations and assessments feed into the planning process?

- Are parents involved in the observation and planning process?

Basic principles of observation

There has been such a focus on observing children that sometimes I find myself wondering whether staff in some settings are actually spending enough time interacting with children. This is not to say that there is not value in observing children – clearly it is fundamental to good practice – but we must not lose sight of why we observe and how to achieve quality observations that are of use. Observations for observations' sake are a total waste of time and so you need to make sure that any observations you organise are genuinely purposeful.

Purposes of observing children

There are many reasons why observation is vital in terms of working effectively with children. You can only work well with children over a period of time if you understand what makes them tick and what to provide to support their developmental progress. Doing it for Ofsted or to create data for government bodies are not reasons that are on my list. Below

are the reasons I would suggest for why it is vital to observe children.

To understand the child

Children come with different temperaments, personalities and interests. Over even relatively short periods of time, children change and develop. The toddler of today may become the setting's superhero of tomorrow. Through sensitive observation of children, we should start to answer the following types of questions.

- How outgoing is this child?

- How does the child cope with changes and new experiences?

- Who does the child like being with?

- What activities, resources or toys seem to engage the child?

- How does the child express fear, frustration and anger?

- Where and in what situations is this child at their most happiest?

- What is this child like when they are at home?

What interests each child? This one is very interested in puppets!

To monitor and support children's progress

Whilst children may not follow exactly the same developmental pattern, we should see that over time children do make progress. We should be able to recognise their developmental progress, and know how to support ongoing progress. By observing children, we should be able to answer these types of questions at any given time.

- How well is this child progressing given their age?

- Are there any areas of development that may need additional support?

- Are there any factors that might affect this child's development?

- What equipment, resources and play opportunities would benefit this child?

To share experiences with parents

Parents usually like to know what their children have been doing whilst they are with us. Quality observations help us to share experiences with parents. It should be a two-way process so that we can also learn about the child at home. If we are working well with parents, we should be able to answer these types of questions:

- How do the parents feel about their child's progress?

- What do they notice about their child at home?

- What do they feel the child will benefit from whilst they are with us?

- What do they feel the child's next steps might be?

- Do they have any particular ambitions for the child?

- Do they have any concerns about their child?

To use for individual and group planning

Just finding out about children is only half of the process. Observations should also help us plan activities and provide resources to ensure that children have an enjoyable and challenging environment. Think about the following questions:

- How are children's interests used to support their learning?

- What do children do at home that they might like to follow up in the setting?

- What experiences do children need in order to further their development?

- What level of support do individual children need and how is this to be provided?

- Do some children need to be grouped together if they have strong friendships?

In addition, we need to have information ready to pass on to others who work concurrently with the child, for example, a child may go to a nursery and then to a childminder. We also need to prepare information ready for when children move on to a new setting, for example, to a school.

Observations can also inform practice

Whilst the focus of most observations is on the individual child, we can also use them to think about what they tell us about our provision. When a whole group of children seems uninterested in activities, a reflective practitioner should be thinking about whether the activity is suitable or sufficiently enjoyable.

How to create an observation process

It is important that you create a system that works for you, the children and the parents when it comes to observing, assessment and planning. Once you have thought about your system, it can be worth showing it as a flow diagram. This means that you can explain it to anyone that needs to know – this might be an Ofsted inspector, a prospective parent or, in group settings, a new member of staff. Putting your system on paper will also help you realise whether you are really connecting your planning with observations. An example of an observation system is shown on p.68.

Storing observations and planning

As you can see in the DVD, I am keen for settings to develop digital records alongside the traditional paper-based ones. You will need to create records for each child that you work with. This could be solely on computer, but being realistic, a combination process is probably the most sensible. Whilst we look at storing digital records on pp.86–88, you also need to ensure that paper records are secure. Parents also have to give permission for observations and you may need to talk about what they are happy to have 'out in the open'. At Lorna's, for example, she keeps the children's individual records in separate folders, but does put out on the wall

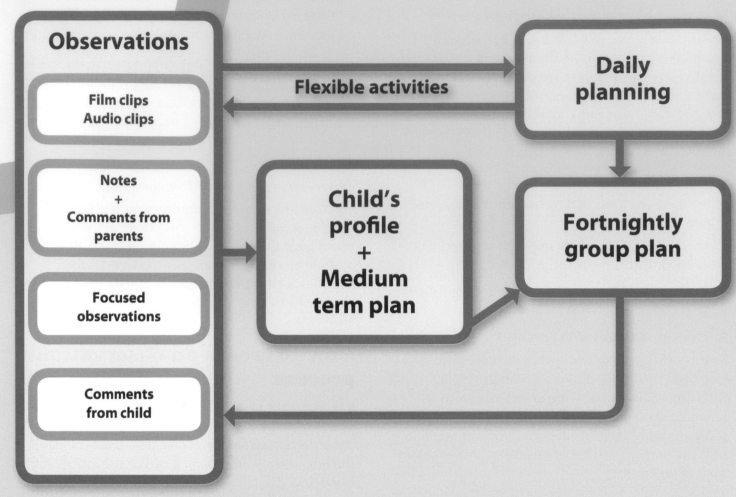

An example of an observation system.

individual planning sheets. Interestingly, I find that most parents are quite relaxed about having notes about their child put up on walls, provided they are not negative or contain particularly personal information. All personal information about children and their families falls under the Data Protection Act and so if you are not sure about how to comply it is worth visiting www.ico.gov.uk.

Creating a tracking system

A good starting point when creating an observation system is to create a tracking sheet. A tracking sheet should save you from duplicating similar types of observations and ensure that you cover the whole range of a child's development.

The sheet should at a glance show the name of the child and what information has already been tracked over a period of time, for example, monthly or three-monthly. The period of time will correlate with how often you put together a summative document which shows the child's overall progress. This might take the form of a report, sheet or overview (see pp. 90–91). For babies, I would suspect that you will need to develop a system whereby you summarise their progress each month or every couple of months. This is because over a course of four to eight weeks their interests and developmental stage will have changed. For toddlers and older children, you might summarise their development in some format every two or three months.

How to create a tracking sheet

A tracking sheet should cover each of the areas of development along with the sub-sections, that is, communication, language and literacy, sub-divided into six aspects as my example below shows. As you complete an observation, work out what aspects have been covered and put a date alongside with a reference which will help you to find the relevant observation later.

In addition, if you are very keen, you can number your observations – this should allow you to find them quickly – so do consider doing this, especially for digital methods. It would also be an idea to include observations that parents have carried out at home, for example, a parent may have brought in a film clip to show you.

I use a coding system on the tracking sheet to ensure that I am using a variety of methods:

- **F** for film clip
- **A** for audio clip
- **TC** for target child method
- **Ch** for checklist
- **S** for Snapshot
- **WR** for written record
- **G** for Group observation.

Observation Tracking Sheet

Name of Child		Key Person		Date	04/07/10

Personal, social and Emotional

1 Dispositions and Attitudes	2 Self-confidence and self-esteem	3 Making relationships	4 Behaviour self-control	5 Self-care	6 Sense of Community
19/7/10F4	16/7/10G7	20/7/10TC5	7/9/10WR3		19/7/10F4 20/7/10TC5

Communication, Language and Literacy

1 (L for communication)	2 (L for Thinking)	3 (Linking Letters and Sounds)	4 (Reading)	5 (Writing)	6 (Hand writing)
19/7/10F4 20/7/10TC5	19/7/10F4	20/7/10TC5			

Observation tracking sheet.

Using the tracking sheet to plan observations

As you can see from the example, a tracking sheet should at a glance show you any areas that need to be observed. This in turn means that you can plan to observe the child in the following week. In some cases, you might even consider organising an adult-led activity which will help you to focus on the child's knowledge and skills. I find that settings that have this type of systematic approach to observing children are more likely to focus on the provision of activities and the environment, which will enable children to access all aspects of the EYFS curriculum.

Observing progress and development

As well as planning observations to ensure that we see all aspects of children's development, it is essential that we know what to look out for. This is where practitioners' personal knowledge of child development comes in. If you are not up to speed on child development or it has been a while since you refreshed your knowledge of milestones, there is a real danger that you may not recognise when children need extra support or, on the other hand, that their behaviours are typical for their age group. Lorna, as you can see in the DVD, was a joy to work with as she had a strong knowledge of child development and was therefore able to look at children accurately and see what was significant about their reactions. When I took out the little white puppet, for example, she recognised that it would be a good tool for one little girl who usually reacts to 'stranger danger' which is common in her age group. Because Lorna knew what is 'normal' for the age range, she did not make comments about the child being shy or see that her behaviour was in any way a problem, which a less experienced practitioner may have done.

Preparing for observations

As well as sometimes planning observations in advance, I would also urge practitioners to look at the normative development for the age group that you work with. Use a book such as Carolyn Meggitt's *Child Development: An Illustrated Guide* (2006) or anything that gives you clear milestones that are age related. This means that before you observe the child you will already have a picture of what is fairly typical for the age range. Anything that the child should be doing, or that is atypical, can then be more easily spotted and you will also get a feel of where the child is in relation to his overall age group. Some practitioners

who have done this also say that this preparation helps them with the actual writing as it can be hard to 'find the words' to express something that you see in an observation.

Below is an excerpt from *Child Development: An Illustrated Guide* by Carolyn Meggitt (Heinemann, 2006) that deals with the behaviour of two year olds – I love these descriptions!

Children:

- are beginning to express how they feel
- are impulsive and curious about their environment
- are eager to try out new experiences
- may be clingy and dependent at times, and self-reliant and independent at others
- often feel frustrated when unable to express themselves – about half of 2-year-old children have tantrums on a daily basis
- can dress themselves independently
- often like to help others, but not when doing so conflicts with their own desires.

Linking the milestones to the EYFS areas of development

Whilst the normative development guides are very useful in helping you to pinpoint a child's development, they do not necessarily link perfectly with the areas of development within the EYFS. The table on p.71 shows how they can fit together.

Using the Development Matters statements

The Development Matters statements in the *EYFS Practice Guidance* were meant to give practitioners a very general idea about what children might be doing. It was impossible for the team creating the EYFS to cover each area of development from 0–5 years in great detail without the document becoming enormous. The ages were widely banded to prevent settings from turning them into checklists. Unfortunately, that is what many settings have done with them. I would advise that you look at the Development Matters statements alongside normative development as the combination will help you to

Table 3: Normative development guides.

EYFS areas of development	Normative development
Personal, Social and Emotional Development	Social and Emotional Development
Communication, Language and Literacy	Speech and Language
Problem Solving, Reasoning and Numeracy	Cognitive Development
Knowledge and Understanding of the World	Cognitive Development
Physical Development	Physical Development
Creative Development	Cognitive Development, Social and Emotional Development

make effective statements about children's progress. It is also useful to use the CD-ROM that comes with the EYFS pack as some of the Development Matters statements are expanded – click on the 'Early Support' button. In the box opposite is the basic statement for Language for Thinking that covers 0–11 months and underneath it is the expanded version using the Early Support button.

This child has clearly mastered using facial expressions!

Language for Thinking

The basic statement:

○ Communicate in a variety of ways including crying, gurgling, babbling and squealing.

○ Make sounds with their voices in social interaction.

The expanded statements:

○ Cries to express needs, for example, when hungry, angry or in pain.

○ Gurgles to get attention.

○ Turns quickly to hear your voice across the room.

○ Listens to familiar voices even if they can't see the person.

○ Vocalises back when talked to (making own sounds) especially to familiar people and when a smiling face is used.

○ Responds differently to different tones of voice (for example, sing-song, questioning, soothing and playful) as the tone of voice helps them to understand the meaning.

○ Uses voice, gesture, eye contact and facial expression to make contact with people and keep their attention.

○ Vocalises more when adults use child-directed speech.

Who should carry out observations?

The majority of observations should be carried out by the people who spend the most time with the child. This is likely to be the child's key person or shared key people as well as the parents. It is also worth asking other staff to contribute to the observations process as quite often they will notice small things on a day-to-day basis. From time to time, it can also be worth getting another member of staff to carry out a comprehensive observation of a child's development – using normative milestones as a basis. This is because it can be hard to be objective when you see a child every day. As a childminder, this may be a little more difficult if you do not co-mind as Lorna does with her husband. There are, however, many drop-in sessions that childminders attend and, providing that you obtain parental consent, it might be worth considering whether you can 'swap' children with another childminder for the purposes of carrying out an observation.

Involving parents in observations

Parents need to be as involved as possible in the observation and planning process. Parents often see things in their child that we miss or notice things that they do at home. As many children are often taken on outings, be they trips to the supermarket or an appointment at the hospital, parents will also see children in different situations. Exchanging information with parents can take the form of a quick chat at handover, a 'home/setting' book or even the odd email. There is no hard and fast rule as to how it should be done, but we should make every attempt to work closely with parents. It is interesting for example to tell the parent about something that you have observed in the setting and see if the child does a similar thing at home, for example, putting shoes on or making rotational marks with a felt tip pen.

On the DVD, we can see how Lorna is very good at involving parents in their child's progress, but I did suggest that she needed to see if parents wanted to be able to contribute their photographs to the child's records; the parent who was filmed that day seemed interested in doing this.

On my travels I have found pre-schools and nurseries that invite parents in from time to time and ask them if they would like to observe their child in the setting. This is a good idea as it can help parents to see their child in an environment very different from the home.

It can also help some parents become aware of just how important play is to children's development.

Frequency of observations

A question that I am frequently asked is how often observations should be carried out on children. This is a hard one to answer at it will depend on the adult–child ratio, how long the child spends in the setting and what type of recording method is being used. I am a great fan of planning observations so that a variety of methods are used and that a quality observation is generated. This prevents staff time being wasted and also ensures that a proper assessment of the child's progress can be carried out. Wherever possible, I believe that observations should not take practitioners 'out of the action' as we know that quality interactions with adults are actually a major factor in promoting progress.

Length of observations

Most observations can be short, but occasionally, it is worth tracking a child's activity over a longer period of time. This works well especially with older children as it is important to assess their concentration span during any given activity and identify whether their play choices are influenced by other factors such as friends. On p. 77, I outline a method whereby you can track children for a longer period.

Traditional methods of observing children

There are several different ways of observing children and formats for doing so. I would always suggest that several different ones are used in order to compile a summative assessment (see pp. 90–91) or for adding to the child's profile. This is because some methods are better than others at catching children's development or interests. At Lorna's, they use a variety of methods with Lorna favouring digital ways and Richard, her co-minder, being what I would call a 'paper and pen' man.

In this section, we look at some of the traditional methods before moving on to explore digital methods.

Day-to day-observations (non-recorded)

If you work well with children, you should be observing them every day. This may not result in you writing anything down, but it is observation nonetheless. These observations are essential and

if they are properly acted on can affect the child's immediate experiences, for example, if you see a child who is looking bored, it's a signal that you should change tack or activity.

Below are some of the points that I suggest you note when children first come into the setting, as they may help you to adjust your way of working to meet the immediate needs of the child.

- How relaxed does the child seem?
- Does the child show signs of tiredness, for example, have dark rings under the eyes?
- Does the child seem distracted or anxious?
- Does the child seem excited?
- How easily has the child separated from their parent or care-giver?

During the session or day you might also like to note the following and again adjust your way of working depending on what you have observed.

- How is the child engaging with other children?
- What has been of interest to the child during the session?
- What resources, toys or activities have held the child's attention?
- How much interaction and adult attention has the child received?
- How tired or hungry does the child seem?

Acting on these day-to day observations

I am a great fan of seeing actions as a result of what has been observed. For me, the actions of staff show that they are using the information they have learnt about the child. Without acting on what we have observed and using our findings to work effectively with children, there is little point in doing them. Here are some ways in which we can turn the day–to-day observation points into possible actions.

Share with parents

Many parents like to know what their child has been doing and will also need to know if we have spotted anything that is likely to affect their child's health and well-being, for example, tiredness or being off their food. A quick word at handover is usually enough or, for babies and toddlers, a note in a home book/email, since they do not have the language to tell their parents what they have been doing.

Share with other care givers

We are meant to be working in collaboration with other professionals and so if the child is going to be with another professional, it is important that we share anything of significance with them. (Note that parents have to give their consent for this.) A quick phone call or email or a regular contact book which goes with the child will allow for better transition.

Planning for the next session using a response sheet

When I was with Lorna, I showed her how to use what I call a 'response sheet' to make a note of anything that had occurred as a result of the day-to-day observations. The idea behind a response sheet is to note down anything that needs to be acted on or is significant during a session, for example, if a child or group of children have really enjoyed using a resource, it is worth making a note of it so that it can be put out on the next session. Ideally, it needs to be put in a location where staff can easily access it. It can be used to note down information that is gained from any observations that have been carried out in the day by using methods such as Post-it® Notes, film and audio clips.

Below is an example of the response sheet that I suggested Lorna might like to try. There is no set format for this and you may like to tinker around to create a sheet that will work well in your setting. I would suggest the following columns though, as a minimum:

- date and time
- name of the child
- what has been observed of significance
- suggestions for action or next steps.

As Lorna knew her way around the EYFS extremely well, I suggested that she might also make links to the curriculum, but this will only work if staff can rattle them off easily. The idea of this sheet is not to stop the action whilst staff go out and find the EYFS *Practice Guidance*. I also suggested to Lorna that she might show on this sheet whether she had evidence of what had been observed, for example, a reference to a film clip or a Post-it® Note. This would allow her to show a link between this short-term planning and her observation process. During the filming, I suggested to Lorna that afterwards, the sheet could be cut into strips so that the notes she made relating to a particular child could be added into their records.

Response Sheet

Date _____

Name of Child	Observed by	What has been noticed	Links to EYFS	Suggested next steps
Nilufer	Penny	Nilufer managed two buttons on her coat	Self-Care (PSED)	Staff to encourage again
Emmanuel	Vicky	Wants to play snap again tomorrow	Dispositions and attitudes (PSED) Calculating (PSRN)	Play again – perhaps with Sarah?
Alicia	Shane	Picked up and looked at Gruffalo for ten minutes	Reading (CLL)	Read this as a group tomorrow? Could do some role play

My suggested response sheet.

Daily records – a daily summary

Parents of young children, especially babies and toddlers who may not be speaking, do like to have a record of what their child has done. Lorna puts together a quick record for parents, which is shown below. If you do this, get some feedback from parents as to what information is important for them. For example, Lorna lets parents know what food was offered to the child alongside the activities that have engaged them. I also like the way that Lorna includes a photograph of the child. I think this is a wonderful touch.

Written methods

There are many different written methods of observing children. Popular ones at the moment include using Post-it® Notes and writing a 'snapshot' of the child which may form part of a child's learning journey. A purist approach to using written methods is to write in the present tense and record only what you are seeing at the time. This is difficult and so I know that many

(2)

Daily Information

Child's name Samuel   Date: 9.3.10

Breakfast Weetabix

Lunch Ham sandwiches, grapes, banana, yoghurt.
Snack Apple and Rice cakes
Dinner Cottage Pie and vegetables. Yoghurt.

Sleep 1pm - 2pm.
Toileting Excellent today - no accidents

Activities Today we played in the garden. Sand and waterplay. Played a shape game.

Additional Information Newsletter given to parent

Parent Signature _____

Samuel joined in with others playing a "shape" game. He matched some of the shapes. He became very interested in Triangles - PSRN

Next Step: Follow Samuel's interest of shapes - starting with triangles

Lorna's daily record.

practitioners watch what has happened first and then write about it afterwards.

Advantages of written methods

The main advantage is that you only need a pen and pad and so you can sometimes organise an observation at short notice.

Disadvantages of written methods

It is a real skill to keep your eyes on the child and manage to turn what you have seen into words and do so accurately. If you struggle with this, do not despair – firstly it is a skill that you can improve with practice and, secondly, you could consider filming instead (see p.84).

Post-it® Note observations

Many settings find it useful to record a 'snapshot' of a child onto a Post-it® Note. These can work well, provided that what has been written down is significant and accurate. Settings also have to be careful that the child's name and the date are put down and that the observations are then looked at to work out next steps. You could consider combining Post-it® Notes with the response sheet. I would also ask practitioners to keep looking at the tracking sheet in order to be aware of what in particular needs to be observed during the week. Otherwise there is a danger of very repetitive observations.

> 26/4
>
> Ayse using left hand consistently whilst playing snap. Right hand used to hold cards.
> P. D

An observation on a Post-it® Note.

Learning stories or journeys

This is a lovely way of both observing children and providing a structure for planning for individual children. This method works well with all age ranges and is popular with parents. If this is going to be the main method that you choose to rely on it will be important that you do plan some of the observations so that you can be sure you are looking at each aspect as well as each area of a child's learning and development. Most learning journeys will include a photograph of the child engaged in the activity and this is what partly adds to their charm.

Below is a suggested sequence for creating a learning journey.

1. Plan what it is that you would like to 'catch'.

2. Take a photograph of the child engaged in the activity.

3. Write a short written record using the 'written record' style. (You may need to copy it out later, if you find writing neatly at speed difficult.)

4. Work out which aspects of development have been observed.

5. Draw some conclusions about what you have seen.

6. Make some suggestions of what the next steps might be for the child and how they are to be supported.

7. Transfer the next steps into the short-term or medium-term planning.

Taking photographs is a quick and easy way of recording activities.

Time samples

I am a great fan of time samples and feel that they are quite under-used in settings. A time sample allows you to track a child's activity over a period of time – I would suggest 40 minutes would be useful. Whilst it is a written method, you do not have to keep recording for the full time and so it does allow you some 'thinking time'. An example of a time sample sheet is shown below.

It is particularly helpful as a way of collecting a lot of information with children who are over 2 years old – especially during child-initiated activities. You can carry out a time sample whilst working with other children provided that your 'target child' does not disappear outdoors whilst you remain inside! Even then, you could ask a colleague to carry on for you.

How to organise a time sample

1. Create a simple grid on a sheet of A4 paper.

2. Wear a watch! Decide on a start time and then aim to record at five-minute intervals.

3. At the start of each five-minute period, make a note of what the child is doing and whom they are with. Then carry on with whatever you are doing – the idea is that you literally sample the child's activity.

4. Analyse the time sheet and consider the following:

   - Did the child engage with other children during this period?

   - Did the child stay at a single activity?

   - What developmental skills did the child show?

   - Did the child have any particular interests?

   - Did the child engage with any adults?

Time Sample Sheet

Name of Child		
Date		Carried out by
Time		Comments
10.00		
10.05		
10.10		
10.15		
10.20		
10.25		

Example of a time sample sheet.

Checklists or tick charts

Checklists or tick charts are simple to use and the observer simply has to decide whether or not the child has developed the skill in question. Few of the Development Matters statements can be used as checklist statements – they were never intended to be – and so the golden rule of using a checklist is to make sure that the statement is relevant. I have never really liked checklists or tick charts, but I have started to change my mind of late. Firstly, many children no longer see health visitors as frequently as in the past. Secondly, I am finding that not all practitioners are confident about age/stage when it comes to language and physical development. This means I now suggest that settings should use some sort of developmental checklist that is age-related from time to time. This might identify some children who need support earlier than if you rely just on either your 'hunch' or the Development Matters statements.

The danger of using the Development Matters statements alone is that, because of their wide banding, you may not pick up that a child is not making expected progress. You can either use commercially prepared developmental checklists or create your own using child development books such as *Child Development: An Illustrated Guide*.

Using a checklist and tick chart

1. Make sure that you read through the statements and check you understand them.

2. Look out for the behaviours listed or set up specific situations whereby the child is likely to show them.

3. Expect that a checklist may need to be completed over a week or so.

4. Recognise that children sometimes do things on one day but not on another.

5. Decide how much support the child has required – the aim is to assess what the child can do unaided.

Physical Development 2–3 years	Date observed
Strings 4 large beads in 4 minutes	
Turns door knobs, handles etc	
Jumps on the spot with both feet	
Walks backwards	
Walks downstairs with aid	
Throws ball to adult 150 cm away	
Builds tower of 5–6 blocks	
Turns pages one at a time	
Unwraps small object	
Folds paper in half in imitation	
Takes apart and puts together snap-together toy	
Unscrews lid on bottle	
Kicks large stationary ball	
Rolls balls out of dough	

Example of a checklist.

Group time samples

In my last book (*Penny Tassoni's Practical EYFS Handbook*), I suggested a way of tracking groups of children in group-care settings. As this has proved popular with many settings I would like to expand upon its uses and also share it with those of you who have not tried it.

The origin of the group time sample began when I was asked to support a pre-school which had difficulties with children's behaviour. I wanted to find a way of establishing exactly what was happening, how engaged children were in the activities and resources as well as the way in which staff were being deployed – a tall order. I decided to create something that was a cross between a target child method and a time sample and use it to focus on eight out of the 24 children. I felt that this would give me a representative sample as I would be looking at a third of the children over an hour. The time sample element allowed me to track children over a period of time whilst using my personal coding system, I could keep a track of the action. If you look at the example provided on p. 80,

you will see that very little is actually written, but I am able to remember quite a lot with the codes and notes that I have used.

What to use this method for

This method can be used to look at how individual children spend their time over a longer period and shows whether children are interacting with other children and with adults. From this observation, you can also consider how engaged children are during activities and why they leave them. In addition, with older children I look to see whether they seem to stay with their friends and whether this appears to dictate their choice of activity.

As I use this method for observing relatively large numbers of children, it gives me an insight as to whether the environment, provision of resources and activities are working well. If one child does not seem engaged, one might assume that it is because this child is having an 'off day', but if eight or nine children seem to be spending most of their time unengaged, there is clearly something wrong.

Time	Jason	Kiera	Molly	Rahima	Bekir	Josh
9.30	Sand C	Role play	Role play	~~7 A ~~7 water	Cars C 5	Puzzle
9.35	5 Digging	Bags Shopping		Water 2 ~~7 → dough	Sorts Cars	Puzzle floor 5 tidies
9.40	Digging Scoop (L.H)	Pushchair	squabble! → A Dough	Dough A → book corner A	ramp C 5	~~7 ~~7 → A computer
9.45	Hiding Shells	Pushchair	Dough ~~7	Stands A	on furniture A	Computer 3 ~~7
9.50	Hiding hands 5	Pushchair	Painting 2 Wash hands	Book → puzzle A A	Cars C mat + bricks	~~7 marking c
9.55	Hiding funnel	Pushchair 5 wrapping up dolly	Wash hands - soap dispenser C	Puzzle A	5	~~7 puzzle A ~~7 book A
10.00	Hiding hands		→ Snack A	Puzzle A	→ snack A	

Example of group time sample sheet.

Steps to producing a group observation

1. Create a simple grid with eight or nine columns, depending on how many children you are hoping to observe.

2. Use the first column for timings – every five minutes works well.

3. Use the other columns to record each child's activity.

4. At the start of each five-minute slot, look to see where the children are.

5. Use the remaining minutes to note down any activities that seem interesting and whether children are leaving activities. (It is always interesting to work out why.)

Keeping it simple

To ensure that I can easily keep track of what children are doing, I tend to write very little. I usually only put the odd word down and tend to limit this to what I feel I might otherwise forget. On the other hand, I do try and use codes as they are much quicker for recording action. Over the years, I have developed my own coding system, for example, a straight arrow downwards indicates that the child is still in the same place, whilst a wiggly arrow means that they are wandering. I have also found it helpful to use a C and A, for the presence of other children and adults. When I spot that there is interaction going on, I put a circle around. In my head, I think of this as an activation!

Observing levels of engagement

One of my main objectives when I use this method is to see not just how long individual children stay at activities, but also how focused they seem. Once I feel that I am 'into' the observation, I will start to notice just how engaged children are in an activity. I then put a score down on a 1–5 measure, with 5 being totally engaged. During the observation, I will often find that children fluctuate according to what they are doing and so when I see a change, I will record this.

Picking up on different children during the observation

I usually find that after ten minutes or so, I start to notice particular things about children. I will then aim to spend a little more of my time following my thoughts. Here are some examples of things that I have noticed about children in the past:

- a child who does not interact with others even though they are alongside

- a child who only stays at an activity whilst an adult is there and chooses activities on the basis of whether or not an adult is present

- a child who has been concentrating well on an activity, but leaves to rejoin a friend

- a child who spends most of the session standing and watching other children at play.

As a result of these observations, staff can go on to explore whether what I have observed about a child is a 'one-off' or whether practice needs to change to meet these children's needs.

Evaluating the observation

This observation can potentially throw up a lot of information about individual children and the way in which the environment and provision are working for them. It is worth taking a copy of the observation to cut up into strips so that an individual child's observations can be put in their records once you have written up some next steps for them.

It is also worth taking some time to have a quick team meeting to share what you have seen. I would hope that this observation is then used to follow up some particular children and also if necessary to make some changes to the routine/provision within the setting.

Using this observation to improve staff performance

The group observation can also help staff to be aware of their practice. This is sensitive and so it is important to agree with the staff team at the outset that this will be a feature of the observation. Teams I have worked with in the past that have been open to this have benefited from getting an overview of a session. When I carry out this kind of observation, I focus on how much interaction the chosen children have had with adults and also where there were missed opportunities with children. In this situation, it worth choosing the children at random although I might incorporate a child with known speech and language delay.

Limitations of this method

As with all recording methods, there are some limitations to this method. Firstly, it does require an adult to be 'out of the action' so this can only work well when you have an additional pair of hands in the setting. Secondly, whilst you will gain plenty of information about the selected children, you are inevitably not focusing on any one individual. This method cannot therefore replace the more focused individual observations that you carry out on children. Finally, as I mentioned earlier, this method works well with children who are engaged in child-initiated play – probably from 2 years old onwards.

Using digital technology

Welcome to the digital world!

One of the reasons that we chose to film at Lorna's was that she uses digital technology and, as you can tell from the DVD, is a real enthusiast. It was great to see someone who is not a 'geek' and who is good at their job using what has become fairly common technology. When I suggest on my courses that the way forward in observing children is to use technology the following comments are often made. So let's look at them one by one.

Lorna uses her iPhone to aid her observations.

Common misconceptions about going digital

You have to be careful with security

Security is an issue, but only in the same way as it is for paper records. Records of children should be kept in a locked environment and so too should any material that we create digitally. There are many ways to keep digital information secure. You can password-protect individual documents or you can obtain software that will password-protect folders. It is also possible to store all material on memory sticks which in turn can be locked either with each child's record or separately in a secure place. Ideally, I would adopt a belt-and-braces approach by storing information directly onto a memory stick and then password-protecting each folder.

In addition, you should consider the following:

- Risk assess the likelihood of a computer or laptop being stolen – if this is a possibility, consider storing information on memory sticks or portable hard drives.

- Do not put information onto a computer that is used by others who do not work directly with the child, for example, if you are childminder and your computer is used by other members of your family.

- Create a password for your computer – one that cannot be guessed!

- Password-protect folders for individual children.

You can't send photographs over the internet to parents

Sharing information over the internet (including photographs) can work very well, as we saw in Lorna's setting. But, before this can take place, parents must give their explicit consent. Many parents will welcome having up-to-date photographs or emails about their child, whilst others may not want to do this. Interestingly, most parents who are online tend to send photographs of their children to relatives and may also use photo-sharing sites.

It's easier to write things down

There are times when writing things down by hand works well, but filming children or recording their speech tends to be more accurate. Few people can accurately record what children say in the tones that they use nor can they write down the actions that children are making over a five-minute period. Being able to write directly onto the computer also has its advantages as it allows for copying and pasting.

I can't 'do' computers

If you are about to retire in the next two years, I would say don't worry – stick to how you have always worked. If, on the other hand, you intend to keep working in this sector, you do need to start using computers. Most of the parents that you will work with over the next few years will expect information to be passed on digitally. The good news is that computers are increasingly easy to use and so too are the gadgets. Try to conquer one skill at a time and once you have been shown how to do something, practise it again immediately until you have got the hang of it.

What about the Data Protection Act?

The essence of the Data Protection Act is that personal information relating to someone should only be collected for a specific purpose, should be accurate and should not be kept unnecessarily. Information also has to be kept securely. In terms of photographs, film clips and sound recordings, you need to make sure that parents are happy for you to take them. For parents to give you informed consent you must explain exactly the purpose of these records and how you intend to use them. Parents should be given the chance to opt out of certain uses, for example, they may be happy for photographs to go into their child's records, but not to appear on the walls or on a website. If you intend to use a child's photograph for a different purpose, for example, to send it into the local newspaper, always ask parents for their permission. You should not keep material when children are no longer in the setting unless parents have given their written consent.

Ofsted won't like it

There are no problems with Ofsted provided your system for observation and planning works. You will need to have a computer available to show them the records of the children. It would also be good to have a print-out of the process showing your systems in regard to observation and planning – but then it is worth having one anyway.

Benefits of combining digital technology with traditional methods

There are a number of clear benefits of using digital technology alongside traditional methods when it comes to observing and planning.

Time

Using technology is a great time-saver. Taking film clips, voice recordings and photographs of children means that you can collect information quickly while still remaining with the children. This is important if you work as a childminder and may not have anyone else with you to take over – instead of writing up observations, you can simply upload recordings.

Partnership with parents

Photographs, recordings and film clips are great ways of engaging parents and making them aware of what their child is doing when they are with you. As we saw in the clip with Lorna, it is also a way in which they can share their observations or special moments at home with you.

Accuracy

One of the things that I find useful about using film clips and voice recordings is that I can watch or listen to them again. This means that I often notice more, as when you are busy writing things down, it is hard to catch everything. I also find that playing back clips a few months later allows me to see or hear the progress that a child has made.

Types of digital technology that you can use

There are many different types of digital technology that you can use, and who knows what might appear in the future. I would like to look at three common items that are not expensive and are fairly easy to use.

Digital camera

Digital cameras are easy to use and relatively cheap these days to buy. In the DVD Lorna used a PoGo™ which is a digital camera with a printer inside it. Many settings find these very useful: not only can they print out an instant picture, they can also save the image on to the camera for later transfer to a computer. One downside of using photographs is that printing costs can be high, although some settings get around this by copying photographs on to a CD-ROM or emailing them to parents from time to time and they can then print out any photographs they would like. If you are buying a digital camera, look out for a model that allows you to take film clips (see p.84).

To aid her observations, Lorna also takes photos on her iPhone which she then emails to her computer. This is an easy way to use everyday technology to help you out.

When to use photographs

Makeover Story 3

Photographs catch a specific moment in time. They are perfect for photographing children's work, for example, models that they have made, collaborative paintings, sand sculptures, etc. Photographs also help to bring children's records alive and parents like seeing special moments in their child's lives being captured. At Funshine Nursery, the staff put photographs of the children onto a laptop in the reception area so that parents dropping off or collecting their children can see what the children have been doing.

When photographing children, aim to catch a mixture of naturalistic shots when children are not aware that you are taking a photograph, alongside shots where children are proud of what they are doing and are keen to be part of the photograph.

Understanding their limitations

Whilst photographs are wonderful, they are only a snapshot of children at a certain moment in their lives. Detailed written notes have to be taken in addition to create a worthwhile observation.

Providing digital cameras for children

Very young children can take photographs with a simple camera. It is always interesting to watch what they choose to photograph as this often reflects their own interests. There is a range of cameras on the market aimed at children, although you may also find that some parents will donate an old model if you put out a request. Using digital cameras with children is a good way of helping young children learn about ICT.

Camcorders/film option on digital cameras

It is worth thinking about either a camcorder or using the video option on a digital camera to create some film clips of children. Whilst camcorders and digital cameras with this option used to be very expensive, they have become relatively cheap and are of course tax-deductible items for childminders and private nurseries. Over the past few years, this has become my primary method for capturing children's activity. I like filming children as I can capture all aspects of their development and afterwards I can replay the clip several times to take notes or to consider their stage of development. I also find that children are fascinated by watching themselves and that parents find the clips very informative.

When to film children

It is easier to film children during their child-initiated play or during an activity that has been set up and that does not require adult support. I only film for one to two minutes at a time, although sometimes I will film the activity later on. One to two minutes may not seem a very long time, but it is amazing just how much you can learn about the child's speech, level of interest and physical skills in this time. You can also involve children in filming by telling them what you are doing and asking them to talk about or show you what they are doing. This can work well because you can hear their explanation and impressions of the importance of the activity.

Limitations

Some cameras do not function well indoors or in poor light. It is also hard to film children if what they are doing requires adult support. I would also suggest that you do not film endlessly as otherwise you are likely to miss out on what children are doing.

Providing camcorders for children

As a parting gift for Lorna, we left her and the children with a camcorder that is designed to be used by young children. These are not cheap, but on the other hand are designed to withstand rough use and also have simplified features. They work well as part of planned adult-led activities and can help children to explore ICT. There is potentially quite a lot of language use involved as children can work with you to plan their 'filming'.

Tips for using digital cameras

○ Wear an overall or garment that has a pocket in it so that the camera is always close to hand.

○ Make sure you set the time and date on the camera.

○ Buy a sufficiently large memory card so that there is plenty of space.

○ Get into the habit of deleting photographs that have not worked straight away or at the end of each session.

○ Develop a routine for charging the battery – for example, for one hour after the end of each session.

○ Transfer the photographs quickly into children's records.

○ Lock the camera away at the end of the session to comply with data protection regulations.

Tips for recording film clips

○ Buy a camcorder or digital camera that is fairly compact and easy to use.

○ Recordings take a lot of memory, so buy a large memory card.

○ Only record in short bursts.

○ For a more interesting clip, try to slowly move around the child or use the zoom feature.

○ Let other adults in the room know that you are recording so that their voices are not picked up.

○ In very noisy situations, disable the sound function.

○ Lock away the equipment when it is not in use.

○ Get into a routine of charging the equipment.

MP3 and recording devices

Whilst filming children can mean children's voices are captured, I also like to use MP3 players specifically to record children's speech. They are very small and so children cannot see that you are recording them. I find that hearing the child's voice alone makes it easy to focus on the clarity and structure of speech. If recordings are regularly taken, it is easy to build a strong profile of individual children's speech. In some cases, it may also alert us to possible speech delay.

Speech recordings also provide a lovely record for parents as it is easy to forget what your child sounded like when they were first speaking. As some MP3 players cost less than £20 at the time of writing, you may also consider having an extra MP3 that you can loan to parents so they can record their child at home. This is useful if the child speaks a different language from the one you use in the setting. It is also helpful when parents report that their child talks a lot at home, but you find the child quiet in the setting.

When to record children

You need to record children when you are close to them and engaged with them. It is hard otherwise to make a good recording. The best recordings are of natural conversations with the adult which may occur during activities or at snack time. It can be useful to record children in similar situations every few months so that you can see how their language has developed, for example, you could show them photographs of themselves and record their commentary. As with film recording, you only need to catch one to two minutes at a time as this will give you plenty of information about their speech.

Tips for using MP3 players

○ Keep the MP3 player in a pocket so that you can use it at any time.

○ Expect to have to talk yourself in order to gain a good recording.

○ Introduce the child's name early in the conversation if you are recording more than one child over the session.

○ When children's speech is still emerging, acknowledge what they have said and recast it back so that afterwards it is clear what the child was attempting to express. This is good language practice in any case.

○ Transfer the recording promptly into the child's records. Name the file with the date and situation/topic of conversation.

○ Aim to record children in similar situations so that you can hear how their language has progressed when playing the same game or talking about objects.

○ Keep the MP3 player for professional use only and lock it away when the session is over.

Limitations

Recording devices do pick up other sounds and so you need to find quiet areas or activities to catch children's speech. If this is impossible in your setting, you should question whether the layout and structure needs changing as loud environments are not good for young children's speech development.

Mobile phones and multifunction devices

In the DVD, Lorna showed me how she uses her iPhone to carry out recordings. With her iPhone she can film, photograph and voice record children before emailing the recordings to her main computer. For some of you this may be a step too far, but do consider it, especially if you are a childminder. Whilst there are issues relating to individual staff in group care using their phones (see the Limitations paragraph below), it might be worth considering a device for professional use that is owned and kept in the setting.

Limitations

There are a few limitations, both practical and relating to child protection issues. Firstly, the use of mobile phones in group-care settings is a matter of great concern given recent cases where staff were accused of abusing and filming indecent shots of children in their care using their mobile phones. If you are working in a nursery or pre-school, you will need to ask for permission to film children to aid observations and it would be sensible to film or record children only when you are alongside other staff. All materials should be deleted from your phone before you leave work.

Tips for using mobile phones and multifunction devices

○ Make sure that you have learnt how to use the device before using it to record children.

○ Activate and use the locking device on it to keep material secure.

○ Keep the device in a locked place when not being used.

○ Delete all material or transfer it to the computer immediately if the device is used out of the setting.

When to use these devices

These devices can be a little unwieldy, but otherwise, you could use them in similar situations to the ones described earlier. In addition, they can be very useful as you can email parents at work with clips or messages more or less in 'real time'. This can be helpful when children are first settling in as parents can feel quite anxious after they have left.

Starting out

Learning to use technology does take a little time. Both Lorna and I are self-taught and so are the majority of people who use computers and technology. What most of us find is that it is much easier than you imagine and that the more you do, the more you can do. These days there are also plenty of people around who can show you a skill or will lend you a hand – but don't become the person who always lets everyone else sort it out.

If you do not use any technology, begin by buying or borrowing a digital camera, preferably one that has a video function. Take some test photographs or a short film clip – nothing of any importance so that it doesn't matter if it disappears or is on view to others. Next you need to learn how to put the photographs or film clips onto the computer. This is quick and easy and once you have acquired this skill you can upload from any device.

Creating a digital folder

As you can see from the DVD, Lorna is very confident when it comes to using the latest in digital technology. I did, however, suggest that she should consider bringing her digital records together in a single folder. For those of you who have not yet done this, here are some practical suggestions and a step-by-step guide to getting started. Because I am self-taught when it comes to technology I cannot always guarantee that I am doing things the fastest way but, interestingly, one thing I have learnt over the past few years is that there seem to be several ways of doing any task.

What you might put in the folder:

- photographs of the child
- sound recordings
- film clips
- professional notes relating to the photographs, sound recordings, film clips
- summative records
- individual planning for the child
- information/photographs from parents.

To create a new folder

Creating a new folder is easy. Here is a step-by-step guide with screenshots you can follow.

This has been done on a laptop running the Windows XP operating system. If your computer is different, don't worry! It is easy to find very straightforward instructions on the internet. Just search for something like 'Creating a folder using Windows 7.'

1. Insert the memory stick that you intend to use into a USB port on the computer. Allow enough time for your computer to 'find' it.

2. Go to **My computer**.

3. Double-click on the icon that shows the memory stick (highlighted in blue in the screenshot below).

4. In the panel on the left, left click on **Make a new folder.** The new folder will appear in the right-hand pane.

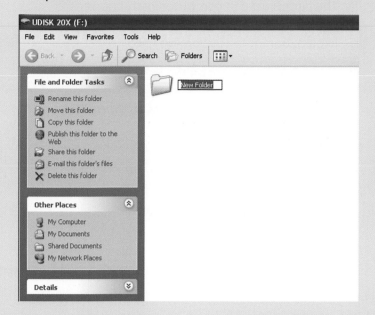

5. Once the new folder is created, you need to rename it, I would suggest using the child's first name as the folder name.

   - If the words 'New folder' are highlighted in blue, you can delete them by pressing the **Delete** key. Then you can then type in a new name.

   - If you have clicked away from the new folder, you just need to right-click over the folder name (New folder) and select **Rename** from the drop-down list of options that appears. You can then type in the new name.

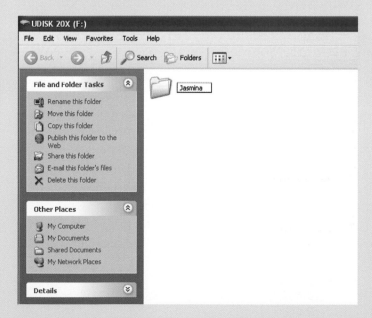

6. Once you have finished, left click in any empty space.

To transfer photographs, recordings etc. from a camera into the child's folder on the memory stick

1. Put the USB lead in the camera and the USB port in the computer.

2. Insert the memory stick that has the folder on it into the computer.

3. Go to **My computer**.

4. Look for the icon for the camera/recording device and double left click on it.

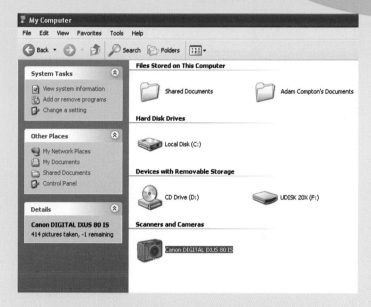

5. Find the photograph, film recording, etc. that you want to move to the child's folder.

6. Right click on it and then select 'Send to' from menu. From the new menu, select the memory stick. This moves the photograph from the camera to the memory stick.

7. Now you have got the photograph onto the memory stick, you need to put it into the right folder. Go to **My computer** and double click on the icon for the memory stick.

8. Right click on the photograph or recording you have just transferred and select **Cut.**

9. Double click on the child's folder, and once you're inside the folder, right click and select **Paste.** The photograph will then be in the right folder.

To see the contents of folders on the memory stick

1. Insert memory stick into computer.

2. Go to **My computer**.

3. Double click on the icon for the memory stick.

4. Double click on the folder that you want to see.

5. Double click on the item in the folder that you wish to look at or work on.

Jargon

The jargon used in computer instructions can seem a bit daunting – but don't panic! Here's an explanation of the jargon I've used.

○ *USB port* – the slot on the side or front of a laptop or computer where you can 'plug in' devices, such as your mouse, camera, memory stick and printer

○ *Double click* – fast-clicking twice on the left mouse button, or mousepad on a laptop

○ *Left click* – clicking once on the left mouse button, or mousepad on a laptop

○ *Right click* – clicking once on the right mouse button, or mousepad on a laptop

Evaluating information gained from observations

One of the main criticisms that Ofsted makes is that whilst settings observe children, some fail to use the information gained to plan for the child. When you are reviewing or creating your system of observing children, you need to evaluate what the observations actually mean in terms of the development of the child and in terms of planning. You should therefore create systems that allow you to input information gained from observations into your planning. I would suggest that you need to do this on a day-to-day or short-term basis and also over the medium term.

Day-to-day/Short term

When you have completed any type of observation, you should always be considering what you think this means in terms of the development of the child and what the next steps might be. Some observation formats, such as the learning journey type, we discussed earlier (see p. 69) have this built in, but you may need to create a format for other methods such as for when you film children or use Post-it® Notes. You may decide that you can use the response sheet for this (see p. 75) or a slip such as the one illustrated below.

Whilst eventually the slip will be filed with the child's records, you will need to find a way of transferring your observations onto the short-term planning tool. At Funshine Nursery, where we looked at their outdoor environment, they use their planning wall for short-term planning. This allows staff during the week to put up notes and also to write next steps for individual children immediately after they have observed something of interest.

Summative assessments

Summative assessments are crucial and should be done every few months. A summative assessment is literally a summary of where the child is, what progress they have made and what support, activities or interests need to be followed up over the coming months. To carry out a quality summative assessment you should spend a little time reviewing what you have learnt about the child over the past few weeks. This is a chance to look back at the observations you have carried out, including daily records if you work with babies, and examples of children's drawings or mark-making. You should also refer back to the previous summaries.

Ideally, you should try and do some or all of this alongside parents, although this will not always be possible. Think about how the child has progressed and crucially whether their progress is in line with expected development. Once you have done this, you need to think about what they might be ready to do next and how you might support them.

Formats

There are plenty of examples of summative assessment sheets around that you can tweak to suit your setting. When deciding on a format, I would always go for something that will allow you to write in detail about each area of a child's development and the particular aspects within it. I would also create a way of showing the evidence for the analysis, such as putting the observation number in brackets. As parents are also meant to be partners with us, you should try to include their comments and ideas on the summative assessments. For best practice, you should also find a way of reflecting the child's thoughts – this might mean encouraging them to tell you what they most like about the setting or what they have enjoyed doing.

Name of Child	Date of Observation	Reference/Type
Aspects of EYFS observed		
Next Steps/Action		
Comments		

Example observation follow-up slip.

a)

Child's name			
D.O.B.		Time in setting	
Date of completion		Practitioner completing this overview	

Area of Development	Comments	Obs. ref
PSED		
CLL		
PSRN		
KUW		
PD		
CD		

Example of a two-sided form: a) Summative assessment b) Medium-term plan.

b)

Child's interests and thoughts	
At home (To be completed with parents)	
Statement of progress	

Medium-term Plan	(Next Steps)
PSED	CLL
PSRN	KUW
PD	CD

Encourage the children to tell you what they think.

At the bottom of the summative assessments there should also be a 'Next Steps' or similarly named section. This is the bit that should feed into the planning process. In this section, you should write about what the child will be doing next and give some examples of activities and resources. In the example of the two-sided sheet that I have provided on pp. 90–91, I have combined the summative assessment with the medium-term plan and you may like to copy this idea.

Bringing it all together

It would be great if you could get everything together on one single sheet – the observations and planning – but this is not likely if you are working with groups of children. Your system is likely to be made up of many different pieces of planning; the trick is to make each piece 'work hard' and also show in any group planning how you are bringing in children's individual needs.

Flexibility is key

Some of the best planning tools that I have seen have spaces or columns to allow extra things to be added. Use large pieces of paper wherever possible so that changes can be made and notes about children added.

As I mentioned earlier in the chapter, Petra and her team at Funshine Nursery use a large planning wall which is filled in each week. Adult-led activities are noted with the children's initials or names alongside, notes are made about what resources are to be put out the next day based on children's interests and a note is made of what particular children in key groups have enjoyed doing over the week. I love this system, although I recognise that it would not work in all settings.

A weekly planning sheet

If you are working with relatively small groups of children or with babies and toddlers whose needs are likely to be different, consider using a weekly planner sheet for each child. Lorna's sheet on p. 94 is an example of this and her ideas come both from the medium-term summaries that she creates and from

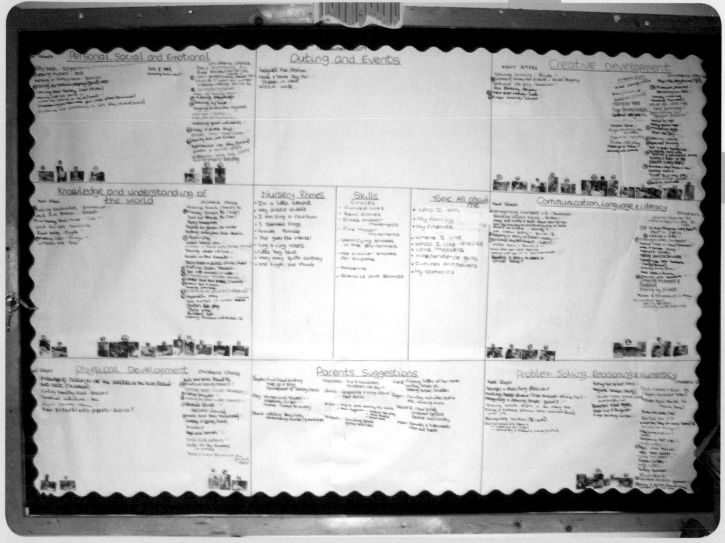

Funshine Nursery uses a planning wall, which staff add to each day.

what she has seen whilst working with the children each day. Again, this is a system that has in-built flexibility.

Daily sheets showing provision and adult-led activities

Many settings find it useful to create each week a series of daily sheets that are only partially completed at the start of the week! The sheets show the adult-led activities which have been planned for particular children and link to these children's recognised needs (taken from observations and medium-term summaries.) They also show what equipment and materials are to be put out to allow for child-initiated activity. In addition they show which children are due to be observed and by whom. At the end of the session or during the session, the planning is added to, based on what has happened, for example, if two

children have found a bird's nest, then it may be decided to put out books about birds and to look for twigs, grass and other materials in case those children wish to make a nest of their own.

Where settings work in this way, it is usually the responsibility of the key people to suggest adult-led activities for their key children. This works well because they should have a good understanding of the child's developmental level, needs and interests. They should also be checking that the whole of the curriculum is being covered.

Suggestions for focused observations

There are some things, some of which are age related, that are really worth focusing on in terms of children's development and needs. In this section, I will be

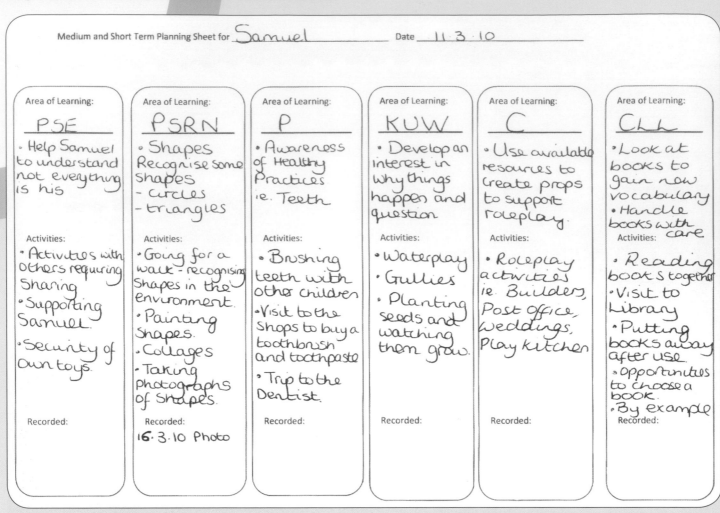

Medium and Short Term Planning Sheet for **Samuel**   Date **11.3.10**

Area of Learning:

PSE

- Help Samuel to understand not everything is his

Activities:
- Activities with others requiring Sharing
- Supporting Samuel
- Security of Own toys.

Recorded:

Area of Learning:

PSRN

- Shapes Recognise some shapes
- circles
- triangles

Activities:
- Going for a walk - recognising shapes in the environment.
- Painting Shapes.
- Collages
- Taking Photographs of Shapes.

Recorded:
16.3.10 Photo

Area of Learning:

P

- Awareness of Healthy Practices ie. Teeth

Activities:
- Brushing teeth with other children
- Visit to the Shops to buy a toothbrush and toothpaste
- Trip to the Dentist.

Recorded:

Area of Learning:

KUW

- Develop an interest in why things happen and question

Activities:
- Waterplay
- Gullies
- Planting seeds and watching them grow.

Recorded:

Area of Learning:

C

- Use available resources to create props to support roleplay.

Activities:
- Roleplay activities ie. Builders, Post office, weddings, Play kitchen

Recorded:

Area of Learning:

CLL

- Look at books to gain new vocabulary
- Handle books with care

Activities:
- Reading books together
- Visit to Library
- Putting books away after use.
- opportunities to choose a book.
- By example

Recorded:

Lorna's weekly planning sheet.

looking at specific observations that you might like to carry out with the children you work with. Some are 'one-offs' and so once done will not need to be repeated.

Observing that children have strong relationships with their key adult (all age ranges)

I think that it is worth checking fairly early on that children have really settled down and have developed a strong relationship with at least one adult. These are some points that you might like to look out for:

- Does the child settle quickly once the parent/carer has left?

- Does the child seem angry or upset when the parent returns?

- Does the child make eye contact with the key person during the session?

- Does the child seem comfortable in the key person's company?

- Does the child notice when the key person is not in sight or has left the room?

Planning

It is not good for the child to be left to settle in and so it is worth thinking about how you can increase the amount of time they spend with the key person each day for a while. It is also worth talking to parents about just how comfortable the child seems when it is time to come to the setting. Finally, we might need to 'think the unthinkable' – does the child need a different key person?

Observing children's handedness (from 2 years)

From 2 years old onwards and before 3 years old, children should normally have developed a hand preference. This is worth looking out for as children need to have developed a consistent hand ready for writing.

There is also some speculation that having a strong dominance is good in terms of some cognitive skills.

- When a small object such as a cork is offered, which hand does the child use?
- Is this fairly consistent?
- Which hand does the child use to open a door, or hold a spoon or a cup?
- Which hand does the child use to hold a paintbrush or pen?

Planning

Whilst you cannot make a child choose a hand to use, there are activities that can be planned to strengthen preference. Look out for activities that can be built into the routine of the day that encourage separate hand functions – that is, a stabilising hand and an active hand. Good examples of this type of activity are washing up, doing up buttons, opening a bottle by unscrewing a lid, using a dustpan and brush.

Checking that children are hearing (all age ranges)

There are two types of hearing loss. One is known as sensor-neural, which is usually detected early on in a child's life and may result in a child wearing hearing aids or having a cochlear implant. The other type is a conductive hearing loss which is very common in young children. (The NHS suggests that 90% of children will have one episode of hearing loss by the age of 10.) Conductive hearing loss is often referred to as 'glue ear' and is mostly caused by fluid building up in the tube that runs from the outer ear towards the eardrum, resulting in children's hearing being significantly reduced. Most children grow out of it by the age of 6 or 7.

Whilst hearing loss is very common in children, its impact can be considerable. Children's speech may be delayed or unclear and there are likely also to be behavioural signs such as poor concentration, aggression and withdrawal. The difficulty is that, unless you are actually looking for it, it can be very intermittent – one week a child may be hearing quite well, but a week later they may not be. This pattern means that it easy for parents and others to think that the child has 'selective hearing' or that they are just 'dreamy'.

- Does the child respond when you make a clicking sound from behind?
- Does the child have unclear speech?
- Does the child often seem to focus intently on your face when you are speaking ?
- Does the child seem to talk in a loud voice or with a 'flat' tone?

Planning

Try to regularly check that all the children that you work with are hearing. Plan games that involve having shakers and sounds out of sight and see if children react to them. Also do things such as whisper very quietly behind or to one side of the child and see if they respond. If you suspect that a child has glue ear, you should talk to the parents and see if they can organise a hearing test. Note that in some cases, a child will be tested when they are having a good spell and so a repeat might be necessary. The good news is that once the glue ear is discovered, treatment is offered and children respond very well.

Checking that babies are tuning in (0–1 years)

The first year of life is crucial in terms of children's language development. It is in this year of life that children start to differentiate between different sounds. They then go on to use only the ones that are needed in the language or languages that they are being exposed to. Some later speech delay can be avoided if observations focus on whether babies are tuning in. Use an MP3 player each month to record the child's vocalisations as well as doing some traditional observations.

- Are the pattern of the child's vocalisations changing month by month?
- Does the child seem to respond when they hear the sound of their parents/key person?
- At ten months does the child seem to understand some of the words that are being used, for example, getting excited when they hear a particular word, or point to objects when asked about them?

Planning

Make sure that there are plenty of times when the key person and the baby spend time facing each other and interacting with eye contact, for example, put the baby facing you on your lap. You should think about how much background noise there is and how easy it is for the baby to focus on a single voice. You should also work out how much time the baby has to interact with their key person and how long these interactions last. If, after intensive work and after talking to parents about the child at home, it appears that the child is not that responsive, suggest to the parents that they may like to talk to their health visitor or GP.

Friendships (from 3 years)

From 3 years, most children have begun to develop friendships with other children. Some friendships are particularly strong and it is worth assessing them to see the impact they may be having. Whilst it is great that children have strong friendships, it is important that each child is emotionally strong enough to cope if the other child is not available. This is particularly important if children are about to be separated because one or both are going to school. It is also important that both children can follow their own play interests at times. Consider carrying out a time sample over a period of a morning or just focusing on the children over a week.

- How much time do the children spend together?
- Is one child dominant?
- Can both children cope when the other is absent for some or all of a session?
- What do they enjoy doing together?

Planning

Consider organising adult-directed activities that involve other children alongside the friends. If children are likely to be separated because one is going on holiday or leaving for school, organise some adult-led activities in which the children are not together so that they become used to spending time apart.

Gender exploration (from 3 years)

Most children begin to explore what it means to be a boy or a girl. This can lead to some children avoiding play opportunities that they do not feel are for them. The level to which children are affected can vary enormously and so it is an area worth looking at. You can use the group tracking observation to note who and what certain children play with or you can keep an

Are there any particularly strong friendships between the children?

eye out for your key children and think about where their interests lie. In addition, you can set up certain activities and resources that are usually associated with gender and see which children avoid or are interested in them, for example, see what happens if you only put out pink beakers at snack time or only put out tractors, cars and trains for small world play.

- How do children's play preferences link to their gender?
- Which children are particularly interested in exploring gender concept?
- Are any children actively avoiding certain resources, toys or activities?
- What do parents say about their child at home?

Planning

If you find that some children have clear gender preferences make sure that they are still accessing all areas of the curriculum and play activities. This might mean adding in some role models or giving signals that an area is not just for boys/girls by putting out key props.

Mouthing (from 12 months – 2 years)

Most children mouth objects as a key way of exploring items until around 18 months. It is therefore worth carrying out some observations to see when children no longer use their mouth and instead tend only to use their hands. This allows a different range of objects to be put out which can open up new challenges. Use a snapshot observation or film the child when you put out objects that they have not seen before. Only use objects that you know are not choking hazards to eliminate any potential risk.

- Does the child take the item immediately to the mouth?

- Does the child explore the item first with hand and eyes before taking it to the mouth?

- Does the child only touch and look at the object before discarding it?

Planning

If you know that children are still mouthing, you must ensure that a range of different, safe objects are put out that can all be explored with the mouth. Talk to parents about the child's need to put things in the mouth and share with them examples of objects that they may have at home that could be used. When you have observed that a child who used to mouth is no longer doing so, repeat the observation over a few more weeks. When you are sure that mouthing is not likely, look out for different sets of objects and toys which can widen the child's learning, for example, different types of paper or dry coloured rice.

Pencil grip (3 years upwards)

A tripod grip (where children hold a pencil between finger and thumb with the middle finger acting as a support) is the most effective hand grip for holding writing implements. It allows the hand to be relaxed whilst controlled and so is important for later joined up handwriting. Unfortunately, some children develop alternative grips which can be difficult to change if they have developed a habit of using them. A snapshot observation or filming will help you to see how a child uses a pen or pencil. Aim to repeat the observation as sometimes children will have a changing grasp, in which case the tripod may come easily.

- Does the child hold a pencil between thumb and forefinger with middle finger as a support?

- Does the child use a palmar grasp to hold the pencil (whole hand clasped around the pencil)?

Planning

Children who are not yet using a tripod grip need plenty of activities that will encourage a pincer grip movement, for example, picking out confetti from a bowl containing dried chick peas, using tweezers to pull out macaroni from a plate and transfer it into a jar. Children can also hang out washing using clothes pegs. Talk to parents about other fine motor movements that could be practised at home which often relate to Self-care, such as doing their own buttons up, using a zip and helping with household chores. You may also look out for mark-making opportunities that do not necessarily involve pens, for example, using sticks in damp sand or painting.

This child is developing a tripod grasp.

Anti-clockwise rotational marks (3 years upwards)

To support children's handwriting, it is helpful if they make rotational marks, or 'circles', that begin at the top of the paper and move around in an anti-clockwise direction. This is the basis of many lower case letters. Some children make these marks automatically, but others do not (for example, some left-handed children make clockwise marks). Carry out a structured task whereby you encourage children to draw a circle with a marker on a whiteboard – aim for the task to use gross motor movement.

- Does the child begin at the top of the page?

- Does the child move anti-clockwise?

- Does the child complete the circle or break off and begin from the other side?

Planning

It is worth planning specific fun activities for those children who have not developed the anti-clockwise rotational movement. Try putting out sponges and water so that they can wash the window – but model the movement first. You can also play 'follow the leader' type games (see the painting wall activity, p. 178). For left-handed children aim to provide them with many large marking opportunities and see if you can provide some writing slopes for them once they start to write individual letters. A writing slope can be made by using an A4 folder turned so that its spine is facing away from the child. The idea of using slopes is not new. Years ago all school desks had slopes and many architects and designers use them. A slope allows children to see more easily as they write, but also keeps their back straighter.

Your questions answered

○ *We have been told that we must observe every child every week?*

Nowhere in the statutory framework does it say how often observations have to be carried out. It is important that you do observe regularly, but not just for the sake of it. Factors such as how often children come into your setting, their age and also the adult–child ratio will affect the frequency of observations. I would expect that if you are working with babies, you might observe them more often as the adult–child ratio in group settings is low whilst babies' rate of development is fast.

○ *Do we have to use the forms on the CD-ROM that come with the EYFS?*

No, these are not statutory and were designed to give people a starting point. The best paperwork and systems that I have seen are always those that have been designed for the setting by the people in the setting.

○ *What should I do if whilst I am observing, other children want to join me?*

This is always a tricky one. Personally, I favour a low eye-contact approach. I tend to keep on with my observation and will not turn to look at the child who is interested or who wants my attention. I might say that I am busy, but invite the child to sit next to me. Most children do this for a bit, but when they see that I am not focusing on them, they tend to get bored and disappear. The other tactic that you could use is to provide similar forms and a few pencils and use this as a way of encouraging mark-making.

○ *Do we have to show parents what we have written?*

The short answer is yes! Parents have a right to know what is being said about their children, particularly when comments are being recorded. This means that the style of writing that you adopt should tend towards the positive and you should avoid a 'deficiency model' if the child is otherwise showing age-related behaviour, for example, you should write things such as 'she can concentrate for short periods which is usual for this age group' rather than 'she cannot concentrate for more that 10 minutes.'

○ *What should we do if things crop up and we don't follow our planning?*

I see this as a good sign as it means that you are using naturally occurring opportunities and are ready to move at children's pace and according to their interests. I would suggest that you simply put a note onto the planning that records what you have done instead, its benefits and a sentence as to why it was important to change tack.

○ *We have a staff member who has difficulty with spelling*

Observation and planning notes that are likely to be seen by parents and other professionals need to be as legible and accurate as possible. Having said this, many people struggle with handwriting and spelling. Consider encouraging this member of staff to learn to use a word processing package on a computer – this might be a goal for staff development.

Outdoor play

One of the main changes that has arisen as a result of the EYFS is the focus on the outdoor area. This was why I wanted to look at an outdoor environment in the DVD. We chose Funshine Nursery to film in because not only were staff interested and keen, but their garden presented some real and typical challenges. Firstly, like many nurseries there were space limitations and there was no access to running water. Secondly, the garden was used by all age ranges. Finally, there was a heavy reliance on toys and plastic resources.

In this chapter, we look at how you might enhance your existing area in order to create a challenging play environment. The areas covered in this chapter are:

- Layout
- Creating challenge outdoors
- Creating an instant garden
- Opportunities for physical challenge
- Sensory opportunities outside
- Creating small enclosed spaces
- Mark-making opportunities
- Creating a digging area
- Loose part play

Layout

It would be great to say that there is one single layout that works for everyone, but sadly there isn't. Layout will depend on the size of your outdoor area, the age range of your setting, availability of storage space and even how much exposure to the sun there is. The following points can be helpful when creating a layout.

Observe children's movements in your current layout

Observing children can often help you understand which areas are working and where there are difficulties, for example, if the tricycles get in the way of the play.

Create areas where children feel out of sight

It is good to deliberately create some areas where children do feel a sense of privacy – cosy corners, for example. Having some areas which are more secluded also has the advantage of helping children to concentrate as they may feel less distracted. (See also Creating small enclosed spaces, pp.117–119.)

Provide areas for babies and toddlers

If babies and toddlers use the outdoor space at the same time as older children, you might like to consider whether to partition off a space for them, as their needs are quite different. Some settings do this with low fences, others use cones and some use soft play cubes. Ideally, babies will need something that they can pull themselves up on so that they can see what is happening around them. Small swings can be good here as they allow babies and toddlers to have physical experiences whilst being able to see what the other children are doing.

Create an area where children feel out of sight.

Try to make play areas coherent

It is important to think about what children will need to do when they are playing, for example, children with a source of water are likely to water the plants, or children who are on tricycles might want to visit the 'petrol station'. It can therefore be helpful to try and get some flow into the layout. At Funshine, for example, the bamboo garden was sited near the existing sand tray as I know from experience that children might take dinosaurs or other small world objects from the sand tray across into another 'landscape'. We also tried to create a sitting area within the bamboo garden and so it was good to have it away from the 'race track' where children were likely to be quite physical. On the other hand, the addition of the tree stumps in the centre of the race track has meant that that part of the garden has clearly become a more physical area.

Aim to create a versatile and varied environment

I am a great fan of materials and resources that can be moved or are inherently flexible. A versatile environment is particularly important, especially if the children in your setting will be clocking up a large number of hours when they are with you. If you have a small environment, think about avoiding too many fixed pieces of equipment. You should also think about creating as many different varied play opportunities as possible, for example, sensory, digging, construction and mark-making.

Be realistic

It is important to be very realistic when working out what you can put into your environment. A good example of this is with tricycles and scooters. Whilst these are great, you will need to have plenty of them and then there must be enough space for children to have a satisfying experience. In small spaces, I would forego these items because they are likely to disrupt other children's play and the amount of physical challenge that can be created with them might be too limited for children to really benefit.

Create your outdoor area in phases

It is very hard to create the 'perfect' outdoor area in one go. It is therefore worth seeing its development in phases. At Funshine Nursery, the garden area is still developing as staff are adding to it after observing how the children are using it. After each new phase, wait a while and see how it is affecting children's play. Some ideas will not work, others will but may need to be re-sited.

Make sure that storage is accessible

Storage is often key to a rich outdoor area with changing resources. Keeping everything inside to bring out is hard work and also consumes space. In some areas, this is the only option because of local vandalism or theft. If you are able to leave things out, you might like to create more than one storage area which has the items, tools and resources needed for the nearby play. For example, next to the role play have storage bins with props and fabrics; next to the mark-making board have storage bins with rolls of paper and pens. Look out for plastic storage bins that are designed as recycling bins. They are often waterproof, yet are easy for children to access. I have found them to work well for items that will not be a target for thieves, for example, strips of fabric, cardboard tubes and pom-poms.

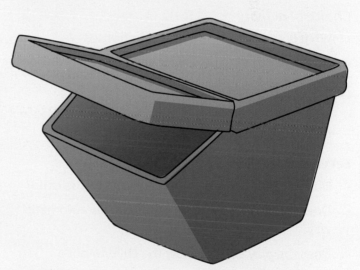

Storage bins are great: they are waterproof yet easy for children to access.

Choosing sheds with easy access

The traditional garden shed (with the door on the narrowest part) does not always work well in settings. Think about a double door shed which opens more like a traditional wardrobe. Whilst this will not have the depth, it does mean that everything can be taken out more easily. Some settings also add ramps so that it is easy for the wheeled toys to be taken in and out.

Creating challenge outdoors

It is important when looking at your outdoor area to consider whether it is sufficiently challenging. This is particularly important as many children today will spend hundreds of hours a year in settings.

So what does 'challenging' mean? For me creating challenge is about a combination of physical and mental challenge. A slide, for example may well be quite challenging at first for a child, but once they have mastered it, it may no longer be much of a challenge. This is not to say that children will not enjoy using a slide afterwards, but I think we need to recognise that the challenge will have disappeared.

Auditing the level of challenge in your outdoor area

A good starting point when looking at your outdoor area is therefore to consider what level of challenge is available for children. To do this, observe a selection of children as they play outdoors over a few days and consider the following questions:

Choice of activity

- What is available for the child to choose?
- Do they choose to do similar activities each session?

Levels of engagement

- What level of concentration and focus is required in their play activity?

Level of mental challenge

- How is the activity mentally challenging the child?
- Does the child seem to be playing in an 'automatic' way?
- Does the play activity allow the child to put a 'personal stamp' on it?
- How does the child's play vary?

Level of physical challenge

- How easily can the child engage in their play activity?
- Does it seem physically demanding?

Reflecting on what you have seen

From your observations of children over a number of days, you may start to detect that whilst some children are perfectly happy, they may not necessarily be having opportunities to develop new ways of thinking or physical skills. Repetitive play may be linked to a child exploring a play pattern or it may be related to the age of the child, but when I see repetitive play, I am also looking to see how engaged and focused a child is in what they are doing.

Creating challenge

Some settings are lucky because their gardens or grounds have natural challenges within them such as trees, streams or slopes. (Whilst the production team laughed at my enthusiasm over Stepping Stones' grass mound, I knew instantly that the pre-school had a wonderful feature that would provide children with many different opportunities.) If your setting is not blessed with such natural features, it will be up to you to create them. There are many ways of doing this and ideally, you should put in several. Over the next few pages, I will look at the areas in the diagram below:

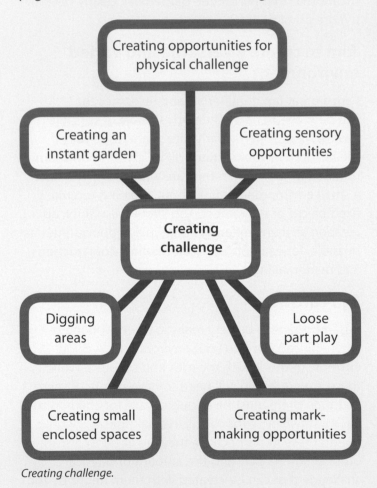

Creating challenge.

Creating an instant garden

Gardens are wonderful places for children. They soften the outdoor area and somehow bring it to life. Gardens can also act as a good backdrop for children's play. I love watching children running around the base of tree or using leaves as substitute food. Sadly in the past few years, there has been a trend to create play areas for children rather than to integrate play into a garden structure. The good news though is that it is possible to create a garden within a play area and on a modest budget, as Petra and her team show in the DVD.

Benefits of creating a garden

Over the past few years, many children have had less opportunity to see, feel and be near plants and natural items such as stones. Creating a small oasis can be a great starting point for children to enjoy nature, but also to experience a range of different play opportunities. At Funshine Nursery, it was amazing to see the transformation in the children's play at all ages. The toddlers enjoyed picking up stones whilst the older children used the environment to enrich their small world play. Once an area has been established, activities can be planned around it such as creating bird feeders or telling stories. Children can also use this area to go in and out of as part of role play. The care and maintenance of plants is also a learning opportunity and additional/seasonal plants can be planted by children, for example, bulbs to go at the base of a container that has a tree in it. (A trick that I have learnt is to plant beans, peas and other climbing plants that can grow up and cling onto taller plants.)

Since the team at Funshine established their garden they have found that parents have been making favourable comments.

An oasis of nature within the play area

As in many settings, there were quite a few constraints when it came to creating a garden at Funshine Nursery. The nursery had an artificial grass surface which they wanted to keep as it was working for them. The outdoor space, although adequate, was not generous and so thought had to be given to ensuring that children could still run and move around. A good solution in such cases is to create a small oasis of garden within the play area. This acts as a contrast to the rest of the space. In some settings this can be put at the heart of the outdoor area, but it can work equally well in a corner.

To create an oasis, you need a minimum of three trees, shrubs or plants that will give some height. For me,

Example of how planting trees can help to create a clearing and pathways for children to play in and explore.

creating height is absolutely crucial so that children have places to hide. Having three tall plants grouped can also enable three pathways and a 'clearing' to be created as the diagram below shows.

I asked Petra to look at bamboos that once planted would give 8 ft of height. By starting off with three, you are likely to be creating some small amount of shade as well. From this as a basis, you can then think about putting in pathways and adding a further texture. I see this as 'flooring' for the area and should be a contrast to whatever surface you have – bark chippings, tree stumps or slab-like stones and cobbles, such as the ones that the team at Funshine used. The ideal is to create an area in which children can hide or weave in and out of.

Creating some further magic

Once you have created a basic oasis, there are plenty of things that over time you might like to add into your instant garden. In some cases, you might just add in more of the same or expand the area by adding more containers or planting directly into the ground. Below is a list of things that can add a little more magic, although as with anything that you bring into your area, make sure that you have done a risk assessment and monitor children's usage.

Solar-powered fairy lights

It is possible to find solar-powered lights and these can give the area a little more magic.

Tinsel

Children like tinsel and so tying tinsel into trees can make the area feel a little more magical.

Additional textures

If you enlarge the area over time, you may be able to create different areas that have their own ground surfaces and therefore introduce children to new or different textures, such as sand, gravel or matting.

Water features

Children love water and there are plenty of very reasonably priced water features on offer, some of which are solar powered or battery operated.

Do some research

There is little point spending time and money in creating a garden that will die. To avoid this, you must do some research first so that you put the right plants in the right places. This is not rocket science and having the right information will enable a garden centre or keen gardener to advise you on what you should plant. Consider the following points.

- Is your site sunny, partially shaded or fully shaded?
- Is your site particularly exposed or windy?
- Will someone be able to do the watering? (Think about this if you are only there in term time.)
- If children will be able to water plants, have you chosen types that will not suffer if overwatered?
- Will you plant directly into the soil and, if so, what type of soil do you have?
- Will you be using containers as a way of creating the garden?

Using containers

Whilst some settings may be able to plant directly into the ground, it can be useful to do some large-scale container planting. Having containers does mean that plants are protected from bottoms that might squash them or feet that might trample over them! An instant garden can be created by using several large containers which can contain several litres of soil or potting compost. These can be bought, but if you look around you might find some in builders' skips. Plumbers, for example, often take out metal water tanks from people's attics and these make excellent containers. Containers have to be large enough to

allow planting of small trees, shrubs or plants such as grasses and bamboos.

Petra and her team decided to use metal dustbins for their instant garden. If you decide to make a garden using containers, make sure that you create good drainage by drilling in a couple of holes and also putting some bricks or large stones at the bottom. You should also get advice as to the best type of soil or compost to use which will vary according to the plants that you choose. In addition, you should also find out about whether you should provide additional nutrients from time to time by, for example, adding in plant food.

Working on a budget

Creating a garden does not have to be expensive. It is surprising how many parents are interested in gardening or know someone else who is. This means that you may be able to get some of the materials or plants by putting the word out. Consider also joining your local freecycle group and putting out a request for plants (see www.uk.freecycle.org for further details). It is also worth building up a relationship with local businesses who may either give discounts or even the odd donation.

What to observe

Your garden area will need to evolve over a few weeks. Watching what children are doing and how their play has changed will help you to work out what to bring in, move or change. Below are some things to consider which may help you on this journey.

- How do children use the area?
- What materials hold their fascination?
- Are any children in particular benefiting from this area?
- Are any play patterns or schemas noticeable?
- What level of engagement are individual children showing?
- Do children bring items into the area?
- Can you identify any additional materials that might enhance children's play?

Links to the EYFS

Links to EYFS will very much depend on what is put out for children and also how good the adults are at creating opportunities such as involving children in the care of the plants or sharing books in the centre part.

Personal, Social and Emotional Development	Children benefit from having an area that is different from the rest of the space outdoors as it can provide new learning opportunities. This in turn can help with children's attitudes towards learning (Dispositions and Attitudes) and with their behaviour (Behaviour and Self-control). There are opportunities for children to gain Self-confidence and Self-esteem as they explore opportunities and help to maintain the garden. Ideally, adults should also involve children in the further development of the space by asking children for their ideas.
Communication, Language and Literacy	With every new texture, environment and material we create, children have the possibility of learning new vocabulary. They also have something new to talk about. This is important as sometimes the language between adults and children can feel quite stagnant. A garden should be something that allows new language opportunities as plants change, grow and require tending. By providing opportunities for new vocabulary and opportunities to talk, children will be covering Language for Communication as well as Language for Thinking. A small garden area can also help children to enjoy sharing books and hearing story telling as well as providing a space for talking together. There are also plenty of opportunities to encourage literacy as children can come out and find 'notes' attached to trees.
Problem Solving, Reasoning and Numeracy	Opportunities for this area of learning will depend on identifying naturally occurring opportunities during children's play. Children who are moving cobbles of different colours and sizes can have their attention drawn to this and so there are good links here to Shape, Space and Measures. Children who are watering plants can count how many times they need to fill up the watering can, so there are opportunities to work on Numbers as Labels and for Counting.
Knowledge and Understanding of the World	Two aspects in particular are likely to link to having a good garden area: firstly, Exploration and Investigation and then Place. Exploration and Investigation can be enhanced if children can play with a range of natural materials within this area. Adults can provide magnifiers and draw their attention to features, for example, the way that stones might be speckled or that the bamboo makes a sound when it is windy. Place is about children developing the language to talk about different environments and to be aware of features in the environment.
Physical Development	An oasis type of garden requires that children move differently through it. This links to the aspect Movement and Space. If opportunities are given for children to water and tend plants, they will also be handling tools and so there is a nice link to the Using Equipment and Materials aspect. If your area creates shade, you can talk to the children about keeping cool and staying out of the sun on a hot sunny day. This is a way of bringing in Health and Bodily Awareness.
Creative Development	The garden area can support Developing Imagination and Imaginative Play. The area will be different from other areas of your provision and so should encourage children to play in different ways thus helping them to use their imagination. At Funshine, children pretended that the stones were stepping stones. Children may bring their small world play into this area and will imagine that different things are happening to them. Depending on the size of the area that you create, you may also be able to enjoy story telling with children and encourage them to act out tales, linking to Developing Imagination and Imaginative Play. For younger children, Creative Development is more about exploring different textures and media (Exploring Media and Materials).

Opportunities for physical challenge

In an age when children are more sedentary than before with many consequences in terms of health, it is important that we think about creating physical challenges within outdoor areas. Whilst some settings turn to fixed pieces of equipment as a solution, I do not see these as being essential if your setting does not have the budget or the necessary space. There are also many limitations to these fixed pieces of equipment. Firstly, I would argue that some of them can limit children's creativity and also that many are not versatile and so play can become repetitive. They may also consume quite a lot of staff time if children have free access to them. I therefore see large pieces of fixed play equipment as 'extras'.

Benefits of physically challenging activities

Part of the enjoyment of being outdoors for children is to engage in activities that are not otherwise possible or available indoors, for example, running around or climbing. Physically challenging activities give children a great sense of achievement and thus confidence. They also help children to develop skills such as co-ordination and balance. Physically challenging activities also help children to gain an understanding about the properties of different materials, but also a sense of space, distance and time. Interestingly, physically challenging activities seem to help children to play co-operatively or to engage them in parallel or on-looking play. I often see toddlers watching in fascination as older children climb or swing.

Looking at the physical challenge in your setting

A good starting point is to look at what is available for children in your setting. If your setting has babies, toddlers or children with additional needs, think about their requirements as well. Consider observing children over a number of days. One thing that I find helpful is to ask staff at a setting what they have to stop children from doing. This might seem strange, but it often gives me clues as to what is missing in terms of challenge for them. The idea is either to turn what they are doing into a safer activity or to provide an alternative, for example, children who are stopped from throwing things over the fence may need a more interesting throwing experience.

Climbing and balancing

Children of all ages enjoy climbing and balancing. Even crawling babies will try and find a way of getting up on something. There are many ways of creating opportunities for climbing in an outdoor space. At Funshine Nursery, we used two easily found materials that can help children to enjoy climbing – tyres and tree stumps – but there are plenty of others that we will consider here.

Tyres

Tyres are great because not only are they often free, but they come in different shapes and sizes. Look out for a selection of tyres and aim if you can to get a tractor tyre. Tyres can be wired together to create further height for children. It is important to wash tyres before putting them out for children and some settings paint theirs. Once you have a collection of tyres, think about getting some planks of wood. Check that the wood is not rough and, if necessary, do some sanding down. The wood can be used to create obstacle courses or 'bridges' as some children will say. Supervision of how the children are using and moving the planks will be necessary, but this should give adults an opportunity to talk to children as they act as facilitators.

Tree stumps

As you can see in the DVD tree stumps were very popular with the children. Ideally, try to get as many as you can at different heights. Check that they are fairly flat, but remember that the odd wobble will actually help older children's balance. Painting the slightly wobbly tree stump will remind children that they would need to take more care. The team at Funshine Nursery hit the phone book and made contact with a couple of local tree surgeons and so obtained the stumps at no cost.

Low walls and railway sleepers

Children love walking on low walls. Having their feet above ground level seems to be very appealing to them. Creating something low for children to walk along is therefore important when considering your outdoor area. If you do not have a low wall, think about looking for alternatives such as railway sleepers. If you can, think also about how to integrate the wall or sleeper into the wider meaning of a child's play.

Shortly after filming, the children and staff at Funshine Nursery were combining planks of wood with the tree stumps.

Some settings use sleepers to create a trail that takes children somewhere, for example, towards the role play area.

Steps

Whilst making settings accessible has been a recent focus, it can be useful too for children to have opportunities to learn to negotiate steps. Although the ideal is to build some steps into the outdoor environment, this is where I would concede that climbing frames can be useful. If on the other hand, you have steps, work out how to make them safer for children to incorporate into their play. This might mean putting up a handrail for young children to hold onto or putting lines on the edges.

Climbing walls

In some countries, climbing walls are used instead of climbing frames for young children to practise their skills. Cheaper than a fixed play system, climbing walls might be an option in a setting that needs something to challenge older children. Climbing walls require children to make decisions about how to climb and so

not only give them a physical challenge, but also assist in their problem-solving skills.

Swings

Children enjoy swinging. It is good for their balance and overall co-ordination. Whilst it might be an 'extra' for children over three years, I would definitely

This climbing wall is used by 3–5 year olds at a nursery in Istanbul.

consider it a priority for settings that have babies and toddlers.

The traditional swings can be worth considering particularly for the younger age group as they do not take up much space. For older children, you would need to consider whether you have sufficient space to incorporate the swings as they will need to be fixed to the ground. It is also important to think about how to prevent children walking by from being knocked over. Some settings will therefore put swings in a fenced-off area.

Tyre and rope

If you are lucky enough to have an established tree in your setting, do consider using it to allow children to swing from. A homemade swing made from a tyre and strong rope is ideal. Accidents can be minimised by making the swing low to the ground.

Hammock

Hammocks can be lovely in outdoor spaces. Traditional hammocks require fixing to trees, but it is possible to buy ones with ready-made frames. To avoid accidents, make sure that your hammock is low to the ground and consider using it as an adult-directed activity where children share stories or books in it.

Garden swinging seat

The old-fashioned garden swinging seat seems to be making a comeback. They can be made entirely of wood or use fabric. They have the advantage that children can sit and look at books or simply chat in them. I would definitely consider one for settings that have babies and toddlers as adults can rock children in them. As with other types of swings, you would need to carry out a thorough risk assessment.

Throwing

One area of challenge that is often neglected is the opportunity for children to throw or to drop things. Again, with a little imagination, it is possible to create an area where throwing can be done safely. Firstly, you need to think about what makes a throwing activity satisfying for children. Having observed children, I suspect that there are a couple of requirements. The object that is being thrown has to 'feel' good and then whatever has been hit has to 'do' something. In the chapter Activities to support children's learning and development, I look at activities that might work well with children, but ideally, when reviewing your outdoor area, it is helpful to identify a space where throwing can take place – a corner perhaps?

Transporting

From quite an early age, children seem to enjoy transporting themselves and objects around. Wheels and children go together in some way. There are many pieces of equipment that you can put out for children to help them as the spider diagram below shows.

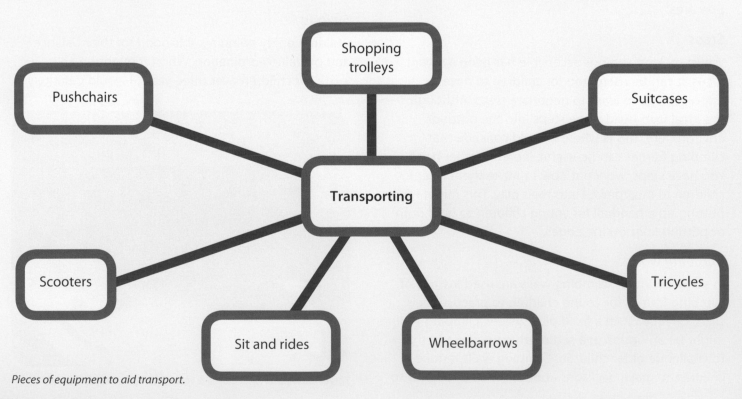

Pieces of equipment to aid transport.

Choosing wheeled resources

There are no 'rights' or 'wrongs' when it comes to choosing which wheeled resources you should use. There are, however, quite a few factors that need to be taken into consideration, as whatever is chosen has to provide children with a satisfying experience and one that is challenging.

Space

How much ground space is available needs to be your starting point. There is little point in having a scooter or a tricycle if children cannot use it over a wide space. Accidents and disputes are more likely to occur and the play itself is unlikely to be challenging. In addition, if babies and toddlers share the outdoor space with older children, thought has to be given as to how to keep them safe. Where space is tight, consider instead other wheeled options, such as pushchairs, which will allow children to transport.

Quantity

Alongside space, thought needs to be given to quantity. Traffic jams spring to mind if too many tricycles or wheeled toys are in too small a space. Buying only two or three can also set up other difficulties as children fight to have a turn. Pushchair or tricycle road rage is quite prevalent in some settings!

Storage

Large wheeled toys have to be stored and this can create problems. This is why thought has to be given to how many to have and which ones to order.

Providing a purpose

When wheeled toys and other transporting resources are working well, children usually have some type of a purpose. They may be using the wheelbarrow to shift something as part of their play or are setting off on their tricycle to 'go shopping'. If you are considering creating a 'track' or 'road' for children to go along, try to create a couple of destinations for children to travel to rather than just going around in circles. The diagram below gives an example of how this might be achieved.

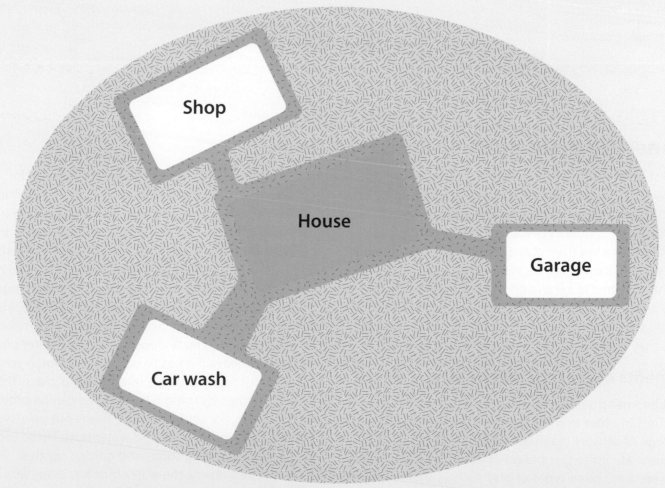

Providing a purpose by creating destinations for children to travel to.

Links to the EYFS

Personal, Social and Emotional Development	Self-confidence and Self-esteem is a key aspect of learning that is delivered when we create areas that are challenging for children. Being able to control one's movements or achieve something such as walking on tree stumps helps children to gain confidence. As children become older, they are also likely to play with other children and so develop the social skills that underpin Behaviour and Self-control.
Problem Solving, Reasoning and Numeracy	The type of resources that I have outlined require that children plan and think. They are also likely to become aware of shape and size, linking to Shape, Space and Measures. Additional understanding of number can be incorporated if adults join children and act as prompts, for example, asking, 'How many times would you like me to push you on this swing?'
Knowledge and Understanding of the World	If resources such as tyres and tree stumps are used, children can explore and investigate what they can do (Exploration and Investigation). It can also be worth taking regular photographs of children as they are engaged in physical play so that afterwards, adults can talk to children about what they can do now compared to what they used to be able to do, linking to the Time aspect.
Physical Development	Creating an environment that has a range of physical challenges will almost certainly cover Movement and Space as an aspect of learning. If adults also talk to children who have been engaged in vigorous activity about how their bodies are reacting, some of Health and Bodily Awareness will be covered.
Creative Development	If we create physical challenges that sometimes have a purpose, for example, stepping stones that lead to a den, children are likely to be Developing Imagination and Imaginative Play. This is why open-ended opportunities are important in outdoor play.

Sensory opportunities outside

Whilst most settings understand the importance of sensory play for children indoors, it is important to think about how it is being provided outdoors. Sensory play outdoors helps children to concentrate and also enriches their play. It is important to expect the sensory materials to 'travel' and also be combined as this is seems to be an important feature of children's play and learning. This means thinking carefully about where to position the materials and also recognising that they will often need renewing or topping up.

Benefits of sensory materials

Children need a range of different sensations and textures in order to stimulate their senses. Providing a range of sensory materials allows children to concentrate for longer periods. Sensory experience can also enhance other types of play such as small world play.

Water

Access to water is a 'must' for children of all ages. Toddlers in particular have a fascination for water and, as you can see in the DVD, they were some of the main beneficiaries when Petra and her team created a water opportunity at Funshine. A good starting point for settings is to see how feasible it is to install an outdoor tap. Having water on hand makes it much easier to create opportunities for water play as water is heavy if it has to be carted about. If you have an outdoor tap that is in the 'wrong' place, think about whether, by using a hose, water can be brought into the area. For settings where this is not possible, consider putting in a covered water butt. These can be found in camping shops and garden centres. At Funshine Nursery, the water butt has been very successful and has created a different type of water play as even very young children have enjoyed serving themselves.

Safety first

Whenever water is provided, we have to be aware of the potential risks associated with it, notably drowning and slipping. We also need to be aware of the danger of standing water that can become contaminated. It would therefore be wise always to supervise water play and not to leave water unattended if there is any possibility that a child could get into a container. It is also important to provide fresh water each day and to make sure that children's hands are washed before they eat.

Ways of presenting water

The usual way of providing water play is via a commercially bought water tray. Whilst this is one possibility, I would argue that you should also consider other ways alongside it as children need opportunities to experience water at different heights and play with water at different depths.

Buckets and metal pails

Buckets and metal pails that children can fill with water or are already filled (in the case of toddlers) can change the dynamics of their play. Ideally, I would go with metal pails just because of the wonderful sound that anything touching metal makes. Buckets and metal pails provide children with the opportunity of having water at a different height from that of the usual water tray. If you provide water in this way, you may notice that children enjoy dropping things in and watching them splash or pushing items down and watching them float to the surface. This type of play is often more cooperative as children seem to take turns and share the space.

Dustbins

If you work with older children consider filling up a small dustbin with water. This will literally create a 'big splash' for children. Stones and other objects can be dropped in so that children can watch and hear them 'plop'. This is a water opportunity that needs constant adult supervision and I would recommend that afterwards the water is immediately drained or siphoned out. I would also suggest that the filling up of the dustbin with water should be done with children to maximise the mathematical learning opportunities, for example, 'How many buckets will it take…?'

Builders' trays

Very shallow trays of water can also be interesting especially if you leave them out in the winter months and the water becomes frozen. Builders' trays can be put at different heights. (At Funshine Nursery, for example, you might just catch sight of a builder's tray on top of a couple of tyres.)

Small containers

Relatively small sized containers of water can give children pleasure and play possibilities and are perfect if you are short of space. Washing up bowls, small storage boxes and even ice cream containers can create some play possibilities for children who wish to play by themselves or want to use water as part of their role play. I have seen children use a small bowl of water outdoors as part of their 'doctor play'. Little by little they spooned the 'magic potion' into bottles with teaspoons!

Items that you might put out alongside water

The props that we put out with water will undoubtedly shape children's play. Consider looking for a range of items – some natural, others from the kitchen – as well as the traditional toys. As the water is to be used outdoors, we can encourage children to transport water from one container to another and so it will be important to provide items that will allow this. Below are a few of my favourite items!

Watering cans

Most toy watering cans are useless as the spout is in the wrong place. Consider using real watering cans where possible, including small ones used to water pot plants.

Small bottles and lids

Small bottles such as those used for food colouring (along with their lids) can provide a source of possibilities for children. Whilst plastic is probably inevitable, some tiny glass perfume bottles can be tough enough depending on how children use them. Putting out some office labels with bottles can give some children the incentive to do some mark-making.

Conch Shells

A couple of large conch shells can be worth considering as children enjoy watching bubbles emerge from them as they are held under water. Removing the water from them is also fun as it requires a twisting motion.

Large cobbles or stones

Petra and her team encouraged children to use water in the garden area that they had created which had stones in it. You can see in the DVD just how much the children enjoyed dropping stones into the metal pail.

Ladles, mashers, wooden spoons

Buckets and metal pails lend themselves to 'pretend cooking' and it is worth looking out for some real kitchen tools so children can stir, scoop and mash the water.

Metal colanders

Children enjoy scooping water, but also watching it fall. Consider, therefore, looking out for a metal colander so that children can watch it 'rain' as they pull it out of the water. Once children have finished, encourage them to dry the colander so that it does not rust.

Sand

Sand is another of those appealing materials for children that is timeless. Ideally sand, like water, should be presented in a variety of ways to avoid children's play becoming unnecessarily repetitive or, worse still, the children becoming bored.

Try to present sand in as many different ways as possible.

Safety first

Sand left outdoors is liable to be treated by local cats and foxes as a lavatory. To avoid health problems, it is therefore important to find a way of covering sand when it is left unattended. In hot weather, some insects can use it to lay eggs in and some micro-organisms can take hold when sand is left moist. This means that sand will need to renewed from time to time and also, if it is damp, it needs to be turned over so that it can dry out.

Ways of presenting sand

Paddling pools

Whilst there are plenty of commercial 'walk or sit in' type of sand trays, if you cannot afford this, consider instead using a robust paddling pool. Paddling pools are not only cheap, but they also have the advantage of being mobile. If you use a paddling pool, consider covering it with a board and some tarpaulin or polythene to avoid the sand becoming wet.

Tarpaulin sheets

Some settings put sand out on tarpaulin sheets to allow children to sit down and play with it. This is once again an option if you cannot afford to build a sand pit. At the end of play, the corners of the tarpaulin need to be gathered and tied up to cover the sand and to keep it dry.

Tyres

Large tyres, if lined, can make wonderful sand pits. Consider putting gravel at the bottom or piercing the lining so that there is some drainage. You can also put two or three tyres together so that children can transfer sand from one place to another.

Builders' trays

Builders' trays are very good if you wish to provide damp sand for children to play in. Their shallowness means that the sand will dry out more quickly than if you add water to a conventional sand tray, thus avoiding problems with smells. As with water, think about putting the trays on tyres or a table so that children can play at different levels.

Sand trays

Commercial sand trays are fine, but I sometimes see staff trying to lift them to take them in and out of doors. This is not a good idea. Sand is very heavy and there is a real possibility of incurring a back injury. If you cannot keep a sand tray outdoors, I would suggest using other alternatives.

Gravel trays

Gravel trays are plastic trays available from garden centres and are used for growing seedlings. They are great because they are bigger than a cat litter tray, but smaller than a builder's tray. They are therefore easily

Children enjoy playing with the gravel tray together.

portable and perfect for two children to play nicely together. You could put a gravel tray in the garden for children to play with. If you put the tray on a wide flat bench, it allows other things to be put alongside it.

Buckets

As with water, children do need opportunities to feel the depth of sand. To do this means looking for a sturdy bucket – or metal pail. Children will gain a lot from digging down and finding or hiding different items.

Bottles of sand

It can be fun for children to find large bottles of sand. Bottles of sand, preferably of different sizes, can be lined up and children can then pour them into different containers. Afterwards sand can be funnelled back into the bottles and put away for another time.

Items that you might put out alongside sand

As with water, there are no 'right' or 'wrong' items to put out with sand, providing of course you have checked that they are safe for children to handle. I often see plastic toys in the sand tray and this seems such a shame as sand is a natural material and there are so many other options that we can use with children. Plastic toys also fade and scratch over time and so tend to lose their visual appeal. Below are some items that prove popular with children.

Large metal spoons

Metal spoons of all sizes work well as children can use them for digging and also for transferring sand into

containers. Look out for serving spoons and consider picking up a catering catalogue, which will have a range of different spoons.

Flower pots

Sturdy flower pots of different sizes can be popular. Some children enjoy watching the sand fall through the holes at the bottom, whilst others will enjoy making sandcastles with damp sand. Find different colours and, most importantly, different sizes.

Providing a range of textures

As well as sand and water, think about incorporating other sensory materials in your outdoor area so that children have a range of textures for their small world play or for scooping. A trip to a large garden centre may provide you with ideas for different textures or areas that you can create. How much you are able to provide will of course depend on the amount of space that you have in your setting and the containers that you have. As with sand, it is worth finding a way of covering these materials when they are not in use in order to keep them clean.

Gravel

Gravel makes a wonderful sound that children will enjoy and they can both scoop it and dig in it. When wet, it also changes colour. It is easy to sweep up which is useful as it will 'travel' if children are enjoying using it. Consider using pea gravel as it does not have sharp edges. Many children will enjoy the combination of sand and gravel. Removing the gravel by sieving is great fun for children and, of course, is an excellent learning opportunity.

Bark chippings

Bark chippings provide a very good contrast to sand and gravel in terms of colour, texture and properties. Bark chippings are fibrous and so children can pull them apart and dig with them. Children will also enjoy putting scoops of bark chippings into buckets of water and trying to mix them in.

Compost

Some settings use clean compost for children to play in. Children are likely to use it in a similar way to bark chippings, and are likely to enjoy digging with it. Compost will 'travel' and so think about how you might create an area to retain it. This might be by creating a wooden pen for it.

Turf

Not all settings have real grass. Whilst I understand the rationale behind using astro turf or hard surfaces, it is still important that children do have opportunities to feel grass. Think therefore about whether you can create a patch of turf – this might be in a paddling pool or in a lined tyre. Ideally, it would be good if there were sufficient space for children to be able to sit in it. If you decide to create a patch of 'lawn', remember that the container will need good drainage. Some garden centres will give you turf remnants, although sowing seeds with children will be a good learning activity.

Links to the EYFS

The links to EYFS will depend very much on the tools, toys and resources that are available for children to use. There are also plenty of opportunities for carrying out adult-led activities using these materials as a starting point. (Some suggestions are included in Activities to support children's learning and development later in this book.)

Personal, Social and Emotional Development	Children gain Self-confidence and Self-esteem from exploring sensory materials. They also gain positive attitudes towards play and learning and in addition they are likely to show greater levels of concentration and perseverance. This links nicely to Dispositions and Attitudes. As children will also be choosing what to use alongside the sensory materials, there will also be a nice link to Self-care.
Communication, Language and Literacy	Many children will talk to themselves and others as they engage in sensory play. Adults should also play alongside children to maximise this in order that children are gaining Language for Communication and Language for Thinking.
Problem Solving, Reasoning and Numeracy	Through their play children are likely to encounter all three of the aspects within this area of learning, especially if adults look for naturally occurring opportunities to encourage counting, for example, talking to children about how many containers they have filled up or noticing that children have separated materials. For children to maximise their learning, it is important to provide many different sizes of containers, scoops etc. so that children can learn about their differences.
Knowledge and Understanding of the World	Children are likely to gain a good understanding of the properties of different materials. This links to Exploration and Investigation. You might also like to consider using magnifying sheets with children for this. If children are busy constructing sand castles or a race track, there is a clear link between this type of play and Designing and Making.
Physical Development	Whilst some children will play using their hands alone, it is most likely that children will want to incorporate some tools into their play. This links to Using Equipment and Materials, which is about encouraging children's fine and gross motor development.
Creative Development	Sensory materials provide an excellent backdrop for small world play, for example, cars, farm animals and play people. If children play with these types of objects, there is a link to Developing Imagination and Imaginative Play. Children will also be Exploring Media and Materials.

What to observe

O Do any children have particular preferences?

O Do you see any play patterns emerging, e.g. children who enjoy filling up or others who like transferring one place to another?

O How do children use the tools, toys and materials in their play?

O How could this play be extended?

O How much speech do individual children use when playing with sensory materials?

O How do adults engage with children as they are playing?

Creating small enclosed spaces

Children of all ages seem to enjoy being in small spaces. At Funshine Nursery, they had two playhouses for the children. One was plastic and on my first visit was in the centre of what I called the 'race track'. The other was a mainly wooden structure and was to the side of the garden. This was the one that I suggested that Petra and her team tried to enclose further as it was in a good position – slightly out of the way so that children would not feel as if they were being seen. The plastic house was re-located into the main building where it has proved to be extremely popular with the children. It also 'looked right' indoors and perhaps is a reminder always to try out equipment and resources in different places as location can sometimes change children's play quite drastically.

Benefits of small enclosed spaces

Being in a small space seems to change the way that children play. Firstly, they are more likely to use language. They may also concentrate for longer periods. This is probably because an enclosed space stops children from being distracted by the movements of others. Small spaces also seem to give children some emotional security.

Successful places for children

It is interesting that many settings, and indeed parents, spend quite a lot of money on playhouses, sheds and other structures which children do not always actually play in. In some ways it is quite amusing to see the children shun the playhouse, but instead try and squeeze themselves behind it or go off and play behind some bushes. As commercial or built-to-measure playhouses are quite expensive, it is worth understanding what children actually need. From watching children over the years, I suspect that the following points need to be considered:

Out of sight

For an enclosed space to work for children, it seems that they must feel as if they are out of sight from adults. This is why children love going behind bushes and dustbins, round corners and sometimes down in the long grass.

Ceiling height

Some structures that are provided for children are simply too high. Whilst an adult may have to bend down to get inside them, the children do not need to. I see time and time again that children like a low ceiling height. Giving children just enough headroom may mean creating an enclosed space that is only a metre high.

Room

It is also important to think about how much room inside the structure children will need. For this, you should think about how many children are likely to use it at the same time. I suspect that sufficient room for six will just about work. If your setting has large numbers of children, think about creating several different spaces.

Supervision

As with all areas of our work, we have to keep children safe and this means keeping an eye on them too. This may mean that the structures that you create may just give children the illusion that they are not being seen. This means that you might put a couple of windows in or look to have a part Perspex® roof. For those 'round the corner' areas that children enjoy hiding in, think about using traffic safety mirrors. These allow children to play without knowing that they are being watched. In addition, you can always listen out or take an interest in what children are doing.

Ways of creating small enclosed spaces

Whilst I have talked about playhouses, there are of course many different ways in which a setting can create small spaces for children, both temporary and permanent. (If you are considering creating a permanent structure for children, it might be worth first creating something similar out of cardboard and fabric in order that you can check its location and its dimensions work for the children. This can avoid costly mistakes.

Tents

Tents appeal to babies as much as they do to older children. If you do not have a grass surface consider using pop-up tents although be aware that they may need fixing down in some way as their lightweight structure can mean that they blow over.

Tipis (Teepees)

Tipis designed for children are a variation on a tent, but it is worth knowing that proper outdoor tipis for children are commercially available. You can also make your own with children.

Children love enclosed spaces.

Cardboard boxes

Cardboard boxes have appealed to generation after generation of children. Look out for some large boxes that are used for packing. It can be worth looking for a retailer who can provide you with a regular supply. As boxes can be folded down, consider whether you can keep a couple in stock along with some rolls of wide parcel tape.

Tables and fabric

A low-tech and temporary structure can be created by simply taking out a table from indoors on a fine day and covering it with fabric or tarpaulin. Tablecloth clips are useful if you decide to do this to prevent the cloth from being tugged off or blown away.

Dens

If you have fencing, especially chain link fencing, then you have the possibility of making a den with the children. Think about tarpaulin or fabric that can be tied or attached to a fence so that it can form the roof.

Playhouses and sheds

If you are sure about the location and size required, a commercially bought playhouse could be a good investment. I would also consider contacting a local shed company to see if you can order one that is made to measure. I would argue against paying for tables and seats to go in it as it is better just to create the space and allow the children to bring things into it.

What to put out alongside an enclosed space

Children often like to make some sort of a home or camp within a structure. It is worth having a range of props available that will allow this to happen. Ideally, it is worth letting children 'find' the props and take them into their house themselves. Below are some of the items that are quite popular with children

Cushions

Children like having somewhere to sit and so a few small cushions seem to be helpful.

Kitchen utensils

A range of kitchen items, including the all-important metal saucepan, are needed as cooking is often a favourite activity for children.

Books

Some children will choose to use a small space as a place to read.

Blankets

A picnic blanket or fabric is nice as children enjoy putting something down on the ground. Look out for plastic-backed ones for days when the ground is damp.

Torches

If you create a small space, consider putting out some torches for children. This could be part of an adult-led activity.

Adult involvement

It is always difficult to give hard and fast rules about how adults should work with children, especially in relation to small enclosed spaces. Babies and toddlers need a lot of adult interaction for their play to be viable and enjoyable. For older children, adults are important too. Some children like to 'report' on happenings within the space and come out from time to time to tell an adult that they like what they are doing and what they are intending to do next. Other children may invite an adult in to inspect their 'work', but do not necessarily want the adult to stay and play. Then again, other children will want and benefit from adults making suggestions and providing them with further props. Whatever role you feel you need to take, it is always worth remembering that the key to this area being successful is that children feel they have ownership of it.

Links to the EYFS

Depending on their age/stage and the way in which children use the space, there are many links to the EYFS.

Personal, Social and Emotional Development	If children feel ownership over their space, they are likely to gain Self-confidence, but also will be learning about Self-care. Small spaces are also opportunities where children learn to be with others and so can gain a Sense of Community. Where children have constructed their own space, there are links to Dispositions and Attitudes.
Communication, Language and Literacy	In a small space, children tend to talk more to each other and can find it easier to listen and concentrate. This links to Language for Communication and to Language for Thinking. If you put out pads and pens, children might be inclined to do some early Writing, whilst if you sometimes provide books, there will be a good link to Reading.
Problem Solving, Reasoning and Numeracy	Some resources that children take into small spaces such as cushions, beakers and spoons can help children learn to count and 'one-to-one' match, for example, each child has their own beaker or cushion. This links to using Numbers as Labels and for Counting. Children often learn about space and size too as they may try to bring into many items inside or realise that some things will not fit.
Knowledge and Understanding of the World	If children create or in some way make their own spaces, there are links to Exploration and Investigation and Designing and Making. This is why it is important not to do too much for children so that they can make their own decisions. If you are making a den or other structure with the children, consider asking them to take photographs at different stages so that they can use ICT. It also means that afterwards they can talk about what they did and so this links to Time.
Physical Development	If the children are making their own space or are making objects to take into their 'homes', there is likely to be a link to Using Equipment and Materials. Adults may also be able to find ways of linking what they are doing to Health and Bodily Awareness by, for example, saying to children that they can have a snack inside the tent, but encouraging them to see the need to wash their hands first.
Creative Development	There are plenty of links to Creative Development as children are likely to be Developing Imagination and Imaginative Play. Where children have created their own space, they will also have been responding to materials and media with also links to Being Creative – Responding to Experiences, Expressing and Communicating Ideas.

What to observe

○ Which children seem to spend a lot of time in enclosed spaces?

○ Do children spend time in pairs or a group in the small space?

○ Are children engaged in imaginative play?

○ What materials and resources do children take into the space?

If children make their own space:

○ What level of concentration and perseverance do they show?

○ Do they seek adult support?

○ Do they work in isolation or with other children?

○ How do they manage disputes?

Mark-making opportunities

It is important that mark-making takes place outdoors as well as indoors. Ideally you should try to provide opportunities for drawing, chalking and painting as well as sensory activities that encourage children to make marks. Outdoor opportunities are easy to provide and can often be very motivating for older children who are not yet doing mark-making inside. At Funshine Nursery, staff were already good at providing for mark-making – in the DVD you might spot their large white board – so this was not an area that I looked at.

Benefits of mark-making outdoors

Mark-making outdoors gives children a great sense of freedom as well as positive experiences of early writing, painting and drawing. Outdoors, we are able to give children larger and often messier opportunities that will often motivate them. Mark-making outdoors in all its forms helps children's fine motor development, creative development and their early writing.

Ways of providing mark-making outdoors

There are many ways of providing mark-making. The key is to make sure that you provide a range of permanent as well adult-directed activities as children will need plenty of different opportunities. It is important that mark-making is linked into creative development and that adults remember that many opportunities will not result in an 'end product'.

Making it satisfying

There are many opportunities which we can use outdoors with children. The key is to make sure that they are satisfying for children. It is disheartening for children not, for example, to see the mark that they have made. This means thinking about providing chalks that do 'chalk' or markers that are not dried up! For young children marking often has to be large for it to be satisfying – another reason why it is important to create spaces outdoors. Below are some ideas that can be used to encourage mark-making, painting and drawing outdoors.

Whiteboards

It is worth investing in a large whiteboard that is fixed to a wall or fence on a permanent basis. Large whiteboards will need markers, of course, and it is important to put out only ones that work. I would suggest putting only a handful out so that they can be 'counted in and out'. Look out for magnetic whiteboards as they can double up as places where children can play with magnetic letters and numbers and with fridge magnets. Think too about providing some small boards which can be taken into a 'writing tent'.

Chalkboards

As well as a whiteboard, think about installing a blackboard where children can chalk, if space allows. Chalkboards and whiteboards can be turned into spaces where children can paint and draw, by simply taping on paper.

Painting wall

In the chapter on Creative development, I explained how to create a large painting wall indoors. It is possible to do the same outdoors. If you decide to do this, choose an area which is not too windy and use very wide masking tape to fix the polythene to the wall.

Paper onto fences

Many settings report great success by pinning up lining paper onto fences for children to paint and decorate. This is of course a temporary activity, but again one that is appealing for children and works well.

Water and brushes

This is a great favourite with many settings. Putting out some buckets and a few large paintbrushes allows toddlers and older children to enjoy painting walls, doors and also the ground. (If there are babies around, remember to empty buckets afterwards to prevent any potential accidents.)

Window washing

Children love washing windows and if slightly soapy water and sponges are used beautiful marks can be made. If windows are not available, perhaps the children can wash the chalkboard or the whiteboard.

Damp sand and sticks

A gravel tray of damp sand and some twigs can provide a great opportunity for children to make their mark. Supervision is desirable though, just in case the twigs are turned into swords.

Writing box

It can be worth developing a writing box; something akin to a tool box would be great. In the box, put small notepads, paper and clipboards. Stamps and other items can be added. Ideally the contents of the box will need to change so that children can always find new inspiration and a challenge.

Writing tents

From time to time, create a writing tent for children. A writing tent will be a covered den which has the writing box within it as well as a table for children to lean on. Writing tents can be themed to suit older children's role play interests, for example, a pirate's map-making den.

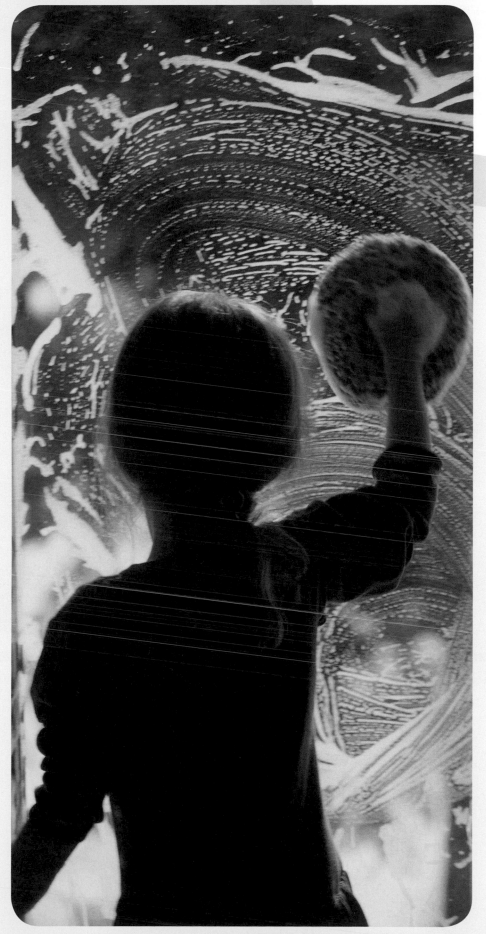

Time to clean!

Links to the EYFS

Mark-making, painting and drawing can link to several areas of development, depending on the tools, resources and materials that children are using.

Personal, Social and Emotional Development	Three aspects are likely to be covered when children of all ages are making marks. Firstly Disposition and Attitudes as children will be concentrating if sensory materials are involved. Children should also be gaining Self-confidence as mark-making can make them feel quite powerful and in control. Finally, where children have chosen for themselves the materials and resources they want to use, they will be showing some aspects of Self-care.
Communication, Language and Literacy	The obvious links are Writing and Handwriting, but it is likely that some children will be mark-making and talking with other children and so showing Language for Communication and possibly Language for Thinking. With babies and toddlers, mark-making experiences may be carried out alongside an adult who should also be drawing out language opportunities.
Problem Solving, Reasoning and Numeracy	The links here will depend very much on what children do as they are mark-making. Some children may talk about the size and shapes that they are producing. Adults should also look out for opportunities to comment about Shape, Space and Measures in relation to the child's mark-making.
Knowledge and Understanding of the World	Mark-making with sensory materials such as paint, water and sand, should support Exploration and Investigation.
Physical Development	Mark-making at all ages links nicely to Using Equipment and Materials in this area of development. If children are making very large shapes and movements by painting on a very large scale, consider also whether their activity links to Movement and Space.
Creative Development	Mark-making, painting and drawing activities are inherently creative so therefore should link to the Being Creative – Responding to Experiences, Expressing and Communicating Ideas. In addition, older children may also use clipboards and other opportunities as part of their imaginative play, e.g. pretending to be a window cleaner and so consider Developing Imagination and Imaginative Play.

What to observe

It is always interesting to see what children enjoy doing outdoors with mark-making opportunities. You might like to consider the following points:

○ Is hand preference observable?

○ Do any children prefer to mark-make out of sight of adults?

○ Which equipment and materials do children prefer?

○ What happens when adults mark-make in front of children?

○ Are any children ascribing meaning to their marks?

○ Do any children show a preference for outdoor marking? If so…

- What do they choose to use outdoors?
- Why do you think that these materials appeal to them?
- Could this be brought indoors?

Creating a Digging area

After years of watching children at play outdoors, I have come to the conclusion that there must be something instinctive about the need to dig. Perhaps we are all farmers? For me this means that we should try wherever possible to provide somewhere for children to dig. At Funshine Nursery, I have suggested that this might be a 'next steps' for them so hopefully when they are ready, they will have a look at this.

Benefits of digging

Digging activities are good for children's physical skills and also their sense of confidence and self-esteem. They are very much 'I can do' activities. Children often find them naturally challenging and usually develop their own imaginative play scripts to accompany their digging.

Satisfying and successful

It is important when creating a digging area to make sure that children have a satisfying and successful experience. This means making sure that they can dig down enough and that the materials used allow them to make a hole. There also needs to be sufficient space as children often tend to dig alongside each other.

Creating a digging area

Some settings will be lucky enough to have some flower beds already which can be converted into digging areas. If this is the case in your setting, move any existing flowers or shrubs to another area and then create some sort of a border so that children know where they can and cannot dig. Think also about putting some bark chippings or gravel on top of where they are allowed to dig so that they can experience different surfaces.

Lifting up a flagstone or creating a hole in the tarmac

In the past, I have visited settings that have tarmac surfaces or areas with flagstones. If this is the case in your setting, you might be able to create a patch for digging. Whilst lifting up a flagstone is quite straightforward, creating a patch in a tarmac surface will require some drilling and so there is a cost implication. I would however argue that it is a 'one-off' and, once done, will provide children with a new resource that is likely to provide them with constant learning opportunities.

Creating a raised bed

If you have a tarmac surface, another option is to create a raised bed. This can be done by building a low wall around an area or by constructing a bed using railways sleepers. This does require more time and effort, but is not necessarily particularly costly especially if you ask for volunteers amongst parents. (Consider also contacting your local FE college and seeing if they run construction courses. If so, they may well take this on as a project to help their students practise their brick laying.) A raised bed also has visual advantages as it can create an 'island' in your setting.

Tyres

Tyres can make good containers. Think about grouping three or four together so that children have plenty of space. Large tyres can be lined with a membrane such as tarpaulin or polythene and then filled with different materials.

What to put out in digging areas

Hand tools

Look out for some hand tools. Many leading manufacturers of garden tools are now producing small versions of proper tools for children and so are worth looking at although you will of course need to do a risk assessment. Plastic hand tools can work providing that the digging material is fairly loose, for example, a gravel and sand mixture. Metal scoops are also worth considering.

Small-scale spades

As with hand tools, it is possible to buy small-scale spades designed for children. They are not toys, and will give children great satisfaction. Consider putting out these tools under adult supervision rather than allowing free access to them.

Containers

Children like to have containers into which they can put soil or other digging materials. Consider putting out some full size builders' buckets as well as small containers. Large containers allow children to experience 'weight' on a large scale and they will enjoy trying to lift something truly heavy.

Wheelbarrows

Providing you are happy for children to 'transport' materials around, think about wheelbarrows. As with garden tools, it is possible to buy a child-sized version of an adult's wheelbarrow, although I would suggest the version that has two wheels and a 'joined' handle.

A scaled version of an adult's wheelbarrow can enhance children's play.

Links to the EYFS

Providing a digging space for children can support their learning across the areas of development.

Personal, Social and Emotional Development	Activities such as digging as part of children's child-initiated play can give them Self-confidence and boost their Self-esteem. There is something rather satisfying about digging a hole by oneself. Toddlers in particular benefit from activities that give them a sense of power and control over the environment. Afterwards, children will need to wash their hands and so you might observe that children are able to show elements of Self-care.
Communication, Language and Literacy	Children often talk to each other when they are engaged in repetitive actions that have a focus. I would therefore expect that many children will be using Language for Communication and Language for Thinking, although adults may need to enhance this. Digging can be part of children's wider imaginative play and so by providing clipboards and markers, some children will pretend to be on a building site.
Problem Solving, Reasoning and Numeracy	If several containers are put out, children might naturally count how many they have filled up. Adults can build on this by creating games that encourage children to count how many scoops of digging material are required to fill the bucket. By putting out different sized containers, children will gain a sense of Shape, Space and Measures. They will of course benefit more if adults comment about the shape and quantity that children are putting in.
Knowledge and Understanding of the World	Digging links to Exploration and Investigation, especially if you provide several different materials for children to use. It will be important also to talk to children about the differences between bark chippings and sand, for example, and for children to talk about how materials change when they are damp or wet.
Physical Development	Digging with tools fits nicely into the using Equipment and Materials aspect of learning within Physical Development. There might also be opportunities to look at Health and Bodily Awareness if you can also encourage children to talk about the effects of digging on their body, for example, saying their hands become tired or start to hurt. Encouraging children to wash their hands and seeing if they understand the reason behind this will also linked to this aspect.
Creative Development	Whilst children are digging, some will be exploring materials. For older children you might find that they incorporate digging into their imaginative play and so this will link to Developing Imagination and Imaginative Play.

What to observe

It is important that this area remains challenging for children and so observing them will help you to work out how to extend their play and also give you early warning signals that you might need to put out new materials.

- O Do children have a clear purpose when digging?
- O Are children co-operating?
- O Are children using this as part of their imaginative play?
- O Which type of tools and movements do children mostly use?
- O Can you see hand preference when children are using one handed tools?
- O How confident are children when handling tools?
- O How persistent are children if items are hidden in the digging area?
- O Do children enjoy engaging with adults?

Loose part play

One of the many ways in which we can make outdoor spaces more interesting for children is to use loose part play on a regular basis. Loose part play is simply a case of putting out objects for children to incorporate into their play or to use as starting points for play. In the DVD, you will see that I gave a few bits and pieces to Funshine nursery. These were items that I had found in my local shops. You may see the following:

- metal jewellery box
- enamel cups
- plunger
- 2 metres of thick rope
- thin fabric.

In some ways there is nothing new in this. Children the world over have always used whatever is in their environment as a basis for play. This has meant that play often used to be quite spontaneous and therefore challenging for children. Nowadays, there is a danger that children know what to expect and so their play becomes quite stale. When I was in China I saw two boys spontaneously playing in a mound of builder's sand at the side of a busy street. Whilst we may not be able to put down a large mound of sand, we can look out for large and small objects that might be of interest to children. Providing that you have considered any possible hazards, there is no right or wrong to the type of items you provide although in general try to avoid toys.

Benefits of loose part play

I would argue that in this age of commercial toys, children need increased opportunities to use their imagination and also to see 'real objects.' The children quickly worked out what they might be able to do with the objects I gave them in the DVD. The plunger for example, was drafted in to 'fix' tricycles, whilst the fabric had the potential to become a dragon, a hiding place and a wedding dress. It is also interesting to see how children can come together to invent new games and how toddlers' language can develop as they want to share their finds with an adult.

Planning loose part play

The key in terms of planning for loose part play is to ensure that the objects you intend to use are safe for the age range of children who will find them. This means checking their size and cleanliness and also whether they have movable parts or sharp edges. As safety is of course a hot topic, it would also be sensible to monitor the way that children use new objects when they are first introduced into the setting.

As well as thinking about safety, we must also focus on the value of the objects themselves. The objects will need to hold children's interest in some way. This may happen because the children have not seen the objects before or because, combined with other materials, they can act as starting points for play. The rope, for example, is something that children may not have as a usual play item, but can be used to step on, to be a magic river or to round up other children. With older children, you may put out objects that are quite small alongside some larger items, for example, a tin of sequins and some shells alongside a kitchen swing bin, some cardboard boxes and a sheet of fabric.

In terms of planning, you will not necessarily be able to guess what children will do with the objects, but as you will see later on, the concept of loose part play has many tangible links to the EYFS areas of development. The number of items that you put out will vary according to how many children are outside at once and of course their ages. If you have a large number of children outdoors, it would be advisable to have several different items so that children who do not pick up or see something at first can go onto find something else later.

Scattering or grouping?

In the DVD, I gave the items in a package. This was partly because it was a present for Funshine Nursery, but also because it can be interesting to see what happens when a collection of objects are available. There are also many benefits in having items scattered or even partly hidden in an outdoor area. Children like 'coming across' or discovering items and this in itself can be a way of boosting children's play. In some settings, objects for loose part play appear as if by magic and fairly randomly when staff feel that children are in need of new challenges and stimulation.

Getting hold of objects

There are no rights or wrongs when it comes to the type of objects that you should look for. Personally, I find building skips a source of many interesting items such as vacuum cleaner hoses or guttering. (Make sure you have permission before taking items from skips.) Hardware shops too can be very useful as can scrap stores. Cardboard tubes and boxes can often be gathered from local companies, whilst different types of fabrics and household objects can be gained from parents.

Children have always played with things that they have found.

Links to the EYFS

Personal, Social and Emotional Development	Loose part play gives children genuine opportunities to discover and do things by themselves. This gives them pleasure, and a sense of agency which in turn can build their Self-confidence and Self-esteem. Older children are also likely to negotiate and turn-take in order to play with others. Whilst there might be the odd squabble, it is interesting to see whether children can control their behaviour and seek a resolution.
Communication, Language and Literacy	Children often want to talk to other children or adults when they find objects. You may observe children talking to each other and discussing what to do or you may find that children want to show and talk to adults. Where adults are involved, there is a great opportunity to develop children's Language for Thinking. Adults can point out features of objects and accurately name them. Adults can also facilitate discussions and explanations.
Problem Solving, Reasoning and Numeracy	Loose part play encourages children to solve problems and to reason. After all they have to think about what they might do with the objects! They may also in a practical way focus on Shape, Space and Measures.
Knowledge and Understanding of the World	There are two key aspects that loose part play is linked to. Firstly, Exploration and Investigation, which it is likely to cover quite nicely, but also Designing and Making if children use the items and turn them into something else, for example, a cardboard box, fabric and a drain pipe might become a house with a chimney. The aspect Time can be covered by taking photographs or videos of children at play so that afterwards children can talk about what happened.
Physical Development	Handling and exploring items will mean that children are likely to use both their gross and fine motor skills. This in turn links to the aspects Movement and Space and Using Equipment and Materials.
Creative Development	Loose part play is a good example of encouraging children to be genuinely creative in their play. There are therefore strong links to this area of development in particular Exploring Media and Materials, and Developing Imagination and Imaginative Play.

What to observe

Watching children use the objects that they find should give plenty of observation material. It is always interesting to see how children react and which children seem to have very high levels of creativity and decision-making. Observing children with loose part play objects can also give you ideas of how to plan further for individual children. Below are some questions that you might use when observing this type of play:

- Is the child confident to pick up and explore objects?
- How quickly does the child find a way of using the object?
- What physical skills does the child use?
- Does the child use the object(s) to engage with others?
- Does the child talk to the adult about what has been found?
- How engaged is the child whilst playing?
- How long does the child play for?
- How could the child's play be enhanced or built on?

Your questions answered

○ *Should we use artificial surface or real grass?*

The ideal would always be real grass, but this is not always possible for all settings. If you have an area of real grass that is often out of action because it becomes muddy, consider putting stepping stones or pathways through it so that children can play out on it. If you do have an artificial surface, I would suggest that you look for ways of creating as many 'natural' areas within it as possible by adding, for example, bark chippings, gravel, sand and real grass left to grow up high. This would create many different textures and thus learning opportunities for children.

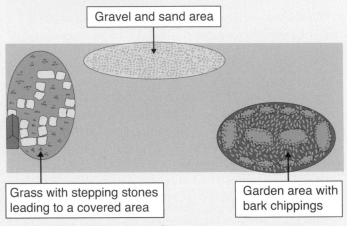

Gravel and sand area

Grass with stepping stones leading to a covered area

Garden area with bark chippings

Example of ideas for outdoor surfaces.

○ *What can we do if our outdoor area does not have any shade?*

In view of the current guidelines relating to sun safety, it is essential that shade is provided for children in the summer months. Many settings tackle this by putting up permanent canopies, but there are other low-cost solutions as well.

Parasols

Think about using commercial parasols – the kind that restaurants use. These have to be properly fixed to avoid them toppling over, but can be a solution.

Planting trees and plants

Shade can be created by planting trees and other plants in groups. Grouping is important as it means that shade is provided regardless of the direction of the sun. In Funshine Nursery, the bamboos will, when established, create a shady area. Until this time, the nursery will be able to throw over some fabric or tarpaulin to create a block of shade.

Using posts

Whilst I would always plump for natural materials, it is possible to create shade by putting a few wooden posts or poles into the ground and cementing them in. Once the poles are in place, strips of fabric or similar can be attached to them so that a tent-like structure is achieved.

Gazebos

Some settings buy gazebos or similar structures. They can work well, although cheaper ones can be buffeted by the wind.

○ *What about outdoor clothing?*

There is an expectation that children should be out in all weathers. To achieve this does mean providing suitable clothing for children. Many settings have tackled this by buying in clothing. This has many advantages: you can be sure that children will be suitably dressed if it is cold or wet and because if a child gets wet or dirty, you are not making work for parents.

Clothing by the door

Think about re-organising the layout indoors in order to put outdoor clothing near the outside door. (I would like to see more hanging rails as children should be learning to hang up clothes.)

Rain ponchos

Rain ponchos can be useful to keep children covered and dry, especially if children are sitting down on damp or wet surfaces. They can be put on easily by the child and are useful if they are doing messy activities. Rain ponchos are not particularly durable, but they are at least cheap. Some settings have even approached theme parks and have been given them for free. Children tend to enjoy them as they do not restrict their movements and they are also useful for superhero play. Watch the length of rain ponchos if children are doing climbing activities though.

Hats and gloves

It is worth asking parents to bring in a woollen hat and some gloves for their child to keep in the setting. These can be kept in a see through plastic wallet with the child's name on. I would not recommend 'communal' hats as many settings do have serious outbreaks of head lice.

'All-in-ones'

These are ideal, especially if your setting has toddlers, but do consider them for older children as well. Look for ones that are easy for children to put on, for example, those that have zips instead of buttons. Consider ordering different colours for each age group so that children know which ones they should put on.

Wellingtons

A good supply of Wellingtons is a must. As with all-in-ones, order different colours for each foot size so that children learn to choose the colour that will fit them.

○ *Should we send children out in the sun?*

Whilst we are meant to be using the outdoor area in all weathers, it is advisable to follow the latest sun advice (www.sunsmart.org.uk.) This might mean creating areas for shade (see p.128). It will also mean making parents aware of the need to use sun cream on their child. Luckily, there are now some long-acting sun creams which can give children several hours of protection. In addition, long-sleeved tops or sun suits should be provided.

○ *Any ideas for keeping the indoors warm if we have free flow play in winter?*

Keeping the indoor space warm in winter can be a real struggle if the outside door is constantly in use or open. Below are some ideas that I have seen settings use as a way to deal with this.

PVC strip curtains

It is possible to buy PVC strip curtains. These are often used in warehouses to keep areas cool. They consist of thick PVC strips that overlay each other. They will not be as effective as closing a door, but may be worth considering if you wish to keep a door open, but reduce heat loss.

Build a porch

If you have sufficient money, consider adding on a porch which can also serve as a clothing area.

Group children into batches

Some settings have few alternatives but to 'batch' children as they go in and out of doors so that the door is not constantly open. Whilst this is not ideal, it might be the only solution in some settings.

○ *How can we incorporate ICT into the outdoor environment?*

ICT in the EYFS is about gadgets and programmable toys rather than computers. Look out therefore for some indoor resources that are robust enough to go outdoors, such as remote-controlled cars, and think also about buying some digital cameras and recorders that children can use. I like showing children battery-operated digital thermometers which can predict the weather. If you create a small space that is quite dark, children can take torches inside as well as other gadgets, such as battery-operated light wands.

Activities to support children's learning and development

In my last book (*Penny Tassoni's Practical EYFS Handbook*, Heinemann, 2008), I chose activities that would clearly illustrate how an aspect of development could be delivered. In this book, I want to show how many good activities will actually support children's development more widely. All of the activities are adult directed. I make no apology for this as good adult-led activities are vital for children's overall development. Having said this, I have indicated how the activities might be developed by children into child-initiated activities.

In this chapter I have provided 10 activities for each of the following age ranges:

- 6–18 months
- 18 months to 3 years
- 3 years plus.

I have also included suggestions for how to develop the activity.

Age ranges

I have grouped the activities into three broad age ranges:

- 6–18 months
- 18 months to 3 years
- 3 years +

I have done this because the play needs and interests of children change quite significantly at different periods in their childhood, that is, 3-year-olds start to use more role play, whilst children under 18 months tend still to be mouthing and quite exploratory. I therefore leave it up to you to decide which activities are the most appropriate for the children with whom you work, as you will know where they are in developmental terms.

Group size

I have not suggested any group size, but I always recommend that children benefit from having as much individual attention as possible. Wherever possible, aim to work individually with babies and toddlers and try hard with older children to keep group sizes down to around four or five. Groups larger than this will result in children missing out on language and therefore learning opportunities. This should be possible for most settings if they run their adult-directed activities alongside the opportunities for child-initiated play (see pp.11–17).

Resources

I have tried to list the essential resources that are needed. In writing activities, I always try to avoid expensive equipment, although in order to embed ICT, I have suggested using a digital camera at times. Note that my essential resources list does not include every last detail or apron as, in my experience, practitioners are totally capable of bringing common sense to bear when thinking about activities.

Health and safety points

Where possible, I have tried to include some health and safety points although I do make the assumption that children will be adequately supervised and that good risk assessments are in place.

Observation points

Observing children during activities is vital so that we can plan further activities and also reflect on how well an activity has worked for individual children. To assist with this observation, I have given some indicators as to what you might consider, but while you are 'on the spot' you may also observe other features of how children are engaging with the activities.

Outdoors

Many activities are suitable for both indoors and outdoors. For each activity, I have suggested how the activity can be taken outdoors although, in some cases, the activity suggested is actually planned for outdoors.

Links to EYFS

I have tried for each activity to signpost possible links to the EYFS. This is not a promise, as it will very much depend on how the activity is delivered and how learning opportunities are maximised, for example, using ICT or encouraging interaction.

Ring-a-ding bells

The sound of bells often excites babies and very young toddlers. With this activity, babies and toddlers can make and explore sounds themselves.

Resources

Bells – as many different ones as possible that are safe, for example

- Cat bells inside small fabric bags or plastic bottles that are sealed
- Sleigh bells that can be attached to a wrist
- Traditional bells with a handle
- Baby toys that include a bell.

Health & Safety

- Risk assess the bells and the way that you intend to present them to prevent them being a choking hazard.
- Do not leave the child unsupervised.

Activity

Collect different types of bells together. Risk assess each type of bell and either discard or find ways of making it safe. Cat bells can, for example, be sealed inside a fabric bag or a plastic bottle.

Take out a different bell and play it in front of the child. Observe their reaction. Allow the child to explore the bell and see if they can make it ring. Try also to play some games by hiding a bell behind your back and making it ring. See if the baby tries to find it.

Think also about making patterns with the bells, e.g. ringing it twice and then stopping and then repeating the pattern again.

Next Steps

Observation points

- How engaged is the child in this activity?
- What is the reaction of the child to the bell?
- How does the child communicate pleasure/ displeasure?
- Does the child understand how to make the bell ring?
- Does the child attempt to touch or hold the bell?
- Does the child have a favourite bell?
- If you make a pattern with the bells, does the child seem to anticipate it?
- What other sounds could be used?

How can we take this outdoors?

This activity can be taken outdoors in different ways. Firstly, the activity could be done outdoors sitting with the child on your lap or on the ground. Baby toys that have a bell inside could be attached to a pushchair so that they can be played with on a walk.

How can we vary/build on this activity?

- You could add bells onto a baby gym so that when the baby kicks or touches the gym they can hear the sound.
- If a mobile baby enjoys this activity, you can hide bells inside boxes and other containers for the baby to find.

How can this become a child-initiated activity?

This becomes a child-initiated activity when the young baby signals to the adult that he would like to hear the bell again. For older babies and toddlers, you can take photographs of the bells so that at another time, they can indicate that they would like to do this again. If bells are part of a safe baby toy, the toy can be left out.

Links to the EYFS

For the baby or young toddler to benefit from this activity, it is important for the adult to interact well with the child and to allow time for the child to respond and react. A young baby can gain confidence and learn about communication when a sensitive adult picks up the cue that the baby wants to hear a sound again. For older babies, being able to make a sound with the bell will help a child to gain confidence and will also help the child to explore.

Personal, Social and Emotional Development	Dispositions and Attitudes Self-confidence and Self-esteem	
Communication, Language and Literacy	Language for Communication Language for Thinking	Handwriting
Problem Solving, Reasoning and Numeracy	Calculating Shape, Space and Measures	
Knowledge and Understanding of the World	Exploration and Investigation Designing and Making	
Physical Development	Movement and Space Using Equipment and Materials	
Creative Development	Being Creative – Responding to Experiences, Expressing and Communicating Ideas	Exploring Media and Materials Creating Music and Dance

Black and white

Putting together a range of black and white objects can help babies and young toddlers to notice colour in a stimulating way.

Resources

Safe objects that are black and/or white – as many as possible, such as

- Black and white checked fabric
- Black and white striped scarf
- Toy zebra
- White plastic plate
- Black plastic tube.

Health & Safety

- Each item should be carefully risk assessed, for example, check that items can be mouthed and that there are no sharp edges.
- Supervise carefully.

Activity

Collect different items together. Aim for different shapes, textures and sizes. Make sure that objects are safe for babies to mouth. Lay out the objects so that they look interesting and dynamic. Take the baby over to them and let them explore the items.

Encourage the baby to touch, mouth and shake items. Talk to the baby about whatever is holding their attention. Pick out some items that the baby has not noticed and show them to them. Name the items and make comments about them.

If possible, take photographs whilst the activity is ongoing. Afterwards print out and laminate the photographs to create a little book.

Next Steps

Observation points

- How engaged is the child in this activity?
- What is the reaction of the child to the items?
- How easily can the child handle the items?
- Are there any items that the child finds particularly fascinating?
- How does the child explore them?
- How long does the child spend with these?
- Can you work out why the child is fascinated by them?
- Does the child try to involve you in their exploration?

How can we take this outdoors?

This could be an indoor or outdoor activity.

How can we vary/build on this activity?

Observe which items the child is especially interested in. Use these items again in different contexts, for example, put them into the treasure basket/heuristic play.

How can this become a child-initiated activity?

Put these items together in a basket so that a mobile child can access them easily. For non-mobile children, take the child over to the basket and carefully observe their reaction.

Links to the EYFS

For the baby or young toddler to benefit from this activity, it is important for the adult to interact well with the child and to allow time for them to respond and react. By grouping items according to their colour, these young children are learning about patterns as well as textures and colours. You should always aim to count items as you tidy up with the baby or child as this helps them to hear counting rhythms.

Personal, Social and Emotional Development	Dispositions and Attitudes	
	Self-confidence and Self-esteem	
Communication, Language and Literacy	Language for Communication	Reading
	Language for Thinking	Handwriting
Problem Solving, Reasoning and Numeracy	Numbers as Labels and for Counting	
	Shape, Space and Measures	
Knowledge and Understanding of the World	Exploration and Investigation	ICT
	Designing and Making	
Physical Development	Movement and Space	
	Using Equipment and Materials	
Creative Development	Being Creative – Responding to Experiences, Expressing and Communicating Ideas	Exploring Media and Materials
		Developing Imagination and Imaginative Play

6–18 months

Fruit and vegetables

Babies and young toddlers learn by mouthing and touching. This simple activity helps them to enjoy the feel, smell and textures of fruit and vegetables.

Resources

Clean fruit and vegetables – choose according to age/stage of child

- Lemon
- Coconut
- Cabbage
- Potato
- Orange
- Pineapple
- Grapefruit

Health & Safety

- Each item should be carefully risk assessed.
- Find out whether children have any allergies relating to fruit and vegetables.

Activity

Collect different types of fruit and vegetables together. Use fruit and vegetables that are firm/hard, for example, lemons. Think about the age/stage of the child that you are working with. Consider whether the child is likely to bite it and consider the consequences in terms of choking hazard. Make sure items are clean.

Put out the different items in a group and let the children explore them. For young toddlers, pick up items and name them. See if later on they can point to items as you name them. Think also about grouping them, for example, three lemons together, one orange by itself. For babies, you may need to pass or hold items for them to feel and mouth.

Try to take photographs of each of the fruits or vegetables. Afterwards, print out the photographs, laminate them and create a book.

Next Steps

Observation points

- How engaged is the child in this activity?
- What is the reaction of the child to the items?
- How easily can the child handle the items?
- Are there any items that the child finds particularly fascinating?
- How does the child explore them?
- Does the child appear to recognise any items?
- Does the child turn to look at you?
- Can the younger toddler point out an item when you name it?

How can we take this outdoors?

This could be an indoor or outdoor activity.

How can we vary/build on this activity?

- For older babies, put out some low baskets or boxes so that they can move items in and out of them.
- Put items in fabric bags so that babies and toddlers can feel and 'find' them.
- Incorporate some fruit and vegetables into the treasure basket/heuristic play.
- Take the child out to a greengrocer or fruit and vegetable section in a supermarket.

How can this become a child-initiated activity?

- Put the items into a basket afterwards so that mobile children can go over to them and use them.
- Regularly offer these items to younger babies so that they can show you whether or not they are interested in exploring them further.

Links to the EYFS

This activity can help babies and young toddlers to gain confidence by exploring. They can also learn to associate these items with sounds in words. Handling the items will also help their physical skills. Touching unfamiliar items also supports children's imagination. As with all activities for this age range, adult interaction and interest is vital. If photographs are taken and a book made, children can begin to understand about reading.

Personal, Social and Emotional Development	Dispositions and Attitudes	Self-confidence and Self-esteem
	Making Relationships	
Communication, Language and Literacy	Language for Communication	Reading
	Language for Thinking	Handwriting
Problem Solving, Reasoning and Numeracy	Numbers as Labels and for Counting	
	Shape, Space and Measures	
Knowledge and Understanding of the World	Exploration and Investigation	Time
	Designing and Making	
Physical Development	Movement and Space	
	Using Equipment and Materials	
Creative Development	Being Creative – Responding to Experiences, Expressing and Communicating Ideas	Exploring Media and Materials
		Developing Imagination and Imaginative Play

Watch the puppet!

Very early on in life, babies and toddlers respond to puppets. This simple activity using a hand puppet is likely to prove great fun.

Resources

Hand puppet – one that you enjoy using, for example

- a glove puppet
- a finger puppet
- a 'pop-up puppet'

Health & Safety

- Do not leave the puppet with the child.
- Make sure that the puppet can be safely touched/stroked.

Activity

Choose a puppet that you are comfortable using. Make sure that it is clean and safe for a child to touch. (This is not an activity where the child will be using the puppet, although a young toddler might like to touch it).

Choose a moment to put the puppet onto your hand. If possible, do this out of sight of the child. Bring the puppet into view. Do not madly wave the puppet or push it towards the child as this is likely to frighten them. Talk to the puppet and make eye contact with it. Try to make slow movements with the puppet and see how the child responds if you take it out of sight and bring it back again – so that the puppet is playing peep. Let the young toddler touch the puppet but do not give it to them as this will spoil the magic. Take a photograph of the puppet so that afterwards the child can have a way of requesting it and you can talk about it together.

Next Steps

Observation points

- How engaged is the child in this activity?
- What is the reaction of the child to the puppet?
- When the puppet goes out of sight, does the child look for it?
- Does the child try and talk to the puppet?
- Does the child try to involve you in this activity?
- Does the child recognise the puppet when it re-appears?

How can we take this outdoors?

This could be an indoor or outdoor activity.

How can we vary/build on this activity?

- Show the child the photograph of the puppet and see if they can recognise it.
- Repeat this activity, but see if the puppet can bring something for the child to hold.
- Repeat this activity with other types of puppet.
- Bring the puppet out at set times in the routine, for example, just after a meal.

How can this become a child-initiated activity?

- Take photographs of the puppet so that the child can show their interest in repeating this activity.
- Have the puppet in view sometimes so that the child can point to it to show that they would like to see it again.

Links to the EYFS

This activity can develop children's language skills as they often react to a puppet. If you play peepo type games, the children will also learn about constancy of objects. They also pick up patterns and even young babies may expect the puppet to re-appear.

If you take a photograph of the puppet, you can incorporate it into a book about favourite toys and activities for the baby to look at. The puppet could also be used at key points in a routine so that the baby begins to learn about time and place.

Personal, Social and Emotional Development	Dispositions and Attitudes	Self-confidence and Self-esteem
	Making Relationships	Sense of Community
Communication, Language and Literacy	Language for Communication	Reading
	Language for Thinking	
Problem Solving, Reasoning and Numeracy	Numbers as Labels and for Counting	
	Shape, Space and Measures	
Knowledge and Understanding of the World	Exploration and Investigation	Place
	Time	
Physical Development	Movement and Space	
Creative Development	Being Creative – Responding to Experiences, Expressing and Communicating Ideas	Developing Imagination and Imaginative Play

Spheres, balls and round shapes

Babies and young toddlers can explore shapes, and balls are particularly popular. In this activity, babies and young toddlers will be able to touch, mouth and roll them!

Resources

A selection of different balls and spheres – choose ones that are safe to mouth and that have different textures, e.g.:

- Ball of string (tie in the end)
- Foam ball
- Plastic ball with an object inside
- Inflatable ball
- Decorations, for example, wooden sphere.

Health & Safety

- Check items carefully and consider whether they are appropriate for the age/stage of child.
- Be aware that heavy balls might be dropped by a baby and so will need supporting.

Activity

Begin by looking out for a range of different sphere-shaped objects. Some will be toys whilst others might have a more decorative function. Consider also fruit and vegetables as well as large cobbles. Make sure objects are safe and clean before putting them out as a group for the child to explore. Aim to put out some duplicate items and group them together.

Follow the child's lead as they explore, but you might also like to roll some items or to play a game of rolling. Heavier items can be safe and useful for a baby to explore, but do be ready to support them.

Next Steps

Observation points

- How engaged is the child in this activity?
- What does the child do with the balls?
- Can they make them move?
- How does the child react when the balls roll?
- Does the child have a favourite item?
- Can the child play a game with you?
- How does the child interact with you?

How can we take this outdoors?

This could be an indoor or outdoor activity. Outdoors, you might consider putting some large balls including a 'Swiss ball', which is commonly used by adults for fitness.

How can we vary/build on this activity?

- Group the balls in different combinations.
- Count the balls and put them in a box.
- Put other shapes alongside the balls, for example, cubes.

How can this become a child-initiated activity?

- Put out balls that do not require supervision so that mobile babies and toddlers can have access to them.
- Observe which balls appeal to the non-mobile baby and play with them.

Links to the EYFS

This activity can give children opportunities to explore shapes and to learn the properties of different materials. Playing with the balls by rolling them can also help babies and toddlers learn to take turns and play games.

As with all activities with this age group, it is important to interact with the child and to maximise any naturally occurring learning opportunities.

Personal, Social and Emotional Development	Dispositions and Attitudes Making Relationships Self-confidence and Self-esteem	Behaviour and Self-control Sense of Community
Communication, Language and Literacy	Language for Communication Language for Thinking	
Problem Solving, Reasoning and Numeracy	Numbers as Labels and for Counting Calculating	Shape, Space and Measures
Knowledge and Understanding of the World	Exploration and Investigation Time	Place
Physical Development	Movement and Space Using Equipment and Materials	
Creative Development	Being Creative – Responding to Experiences, Expressing and Communicating Ideas	Developing Imagination and Imaginative Play

Hard and soft!

Young children learn a lot through feeling items. By collecting together hard and soft items and putting them together, children can begin to learn about contrasts.

Resources

A range of items that are safe for children to handle/mouth that are either hard or soft, e.g.:

- large cobbles
- fabric
- sponges
- a rubber duck
- a metal spoon.

Health & Safety

- Check items carefully and consider whether they are appropriate for the age/stage of child.
- Supervise children carefully.

Activity

Collect together a range of items – anything that is safe and clean that is either hard or soft. Put in some familiar and some unfamiliar objects for the child. Do not include toys and, if possible, avoid plastic items. Aim also to have some items that are similar but maybe different in size, for example three wooden spoons, so that they can be grouped.

Put out the items and allow the child to explore them. Make comments about what the child is touching or is interested in. At the end of the activity, put out a basket or storage container and one by one drop the items in to it. Aim to count the items as they are put inside.

Next Steps

Observation points

- How engaged is the child in this activity?
- How long does the child remain interested in the activity
- Which items take the child's interest?
- How does the child explore these items?
- Does the child mouth or touch the items?
- Does the child group any items?
- How does the child interact with you?

How can we take this outdoors?

This could be an indoor or outdoor activity. You may include large-sized items outdoors and things that toddlers might like to throw.

How can we vary/build on this activity?

- Group the hard objects and soft objects into two piles.
- Put out the objects that interest the child in other play situations.
- Find some objects, such as a dish mop, that are both hard and soft.
- Repeat the activity, but put in new objects that are either hard or soft.

How can this become a child-initiated activity?

- Put out these items into a basket at low level so that a mobile child can access them independently.
- Show the items to a non-mobile baby and note how interested the child seems in them.

Links to the EYFS

This activity can give children opportunities to learn the properties of different materials. By touching the objects, children will be developing spatial awareness and hand–eye co-ordination whilst becoming familiar with new objects in their environment. As with all activities, you need to be interested and interact with the child so that they can gain maximum language from this activity. Counting objects as they are put away can also help children hear number being used. Grouping objects together can also link to the calculating aspect of Problem Solving, Reasoning and Numeracy.

Personal, Social and Emotional Development	Dispositions and Attitudes	Behaviour and Self-control
	Making Relationships	Sense of Community
	Self-confidence and Self-esteem	
Communication, Language and Literacy	Language for Communication	
	Language for Thinking	
Problem Solving, Reasoning and Numeracy	Numbers as Labels and for Counting	Shape, Space and Measures
	Calculating	
Knowledge and Understanding of the World	Exploration and Investigation	
	Designing and Making	
Physical Development	Movement and Space	Using Equipment and Materials
Creative Development	Being Creative – Responding to Experiences, Expressing and Communicating Ideas	Exploring Media and Materials
		Developing Imagination and Imaginative Play

Row, row, row the Boat

Nursery rhymes are an excellent way of helping babies and toddlers to bond with their key person whilst also developing other skills.

Resources

- Knowledge of the nursery rhyme!
- Video recorder or camera

Health & Safety

- Handle children firmly, but gently – do not shake babies and toddlers.

Activity

Familiarise yourself with the nursery rhyme. If necessary, find a recording and play it if you feel that you cannot sing it. Sit on the floor with the baby or toddler on your lap. Sing the song and at the same time hold their hands. Make a slow rowing action with them.

Once you are comfortable, try to ask someone to record you and the child engaged in this activity. (This may be embarrassing but is wonderful for the child.) Afterwards, show the clip back to the child and watch their reaction.

Next Steps

Observation points

- How engaged is the child in this activity?
- How long does the child remain interested in the activity?
- Does the child seem to recognise the rhyme when it is repeated?
- Does the child anticipate the rhythm of the rhyme?
- Does the child attempt to vocalise when you are singing?
- How does the child interact with you?
- Does the child recognise themselves when you play the video clip back?

How can we take this outdoors?

This could be an indoor or outdoor activity. You may like to create a boat with cushions or boxes outdoors.

How can we vary/build on this activity?

- Find other action rhymes that you can enjoy with the child.
- Put out a toy boat in water, for example, at bath time or in a paddling pool.
- Repeat the activity, but put out shakers so that the child can mark the beat with a sound.
- Sing the rhyme very quickly or slowly.

How can this become a child-initiated activity?

- Offer this rhyme and see if children would like to respond.
- Watch out for signs that the child would like to repeat it.

Links to the EYFS

Singing this and other rhymes can help many aspects of a child's development. Children can establish a strong relationship with their key person and any other children that join them. They develop a knowledge of music and rhythm, and this in turn supports Linking Sound and Letters. The children are also gaining a sense of movement and spatial awareness. If children can watch clips of this activity, they are seeing the 'past' and so beginning to understand about Time.

Personal, Social and Emotional Development	Dispositions and Attitudes	Behaviour and Self-control
	Making Relationships	Sense of Community
	Self-confidence and Self-esteem	
Communication, Language and Literacy	Language for Communication	Linking Sounds and Letters
	Language for Thinking	
Problem Solving, Reasoning and Numeracy	Shape, Space and Measures	
Knowledge and Understanding of the World	Exploration and Investigation	ICT
	Designing and Making	Time
Physical Development	Movement and Space	
Creative Development	Being Creative – Responding to Experiences, Expressing and Communicating Ideas	Music and Dance
		Developing Imagination and Imaginative Play

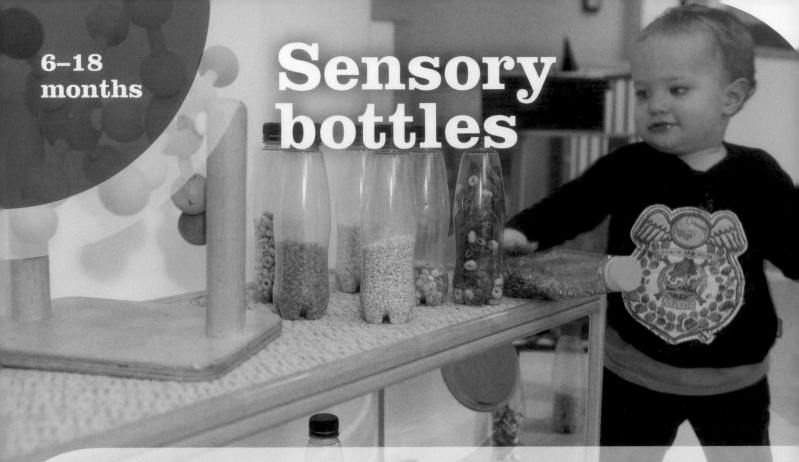

Sensory bottles

Babies and toddlers like looking at things and they also like shaking. This simple activity will help children to explore sounds and sights.

Resources

- A few small, empty water bottles
- Cat bells
- Food colouring
- Rice
- Chick peas
- Paper clips
- Buttons
- Dry sand
- Adhesive that is suitable for gluing plastic.

Health & Safety

- Make sure that the lids on the bottles are tightly screwed and glued.

Activity

This activity requires a little bit of simple preparation. Begin by collecting some items that could be put inside the small empty water bottles. Choose items that will either look interesting or make an interesting sound, for example, rice or a teaspoon inside a bottle.

Consider colouring items such as rice, pasta or chick peas by putting a couple of drops of food colouring onto them, shaking them and, once dry, placing them inside the bottles. Ideally, it would be good to have at least five different bottles made up. Once you are happy with a bottle, glue the inside of the lid and tightly screw it on. Leave it to dry.

Once the bottles are ready, double check that they cannot be unscrewed easily and then put them out for the child to explore. As the child is playing, talk to them about what is inside and join in with them.

Next Steps

Observation points

- How engaged is the child in this activity?
- Which bottles seem to hold the child's interest?
- How does the child use the bottles?
- How easily does the child handle and hold the bottles?
- Does the child try to shake the bottles?
- How does the child interact with you?

How can we take this outdoors?

This could be an indoor or outdoor activity. With toddlers, you might also like to turn this into a game of skittles.

How can we vary/build on this activity?

- Create new bottles with other items inside.
- Create pairs of bottles and see if children notice the pairs.
- Stand the bottles up so that the child can knock them down.

How can this become a child-initiated activity?

- Put these bottles out in a basket or storage container for mobile children to access independently.
- Have the bottles available and show them to non-mobile babies and observe whether they are interested in them.

Links to the EYFS

This activity helps children to look at objects independently and also learn about their properties. Children are likely to shake, rattle and even roll the bottles and so learn about movement, develop spatial awareness and hear sounds.

If several bottles are made up identically, some children may also notice this and so will be learning about number. Adults need to support this activity by joining in and interacting with the child.

Personal, Social and Emotional Development	Dispositions and Attitudes	Self-confidence and Self-esteem
	Making Relationships	Behaviour and Self-control
Communication, Language and Literacy	Language for Communication	Handwriting
	Language for Thinking	
Problem Solving, Reasoning and Numeracy	Numbers as Labels and for Counting	Shape, Space and Measures
	Calculating	
Knowledge and Understanding of the World	Exploration and Investigation	
	Designing and Making	
Physical Development	Movement and Space	Using Equipment and Materials
Creative Development	Being Creative – Responding to Experiences, Expressing and Communicating Ideas	Creating Music and Dance
		Developing Imagination and Imaginative Play
	Exploring Media and Materials	

Brushes!

This activity gives children a great opportunity to explore different textures with their fingers, or by mouthing.

Resources

Different types of clean brushes, for example

- toothbrush
- soft hair brush
- clothes brush
- shoe brush.

Health & Safety

- Make sure that brushes are clean and suitable for mouthing.

Activity

Begin by looking out for as many brushes as possible. They need to be clean and you will need to think about whether they can be mouthed safely. Try to get plenty of brushes made from natural materials, for example, a wooden nail brush or a clothes brush. Once you have a collection, put it out.

Encourage the babies and toddlers to explore the brushes.

For non-mobile babies, you might like to gently stroke their hands with different brushes whilst toddlers might enjoy tickling you. Toddlers may also want to use the brushes.

Next Steps

Observation points

- How engaged is the child in this activity?
- Which brushes seem to fascinate the child?
- How does the child use the brushes?
- How easily does the child handle the brushes?
- Does the child try to sweep with the brushes?
- How does the child interact with you?

How can we take this outdoors?

This could be an indoor or outdoor activity. With toddlers, you might like to find some short-handled brooms that they can sweep outside with.

How can we vary/build on this activity?

- Look out for other brushes.
- Combine brushes and other materials for toddlers, for example, put out something that they could sweep up or put out water with the paint brushes.

How can this become a child-initiated activity?

- Put the brushes out in a basket or storage container for mobile children to access independently.
- Have the brushes available and show them to non-mobile babies and observe whether they are interested in them.

Links to the EYFS

This activity helps children to look at objects independently and learn about their properties. If a range of textures are available, children will start to show preferences. Toddlers will also try to model the use of brushes, for example, sweeping up things. You could talk about the length, texture or shape of the brush. With younger babies, you can use the brushes to tickle and play with babies.

Personal, Social and Emotional Development	Dispositions and Attitudes	Self-confidence and Self-esteem
	Making Relationships	Behaviour and Self-Control
Communication, Language and Literacy	Language for Communication	Linking Sounds and Letters
	Language for Thinking	
Problem Solving, Reasoning and Numeracy	Numbers as Labels and for Counting	Shape, Space and Measures
	Calculating	
Knowledge and Understanding of the World	Exploration and Investigation	
	Designing and Making	
Physical Development	Movement and space	
	Using Equipment and materials	
Creative Development	Being Creative – Responding to Experiences, Expressing and Communicating Ideas	Exploring media and materials
		Developing Imagination and Imaginative Play

What's inside the ice cube?

Putting ice cubes into water provides a wonderful sensory experience for babies and toddlers. In this activity, the ice cube holds a surprise!

Resources

- Washing-up bowl/builder's tray
- Water
- Empty margarine container
- Rattle or other object
- Cloth to wipe up spills
- Towel

Health & Safety

- Make sure that the water is not hot.
- Allow the ice block to begin to melt to avoid dry-ice burns.
- Check that the children's fingers do not get too cold.
- Do not leave children unsupervised with water.

Activity

Fill a margarine tub or similar sized container with cold water. Drop a rattle or another similar sized object inside. Put the container in the freezer. Once frozen, fill up a washing-up bowl or builder's tray with tepid (very slightly warm water) and put the block of ice in it. Put the bowl onto the floor.

Bring the child over to it and let them explore. Expect that the child will put some of the water onto the floor or that they might try to climb into the bowl! Talk to the child about how the water feels and how the ice feels. As the ice block melts, see if the child notices the object inside it.

Next Steps

Observation points

- How engaged is the child in this activity?
- How does the child play with the water?
- What is the child's reaction on touching the ice block?
- Does the child notice the object inside the block?
- How does the child react when the object can be touched?
- How does the child interact with you?

How can we take this outdoors?

This could be an indoor or, in warm weather, an outdoor activity.

How can we vary/build on this activity?

- Create ice blocks with other items inside, for example, a teaspoon, shell or cork.
- Freeze several small cubes of ice.
- Put food colouring into the ice cubes.

How can this become a child-initiated activity?

This is not an activity that children can access independently, but if you take photographs of the activity, children will be able to indicate their interest in repeating it.

Links to the EYFS

This activity can support children's learning across different areas of development. Children are likely to interact with you as this may be a new experience for them. They are also likely to want to touch the water and ice block and play with the item inside.

If several blocks are made at once, you can count how many there are and talk to the children about how the blocks are changing in size. As with any activity, the key is to ensure that you respond to children sensitively.

Personal, Social and Emotional Development	Dispositions and attitudes	Self-confidence and self esteem
	Making Relationships	Behaviour and Self-Control
Communication, Language and Literacy	Language for Communication	Handwriting
	Language for Thinking	
Problem Solving, Reasoning and Numeracy	Numbers as Labels and for Counting	Shape, Space and Measures
	Calculating	
Knowledge and Understanding of the World	Exploration and Investigation	
	Designing and Making	
Physical Development	Movement and Space	
	Using Equipment and Materials	
Creative Development	Being Creative – Responding to Experiences, Expressing and Communicating Ideas	Exploring Media and Materials
		Developing Imagination and Imaginative Play

Posting potatoes

Many toddlers are fascinated by posting. They love pushing things into holes, watching them disappear and, better still, reappear somewhere else. This simple activity helps children to explore posting in a satisfying way.

Resources

- Cardboard tubes – different lengths and widths
- Bag of potatoes

Health & Safety

- When you're using potatoes, remove any green ones and wash the others.
- If children are still 'mouthing', only put out objects that are too large to swallow.
- Keep an eye on children when they are moving tubes so as to prevent other children from being knocked.

Activity

Put out a cardboard tube and some potatoes. The potatoes need to be of different sizes and should be washed first. Hold a tube and pass a potato to a toddler. Encourage them to put the potato down the tube. Observe the child's interest as it rolls down.

If the child is interested in the activity, comment about what is happening and draw the child's attention to the link between the size of potatoes and whether they fit in the tube.

Next Steps

Observation points

- How engaged is the child in this activity?
- Does the child consistently use the same hand to post with?
- Does the child consciously choose potatoes that will fit?
- How much language does the child use?
- Does the child notice that the angle of the tube makes a difference to how fast the potato travels down it?
- What does the child do if the object become 'stuck' in the tube?

How can we take this outdoors?

This activity is ideal for outdoors as children can benefit from longer tubes and can post natural materials that they find. Look out as well for other types of tubing, for example, vacuum cleaner hoses or guttering.

How can we vary/build on this activity?

There are plenty of other objects that toddlers will enjoy posting. Try some of these:

- Pompoms
- Pine cones
- Shells
- Fruit and vegetables
- Toy cars
- Toy dinosaurs and farm animals
- Rubber balls

Think also about putting out containers, such as a metal saucepan, so that toddlers can carry and collect objects that they are interested in.

How can this become a child-initiated activity?

Once children have tried out this activity, they are likely to want opportunities to repeat it. Make sure you sometimes leave the tubes out in the indoor/outdoor environment. Children can then choose to play with them in the way that they wish. They will probably also look for their own objects to post.

Links to the EYFS

This activity should cover a range of aspects of learning provided that you interact well with the child. It is important for Problem Solving, Reasoning and Numeracy that you count the objects and draw the child's attention to the objects' size and shape.

You could also take a photograph or, better still, a film clip of the child 'at work' and show it to them later on. This should stimulate further language and so links to Language for Communication and Language for Thinking, as well as to ICT.

Personal, Social and Emotional Development	Dispositions and Attitudes Self-confidence and self-esteem	
Communication, Language and Literacy	Language for Communication Language for Thinking	Handwriting
Problem Solving, Reasoning and Numeracy	Numbers as Labels and for Counting Calculating	Shape, Space and Measures
Knowledge and Understanding of the World	Exploration and Investigation Designing and Making	ICT
Physical Development	Movement and Space	
Creative Development	Being Creative – Responding to Experiences, Expressing and Communicating Ideas	

Time for tea

There's something about pouring that toddlers enjoy. They also love water. This simple activity allows toddlers to enjoy filling up a container with water and pouring it into another.

Resources

- Bucket, half filled with water
- Metal teapot – any size
- Ice cream tub or similar
- Kitchen tray

Activity

Half fill a bucket of water. Put out a tray with the ice cream tub on a low table or surface next to the bucket of water. Show the toddler how you fill the teapot and pour the water into the ice cream tub. Stand back and see if the toddler wants to copy.

If the child has good pouring skills and is enjoying the activity, get out a range of other containers and put them onto the tray so that they can fill them.

Health & Safety

- Do not leave children unattended with water.
- Check that the metal teapot has no sharp surfaces.
- Use fresh water each time and clean containers as some children will try to sip the water.

Next Steps

Observation points

- How engaged is the child in this activity?
- How easy is it for the child to fill the teapot up with water?
- Does the child consistently use the same hand to pour with?
- Does the child try to stop pouring when the container is full?
- What does the child do with the container once it is full?
- If several containers are put out, does the child line them up?

How can we take this outdoors?

This activity can be done indoors on a hard floor, but will also be a good one to do outdoors. If you take this activity outdoors, you can consider encouraging the toddler to water the plants with the teapot or to fill up other containers.

How can we vary/build on this activity?

There are plenty of other objects that toddlers will enjoy pouring with. Try some of these:

- Jugs
- Bottles
- Scoops
- Ladles.

Think also about putting out a range of different types of containers for children to pour into, for example, saucepans, small bottles or cups.

How can this become a child-initiated activity?

Most toddlers will automatically wish to repeat this activity. The key is to make sure that you put out the same equipment in the same place. As the activity does involve water, you will need to supervise the water. If you put out a range of pouring equipment, children can begin to choose their own 'pourer'.

Links to the EYFS

This activity should cover a range of aspects of learning provided that you interact well with the child. It is important for Problem Solving, Reasoning and Numeracy that you draw the children's attention to the size of container and how much it has been filled up. It is also important to use words such as 'full' and 'empty'. You could take a role in the activity by bringing new containers for the child to fill. If you pretend to drink the 'tea', this should help the child's language and imagination. Children can also be encouraged to wipe up spills and so gain some Self-care skills.

Personal, Social and Emotional Development	Dispositions and Attitudes	Self-care
	Self-confidence and Self-esteem	
Communication, Language and Literacy	Language for Communication	Handwriting
	Language for Thinking	
Problem Solving, Reasoning and Numeracy	Shape, Space and Measures	
Knowledge and Understanding of the World	Exploration and Investigation	
	Designing and Making	
Physical Development	Movement and Space	
	Using Equipment and Materials	
Creative Development	Being Creative – Responding to Experiences, Expressing and Communicating Ideas	Developing Imagination and Imaginative Play

Playing with ducks

Rubber ducks floating in water have great appeal for toddlers. Toddlers also love water and so building an activity around these items is likely to be a great success. As toddlers like taking things from one place to another, be prepared for both the ducks and water to travel!

Resources

- Bucket, half filled with water
- Ladle or equivalent
- 5–10 rubber ducks – at least one that is different in size and colour
- Saucepan or other container

Health & Safety

- Do not leave children unattended with water.
- Make sure that the ducks are safe, for example, make sure that children cannot bite into them.
- Use fresh water each time as some children will try to sip the water.

Activity

Half fill a bucket of water. Put out a large saucepan or another container nearby. Find a ladle or another utensil that is large enough to scoop out the ducks. Put the ducks into the water. As most toddlers love transporting things, you should find that the toddler starts to move the ducks from the bucket to the other container using the ladle. Do not worry if they only want to transport water instead!

It is important that the ducks 'swim' and also that at least one is different in terms of size and colour. This allows children to pick out the differences. If appropriate, count the ducks or draw the child's attention to the 'odd' ducks.

Next Steps

Observation points

- How engaged is the child in this activity?
- How easy is it for the child to use the ladle?
- Does the child consistently use the same hand to hold the ladle?
- Does the child notice the duck or ducks that are different?
- Does the child attempt to transport the ducks or water into the other container?
- Does the child use any language?

How can we take this outdoors?

This activity can be done indoors on a hard floor, but will also be a good one to do outdoors. If you take this activity outdoors, the toddlers may walk around with the ducks and so you may find that they turn up in odd places.

How can we vary/build on this activity?

There are plenty of other objects that toddlers will enjoy playing with. Try some of these:

- Jugs to transport the ducks, for example, large beakers
- Different animals, for example, dinosaurs
- Inflatable toys
- Other objects that submerge, float or sink.

Think also about organising a trip to feed ducks if you have any nearby.

How can this become a child-initiated activity?

Most toddlers will automatically wish to repeat this activity. The key is to make sure that you put out the same equipment in the same place. As the activity does involve water, you will need to supervise the water.

Links to the EYFS

As with all activities for this age range, adult interaction is important. It is important for Problem Solving, Reasoning and Numeracy that you draw the children's attention to the 'odd' duck and take the time to count the ducks when they are first given to the child to drop in the water. You could also take a role in the activity by pretending to talk to the duck. The children can be encouraged to wipe up spills and so gain some Self-care skills.

Personal, Social and Emotional Development	Dispositions and Attitudes Self-confidence and Self-esteem	Self-care
Communication, Language and Literacy	Language for Communication Language for Thinking	Handwriting
Problem Solving, Reasoning and Numeracy	Numbers as Labels and for Counting Calculating	Shape, Space and Measures
Knowledge and Understanding of the World	Exploration and Investigation Designing and Making	
Physical Development	Movement and Space Using Equipment and Materials	
Creative Development	Being Creative – Responding to Experiences, Expressing and Communicating Ideas	Developing Imagination and Imaginative Play

Dropping down

Many toddlers are fascinated by dropping toys and other items into large containers. They like to watch items descend and to hear the noise that is made. This simple activity takes its inspiration from the kitchen!

Resources

- Clean tall kitchen bin with pop-up lid or swing lid – consider buying one for this purpose
- Basket containing 10 bean bags or balls or other items that can be dropped safely

Health & Safety

- Carry out a thorough risk assessment on the bin.
- Do not leave children unattended with the bin.
- Make sure that the items used for dropping will not break.

Activity

Do a risk assessment on the type of bin that you hope to use. Check that fingers or heads cannot be trapped! Model the activity by taking a bean bag or ball out of the basket, open the bin and drop the item in.

Hold out the next bean bag or ball to the toddler and smile. This will give the child the understanding that it is their turn to play. Clap or say, 'well done' as the child drops the item into the bin. Keep repeating until there are no more items and work with the child to retrieve the items from the bin. Playing this game with two toddlers can help them to take turns.

Next Steps

Observation points

- How engaged is the child in this activity?
- Does the child make eye contact with you?
- How quickly does the child work out the nature of the game?
- Does the child manage the process independently?
- Does the child use a consistent hand to pick up the bean bag?
- How long does this activity hold the child's interest?

How can we take this outdoors?

This activity works well outdoors and you might consider putting more than one bin side by side so that the child makes a choice as to which bin they use. You may also find that older children will want to join in or 'help' the younger child.

How can we vary/build on this activity?

The essence of this activity which is about 'dropping' is easy to recreate in other ways.

- Look out for different items that are safe to drop into the bin, for example, corks.
- Consider doing this with sensory materials, for example, dropping sand.
- Look out for other containers that are tall.
- Use other sized kitchen bins, for example, small pedal bins.

How can this become a child-initiated activity?

Most toddlers will automatically wish to repeat this activity. The key is to make sure that you put out the same equipment in the same place. As the bin itself can be a potential danger, you should always supervise.

Links to the EYFS

As with all activities for this age range, adult interaction is important. Children will need to hear phrases such as, 'here's another one for you' as you hand over the next item to be dropped.

You should also count the objects as you retrieve them from the bottom of the bin and encourage the child to put them back in the basket.

Personal, Social and Emotional Development	Dispositions and Attitudes Self-confidence and Self-esteem	Self-care
Communication, Language and Literacy	Language for Communication Language for Thinking	Handwriting
Problem Solving, Reasoning and Numeracy	Numbers as Labels and for Counting Calculating	Shape, Space and Measures
Knowledge and Understanding of the World	Exploration and Investigation	
Physical Development	Movement and Space Using Equipment and Materials	
Creative Development	Being Creative – Responding to Experiences, Expressing and Communicating Ideas	Exploring Media and Materials

Making a splash!

Many toddlers enjoy throwing items. Having activities that allow children to do this safely with an adult can be beneficial. This activity requires a non-carpeted area, so consider taking it outside to start with.

Resources

- Plastic storage box – large
- 5 small potatoes or other small but weighty items
- Fabric bag or shopping bag
- 2 cloths to wipe up spills
- Apron for toddler

Health & Safety

- Position this activity carefully so that other children cannot be hit by objects.
- Make sure that the items used for throwing will not break.
- Tip out the water immediately after use.

Activity

Look for a corner or place indoors where other children will not be able to walk by. The area needs to be non-carpeted as the children will be making a splash! Quarter fill a storage box with water. Put the potatoes into the fabric bag or use other items which, when thrown, will create a good splash.

Model the activity by taking out an item and throwing it into the water. Hold the bag open so as to invite the toddler to join in. Once all of the five items have been thrown, help the toddler to pick them out of the water. Model wiping the floor and give the toddler a cloth so that they can join you.

Next Steps

Observation points

- How engaged is the child in this activity?
- How quickly does the child work out the nature of the game?
- Does the child make eye contact with you?
- Does the child manage the process independently?
- Does the child use a consistent hand to throw items?
- How long does the activity engage the child for?

How can we take this outdoors?

You might begin by making this an outdoor activity and then bringing it indoors. If you find it successful, think about providing a range of different containers outdoors.

How can we vary/build on this activity?

There are many ways in which you can vary the activity.

- Look out for items that will respond differently when thrown, for example, sponges, corks or a light plastic ball.
- Use other materials instead of water, for example, autumn leaves or shredded paper.
- Use different sizes of container.

How can this become a child-initiated activity?

Most toddlers will automatically wish to repeat this activity. The key is to make sure that you put out the same equipment in the same place. As water is involved, you must supervise the activity well – some children may try to climb inside the container.

Links to the EYFS

As with all activities for this age range, adult interaction is important. Children need to hear language such as 'splash' or 'all gone'.

You can also count the objects as they are thrown. Children should be encouraged to clear up the spills afterwards and to dry the objects.

Personal, Social and Emotional Development	Dispositions and Attitudes Self-confidence and Self-esteem	Self-care
Communication, Language and Literacy	Language for Communication Language for Thinking	Handwriting
Problem Solving, Reasoning and Numeracy	Numbers as Labels and for Counting Calculating	Shape, Space and Measures
Knowledge and Understanding of the World	Exploration and Investigation	
Physical Development	Movement and Space Using Equipment and Materials	
Creative Development	Being Creative – Responding to Experiences, Expressing and Communicating Ideas	Exploring Media and Materials

Let's go shopping!

Toddlers love moving things from one place to another. Providing children with a shopping trolley that they can put items in is likely to be a success.

Resources

- 2–3 shopping trolleys – fabric ones with wheels
- 5 baskets of packets, vegetables and other items associated with shopping

Health & Safety

- Risk assess the shopping trolley, for example, assess how easily it can tip over or whether it might trap fingers.
- Put out objects that have been risk assessed.
- Make sure that any vegetables are clean and safe to be 'nibbled'!

Activity

Scatter the five different baskets around at different points. Model the play by going over to one basket, picking up an item and dropping it into the shopping trolley before going across to another. Watch to see if the toddler soon wants to take over from you.

Expect to see toddlers who empty one basket before going on to do the same at another. Look interested in what they have 'found' to put in their shopping trolleys. Be ready to look for other items that they can collect to put inside.

Next Steps

Observation points

- How engaged is the child in this activity?
- What reaction does the child have when they find items to put in their shopping trolley?
- How easily does the child manage to move the shopping trolley?
- Does the child make eye contact with you?
- How long does the activity engage the child for?
- What does the child do with their 'finds' afterwards?

How can we take this outdoors?

This activity can be set up in the same way outdoors, although you might find that children enjoy using a wheelbarrow to put their shopping in.

How can we vary/build on this activity?

There are many ways in which you can vary the activity.

- Put out items of clothing for children to find, for example, hats and shoes.
- Put out soft toys for children to find, for example, teddies and dolls.
- Use other wheeled toys, for example, pushchairs.
- Use shopping bags.
- Use small suitcases.

How can this become a child-initiated activity?

Most toddlers will automatically wish to repeat this activity. You may put out the shopping trolleys for play as part of your wheeled toys.

Links to the EYFS

As with all activities for this age range, adult interaction is important. Talk to the children about the 'finds', offer them additional items and name the items that have been put out. Look in their shopping trolleys and count the number of items that they have found. Talk about size and shape of items.

Personal, Social and Emotional Development	Dispositions and Attitudes Self-confidence and Self-esteem	Self-care
Communication, Language and Literacy	Language for Communication Language for Thinking	Handwriting
Problem Solving, Reasoning and Numeracy	Numbers as Labels and for Counting Calculating	Shape, Space and Measures
Knowledge and Understanding of the World	Exploration and Investigation	
Physical Development	Movement and Space Using Equipment and Materials	
Creative Development	Being Creative – Responding to Experiences, Expressing and Communicating Ideas	Exploring Media and Materials Developing Imagination and Imaginative Play

Washing up

Toddlers enjoy water and also enjoy copying adults. This simple activity can give toddlers a sense of independence as well as helping them to learn a new skill.

Resources

- Washing-up bowl
- Sponges and clothes
- Draining rack
- Tea towels
- Cloth to wipe up spills
- Items to be washed up

Health & Safety

- Find out if any children have skin allergies or skin care needs.
- Check the temperature of the water.
- Do not leave water standing unsupervised.
- Risk assess the objects that you intend to wash up.

Activity

Put out the draining rack and the washing bowl. If you do not have a sink at child height, place the items on a low table. Consider putting plastic sheeting underneath the bowl and the draining rack. Put a little washing-up liquid and some lukewarm water (almost cool) in a washing-up bowl. Find some objects that you feel are suitable for children to wash, for example, snack time beakers or metal spoons.

Ask one or two children to come and join you. Model the process of washing up one item then see how the children do. Expect that they will enjoy playing with water and exploring the sponge and cloth!

Next Steps

Observation points

- How engaged is the child in this activity?
- How well does the child manage the process of picking up items and washing them?
- Which hand does the child use to hold the sponge/cloth?
- Does the child try to talk during the activity?
- How long does the activity engage the child for?
- In what other ways does the child try and play with the water?

How can we take this outdoors?

This activity can be set up in the same way outdoors, although you might put other items out, such as toys to be cleaned. Children are also likely to go off and wash other items that they can see.

How can we vary/build on this activity?

There are many ways in which you can vary the activity.

- Put out items of clothing for washing.
- Put out small toys for washing.
- Make this a drying-up activity.

How can this become a child-initiated activity?

Most toddlers will automatically wish to repeat this activity. Put out the objects, bowl and drainer again. Always supervise the water carefully and remove after use.

Links to the EYFS

Children will enjoy doing a 'grown up' activity with an adult. Talk to the children about the items that they are washing. Let them hear the words 'dirty' and 'clean'. If you put out items such as beakers, talk to the children about 'filling' them up and 'emptying' them. You could also count the items on the drainer that have been washed up.

Personal, Social and Emotional Development	Dispositions and Attitudes	Self-care
	Self-confidence and Self-esteem	
Communication, Language and Literacy	Language for Communication	Handwriting
	Language for Thinking	
Problem Solving, Reasoning and Numeracy	Numbers as Labels and for Counting	
	Shape, Space and Measures	
Knowledge and Understanding of the World	Exploration and Investigation	
Physical Development	Using Equipment and Materials	
Creative Development	Being Creative – Responding to Experiences, Expressing and Communicating Ideas	Exploring Media and Materials
		Developing Imagination and Imaginative Play

Boxes and treasures

18 months to 3 years

Many toddlers are fascinated with working out how things open and close. They also like putting objects in and out of boxes. This activity combines both of these play interests.

Resources

- Assortment of boxes, for example, wooden, hinged, gift, musical
- Treasure, for example, large shiny buttons
- Coloured feathers
- Strips of coloured foil or cellophane/sweet wrappers

Health & Safety

- Risk assess the boxes – for example, do they have sharp edges or could they trap fingers?
- Risk assess the 'treasure' to avoid a choking hazard.

Activity

Put small amounts of 'treasure' inside some of the boxes and put the boxes inside a shopping or fabric bag. Ask one or two children if they would like to see what is in your bag. Take the boxes out and put them on the floor. Encourage the children to explore and see if they can open them.

Talk to the children about what have found in the boxes whilst they are playing with them. If you have included a musical box, show the children how it winds up.

Next Steps

Observation points

- How engaged is the child in this activity?
- How easily does the child work out how to open and close the boxes?
- How does the child react to the treasure in the boxes?
- Does the child transfer treasure from one box to another?
- Does the child talk about their 'finds'?
- Does the child make eye contact with you?
- How long does the activity engage the child for?

How can we take this outdoors?

This activity can be set up in the same way outdoors, but you may wish to find larger boxes and put in different types of 'treasure'. Expect that the children may be inclined to walk around with their treasure boxes.

How can we vary/build on this activity?

There are many ways in which you can vary the activity.

- Look out for different types of boxes.
- Put out 'treasure' so that children can choose what they would like to put in the boxes.
- Look out for some boxes that are difficult to open, for example, that require a key.
- With the children, decorate plain boxes.

How can this become a child-initiated activity?

Repeat this activity with different types of boxes, for example, gift boxes or jewellery boxes.

Links to the EYFS

This activity should allow children to explore different textures and materials. Use a chatty style to show children the different features of the boxes.

Try to find a musical box so that children can see something that is a gadget, which would link to ICT.

Personal, Social and Emotional Development	Dispositions and Attitudes Self-confidence and Self-esteem	Self-care
Communication, Language and Literacy	Language for Communication Language for Thinking	Handwriting
Problem Solving, Reasoning and Numeracy	Numbers as Labels and for Counting Shape, Space and Measures	
Knowledge and Understanding of the World	Exploration and Investigation Designing and Making	ICT
Physical Development	Using Equipment and Materials	
Creative Development	Being Creative – Responding to Experiences, Expressing and Communicating Ideas Exploring Media and Materials	Creating Music and Dance Developing Imagination and Imaginative Play

Treasure hunt photos

Toddlers are interested in photos of themselves and they also like 'finding' things. This activity requires some preparation, but the resources created can be used several times.

Resources

- Photographs of the toddlers – laminated
- Hole punch and ribbons

Activity

To prepare this activity, laminate some photographs of the children. You will need three or four photographs of each child. Punch a hole in the corner of each photograph and thread a ribbon through it. Hang the photographs around the room and then see if the children can find them. As children find the photographs, talk to the children about them.

Health & Safety

- Make sure that the laminated photographs do not have sharp edges.
- Supervise children to check that they do not twist the ribbon around their fingers.

Next Steps

Observation points

- How engaged is the child in this activity?
- How easily does the child find 'their' photographs?
- What does the child do if he finds a photograph that is not his?
- Does the child show their photographs to other children?
- How much language does the child use?

How can we take this outdoors?

This activity will work well outdoors, especially if you have a low tree or bush in your area.

How can we vary/build on this activity?

There are many ways in which you can vary the activity.

- Put out photographs of animals for toddlers to collect.
- Put out photographs of children's parents.
- Involve the children in 'hiding' the photographs.

How can this become a child-initiated activity?

Most toddlers will automatically wish to repeat this activity. Put out the photographs and see if children try to 'hide' them.

Links to the EYFS

This activity links nicely to many aspects within the EYFS if you use the potential learning opportunities. It is important to talk to children about their photographs and about what they were wearing or doing in the photographs. This activity should also help children to gain a sense of belonging.

Personal, Social and Emotional Development	Dispositions and Attitudes	Self-care
	Self-confidence and Self-esteem	Sense of Community
Communication, Language and Literacy	Language for Communication	Handwriting
	Language for Thinking	
Problem Solving, Reasoning and Numeracy	Numbers as Labels and for Counting	
	Shape, Space and Measures	
Knowledge and Understanding of the World	Exploration and Investigation	Communities
	Time	
Physical Development	Using Equipment and Materials	
Creative Development	Being Creative – Responding to Experiences, Expressing and Communicating Ideas	Developing Imagination and Imaginative Play

Let's make gloop

Most toddlers find playing with gloop very satisfying. They also enjoy stirring and being involved in simple cooking activities. Preparing and then playing with gloop is therefore likely to be a success.

Resources

- Packet of cornflour
- Metal teaspoons
- Small jugs of water
- Aprons
- Small bowls

Health & Safety

- Check that children do not have an allergy to corn (maize).
- Supervise in case children try to eat the gloop.

Activity

Work with children in pairs or individually. Put some cornflour into the bowls. Give each toddler a spoon and a bowl. Encourage them to touch and stir the cornflour. Model how to pour in water by having your own bowl and adding a little water at time and stirring it. Ideally the mixture should be liquid when stirred, but solid when squeezed. If children add too much water, don't worry as the aim of this activity is for children to explore. Once the mixture is ready, put out a tray and encourage each child to pour their mixture into it.

Next Steps

Observation points

- How engaged is the child in this activity?
- How easy does the child find it to use the teaspoon?
- Is the child able to follow simple instructions?
- Does the child enjoy the experience of touching the gloop?
- How much language does the child use?

How can we take this outdoors?

This activity will work well outdoors, although you might find that children will transport the gloop into other areas!

How can we vary/build on this activity?

There are many ways in which you can vary the activity.

- Put out coloured water for children to use.
- Put out a range of small beakers and spoons alongside the gloop.
- Try using whisks to mix soap flakes and water.

How can this become a child-initiated activity?

Although making the gloop mixture needs to be an adult-led activity, gloop can be left out with a variety of toys and resources for children to play with.

Links to the EYFS

This activity can help deliver many aspects of the EYFS especially if you take some photographs or film clips of the children as they make and play with the gloop.

Adult interaction will also be important as children need to hear the language of cooking, for example, bowl, spoon and stir.

Personal, Social and Emotional Development	Dispositions and Attitudes Self-confidence and Self-esteem	Self-care
Communication, Language and Literacy	Language for Communication Language for Thinking	Handwriting
Problem Solving, Reasoning and Numeracy	Numbers as Labels and for Counting Shape, Space and Measures	
Knowledge and Understanding of the World	Exploration and Investigation Designing and Making	Time
Physical Development	Using Equipment and Materials	
Creative Development	Being Creative – Responding to Experiences, Expressing and Communicating Ideas	Exploring Media and Materials Developing Imagination and Imaginative Play

Making cheese scones

Children enjoy cooking and making cheese scones is an easy activity. This activity is a 'talking' as well as a 'doing' activity and so should be done with pairs or very small groups of children for maximum learning and enjoyment.

Resources

- 200g Self-raising flour
- 25g Butter
- Grated cheese
- Milk to mix
- Mixing bowls
- Spoons
- Rolling pins
- Cutters
- Digital camera

Health & Safety

- This activity is not suitable for children who have a wheat or dairy allergy. (Consider an alternative cooking activity/ask parents about substitute ingredients.)
- Adults should put the scones into the oven.
- Wait for the scones to cool down before eating them.

Activity

Ask children to wash their hands and to put aprons on. Show them how to measure out the flour and butter into their bowls. Show the children how to rub the butter into the flour so that it eventually resembles breadcrumbs. Let the children take turns to grate their pieces of cheese. They then need to put the cheese into their bowl. Let them measure their milk and then show them how to mix it into the flour, butter and cheese. Encourage the children to knead the dough so that it becomes soft. Show them how to roll out their dough. They can then use cutters before putting the scones onto a baking sheet. Using a pastry brush, they can coat them with a little spare milk. You will then need to put the scones in a hot oven (200°C) for 12–15 minutes or until golden. The children can set the timer! Once the scones are cool, the children can eat them. As you are doing this activity, try taking photographs at each stage. These can be used to create recipe cards and also to help the children talk about what they have done.

Next Steps

Observation points

- How engaged is the child in this activity?
- How does the child cope with measuring out the ingredients?
- How well does the child use the tools, such as the grater or rolling pin?
- Does the child work well with other children?
- How much language does the child use during the activity?
- Is the child able to talk about making scones afterwards?

How can we take this outdoors?

The making part of this activity will have to be done indoors, but you could take the cheese scones outside to eat and turn it into a little picnic.

How can we vary/build on this activity?

There are plenty of ways in which this activity can be built upon.

- Use the scone mix to make a pizza.
- Look at different types of cheeses and breads with the children.
- Make fruit scones.
- Use the photographs to help children talk about the activity.

How can this become a child-initiated activity?

After children have had the experience of making scones, they can build this into their role play. Make sure that you have similar equipment available for children to put into a role play kitchen, for example, dough, pastry brush, cutters, baking sheet.

Links to the EYFS

Cooking activities are wonderful as they cover a range of aspects of learning provided that the adult interacts well with the child. The key to this activity is that children should do as much of the activity as possible so that they can gain a sense of achievement whilst also gaining fine motor skills. It also important to talk to the children about changes to the food that they can see and to use the opportunity to talk to them about foods that they like.

Personal, Social and Emotional Development	Dispositions and Attitudes	Behaviour and Self-control
	Self-confidence and Self-esteem	Self-care
Communication, Language and Literacy	Language for Communication	Reading
	Language for Thinking	Handwriting
Problem Solving, Reasoning and Numeracy	Numbers as Labels and for Counting	
	Shape, Space and Measures	
Knowledge and Understanding of the World	Exploration and Investigation	Time
	Designing and Making	Communities
Physical Development	Movement and Space	
	Using Equipment and Materials	
Creative Development	Being Creative – Responding to Experiences, Expressing and Communicating Ideas	

Sand pies

Making mud pies out of sand is a wonderfully sensory experience for children. With some adult input, it can also be a good learning opportunity for counting and number.

Resources

- Plastic plates
- Kitchen trays
- Damp sand
- Knives and forks
- Shells
- Straws
- Scissors

Health & Safety

- Use children's knives and forks.
- Keep an eye on children in case they wave the knives.

Activity

Sit with the children and make a large sand pie with the damp sand on a kitchen tray. Ask children if they would like to make one as well. Encourage the children to decorate their pie with shells and also by cutting up straws. Some children may pretend that they have made a birthday cake.

Get out the knives and forks and plastic plates. Cut your pie into pieces using a knife. Encourage the children to cut theirs into pieces. You may find that children enjoy the sensation of the knives and may need time to experiment with them. Draw children's attention to the size of their pieces. You might also repeat this and talk about 'half' or 'quarter'.

Next Steps

Observation points

- How easily does the child make the sand pie?
- How co-ordinated is the child when using the knife?
- How much language does the child use?
- Does the child talk about the size of the slices of pie?

How can we take this outdoors?

This activity can take place on a bigger scale outdoors, especially if you have a large sand area. You could make a huge sand pie with all of the sand and the children could decorate it with stones.

How can we vary/build on this activity?

There are plenty of ways in which this activity can be built upon.

- Look out for different sizes of containers to put the pieces of the pies in.
- Put out a range of different items to decorate the pie with.
- Set up a sand pie shop in the role play area along with prices.

How can this become a child-initiated activity?

Leave out the items that you have used in the sand area so that children can make this activity their own. If you do not feel that you can leave the knives out without close supervision, consider putting out large serving spoons instead.

Links to the EYFS

This activity can be linked to several aspects of the EYFS. You will need to draw the children's attention to the size, shape and quantity of the pies that are made.

It is also important that children are given opportunities to enjoy cutting so that they are learning to use a knife.

Personal, Social and Emotional Development	Dispositions and Attitudes	Behaviour and Self-Control
	Self-confidence and Self-esteem	Self-care
Communication, Language and Literacy	Language for Communication	Handwriting
	Language for Thinking	
Problem Solving, Reasoning and Numeracy	Numbers as Labels and for Counting	Shape, Space and Measures
	Calculating	
Knowledge and Understanding of the World	Exploration and Investigation	Communities
	Designing and Making	
Physical Development	Using Equipment and Materials	
Creative Development	Being Creative – Responding to Experiences, Expressing and Communicating Ideas	Exploring Media and Materials

Follow my leader

Children enjoy painting. This is a game that you can use on the painting wall to help children learn about number and shape as well as handwriting.

Resources

- Small trays for children to hold (see p.43)
- Primary coloured and white ready-mixed paint
- Brushes
- Roll of paper
- Masking tape
- Aprons

Health & Safety

- Keep an eye out for children 'colliding'.

Activity

Prepare a painting wall or cover a long table with paper. To begin with, this activity is worth doing with one or two children until they understand the game. Pick up a brush and tray and paint a circle on the wall (aim to do this anti-clockwise, starting at the top, as this is the basis of many lower case letters). Ask a child to put a circle outside of yours. Move along the wall and repeat. Think about painting small circles and large circles. Put some up high and others low.

Swap over so that the child becomes the leader. If more than one child plays, they will add a further circle to each circle. If you have created a painting wall, several children can play at the same time in pairs.

You can repeat this game, using other positional instruction, for example, 'put a circle inside mine' or 'above it'.

Next Steps

Observation points

- How engaged is the child in this activity?
- How easily does the child make their circle?
- Does the child use an anti-clockwise rotational movement starting at the top?
- Does the child enjoy being the leader?
- Is the child able to follow instructions?
- How much language does the child use?
- Does the child enjoy mixing the colours?

How can we take this outdoors?

Think about putting a painting wall outdoors or do the activity using paintbrushes and water on the ground or a wall.

How can we vary/build on this activity?

There are plenty of ways in which this activity can be built upon.

- Turn it into a roll-a-dice game – the number on the dice indicates how many circles have to be painted.
- Use sponges and make patterns of different colours for children to copy.
- Paint a vertical line and see if children can put a line the same length or longer than yours.
- Use a brush to make wavy lines.

How can this become a child-initiated activity?

Encourage children to use the paints and materials independently. If a roll-a-dice game is used, remember to put out dice.

Links to the EYFS

This activity is particularly good at encouraging children to have fun whilst thinking about shapes and space as well as helping them to learn key handwriting movements. For children to benefit, you must draw the children's attention to the colours that they are using and the sizes of the circles that they are drawing. Remember to count circles as well.

Personal, Social and Emotional Development	Dispositions and Attitudes	Behaviour and Self-Control
	Self-confidence and Self-esteem	
Communication, Language and Literacy	Language for Communication	Handwriting
	Language for Thinking	
Problem Solving, Reasoning and Numeracy	Numbers as Labels and for Counting	Shape, Space and Measures
	Calculating	
Knowledge and Understanding of the World	Exploration and Investigation	
Physical Development	Movement and Space	Using Equipment and Materials
	Health and Bodily Awareness	
Creative Development	Being Creative – Responding to Experiences, Expressing and Communicating Ideas	Exploring Media and Materials

Hidden Objects

Children enjoy finding items. They also like playing with sensory materials. So here is a game that can help children count whilst they have fun in the sand.

Resources

- Sand tray or storage box with sand
- Teddy
- Items to hide, for example, buttons, shells, fake jewellery
- Teaspoons
- Marker
- Paper plate

Health & Safety

- Think about whether any children are likely to mouth any items.
- Make sure that children do not throw sand.

Activity

Hide five items in the sand tray. Using the marker, draw five circles on the paper plate. Tell the children that Teddy says that he has hidden five things in the sand. Can they find them using the teaspoons to dig with?

As they find the objects, encourage the children to put the objects on the circles on the plate. This will encourage more accurate counting and helps children with one-to-one correspondence. Repeat the activity, but this time create a mismatch, for example, Teddy says that there are four items, but you have actually hidden six. Ask the children what you should do with the extra items.

Next Steps

Observation points

- How engaged is the child in this activity?
- How easily does the child find the items?
- Can the child count the items accurately?
- Can the child one-to-one match?
- What language does the child use?
- Does the child have a solution when there is a mismatch between the number of items that Teddy says he has hidden and the number of items found?

How can we take this outdoors?

Use a sand tray outdoors or hide objects in areas within your outdoor area. Consider hiding larger items for children to find, for example, pine cones.

How can we vary/build on this activity?

There are plenty of ways in which this activity can be built upon.

- Encourage the children to hide items and tell you how many Teddy has hidden.
- Use other sensory materials for hiding, for example, dried pasta, couscous or bark chippings.
- Hide twenty or so items – children take it in turns to roll a dice which tells them how many they should look for.

How can this become a child-initiated activity?

Put out the objects that you have used for hiding along with the paper plates and markers so that children can take them over to the sand tray and create their own version of the game.

Links to the EYFS

This activity is particularly good at encouraging children to count and match objects. If you choose unusual objects for the children, you can develop their vocabulary. It is also important to encourage children to use Language for Thinking, for example, 'How many more items do you think there are?' Aim, as well, to put in some matching objects, for example, same colours or shapes. Putting out scoops or teaspoons also means that children are using tools.

Personal, Social and Emotional Development	Dispositions and Attitudes Self-confidence and Self-esteem	Behaviour and Self-Control
Communication, Language and Literacy	Language for Communication Language for Thinking	Handwriting
Problem Solving, Reasoning and Numeracy	Numbers as Labels and for Counting Calculating	Shape, Space and Measures
Knowledge and Understanding of the World	Exploration and Investigation	
Physical Development	Movement and Space Using Equipment and Materials	
Creative Development	Developing Imagination and Imaginative Play	

Create a photo frame

Children enjoy making and giving presents. This simple activity will engage children and help them to learn several skills whilst also solving the problem of what to do for Mother's Day or Father's Day, or other such occasions.

Resources

- Digital camera
- Printer
- Card
- Items for collage
- Paint
- Glue
- Markers e.g. felt-tipped pens, crayons
- Wrapping paper
- Scissors
- Plain office stickers

Health & Safety

- Show children how to use scissors/tools.

Activity

This activity will work best with pairs or very small groups of children.

Show the children how to use the digital camera and see if they can take photographs of each other. Children could also take photographs of flowers, plants or anything else that the person receiving the gift might like. Show the children the photographs on the computer and encourage them to choose their favourites to be printed out.

Once children have decided which photograph they would like, they can then make their photo frame. This can be made from a sheet of card or you could buy card frames. Encourage the children to collage, crayon, paint or draw so that their frame is truly unique. Then paste the photograph onto it. Once the frames are complete, the children can wrap up the present using paper and scissors. Children can also write a note onto a sticker and then pop it onto their present.

Next Steps

Observation points

- How engaged is the child in this activity?
- How interested is the child in other children's photographs?
- What language does the child use?
- What ideas does the child have?
- Which items does the child choose to use?
- How well does the child use the tools?
- How much adult input does the child need?

How can we take this outdoors?

Children can choose to take photographs outdoors of people, places and plants that take their interest.

How can we vary/build on this activity?

There are plenty of ways in which this activity can be built upon.

- Create photo albums with the children.
- Create a 'gift shop' role play area.
- Encourage the children to take photographs.

How can this become a child-initiated activity?

Many children will want to repeat this activity. Provide children with the same materials and act as a facilitator so that they can take photographs and print them out.

Links to the EYFS

This activity links to many aspects of the EYFS providing the children take ownership of the activity and are given opportunities to extend their ideas. Children will also gain some mathematical concepts if you talk about size and shape whilst wrapping up the present. Talking with children about photographs can also encourage them to talk about what they like doing at home and with their family.

Personal, Social and Emotional Development	Dispositions and Attitudes	Behaviour and Self-Control
	Self-confidence and Self-esteem	Sense of Community
Communication, Language and Literacy	Language for Communication	Writing
	Language for Thinking	Handwriting
Problem Solving, Reasoning and Numeracy	Numbers as Labels and for Counting	Shape, Space and Measures
	Calculating	
Knowledge and Understanding of the World	Exploration and Investigation	ICT
	Designing and Making	Time
Physical Development	Movement and Space	
	Using Equipment and Materials	
Creative Development	Exploring Media and Materials	

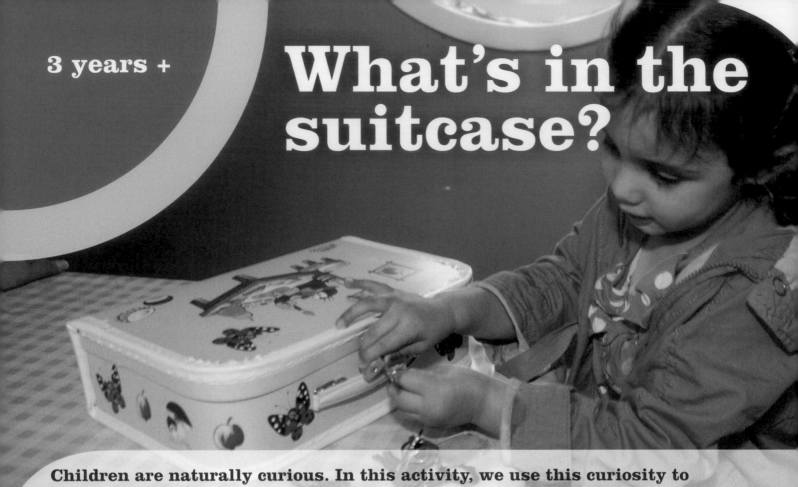

What's in the suitcase?

Children are naturally curious. In this activity, we use this curiosity to stimulate children's language and imagination.

Resources

- Small suitcase that can be locked
- Selection of keys
- Items that might interest children

Health & Safety

- Put items in the suitcase that are safe for children to handle.

Activity

Put a few items that you think will interest children into the suitcase. These are likely to be used afterwards to support their play. Lock the suitcase and hide the key in an envelope along with a selection of other keys.

Put the suitcase outdoors and hide the envelope. Watch as the children 'discover' the suitcase and use this as an opportunity to engage in some discussion. If the children do not find the keys, you might like to give them some hints. Once the keys have been found, children will need to work out which key will fit the lock. When the suitcase is opened, children can talk about what is inside and then go on to use the objects.

Next Steps

Observation points

- How engaged is the child in this activity?
- How good is the child at problem solving?
- What language does the child use?
- What ideas does the child have?
- Which items does the child choose to use?
- What does the child do with the items inside?
- How much adult input does the child need?

How can we take this outdoors?

This is a good outdoor activity, but is also flexible enough to organise indoors.

How can we vary/build on this activity?

There are plenty of ways in which this activity can be built upon.

- Put in collage items and paper to prompt children to make items.
- Put dressing up and role play props in the suitcase.
- Encourage children to pack the suitcase so that they can 'surprise' other children.

How can this become a child-initiated activity?

Many children will want to repeat this activity. Put out other suitcases so that children play out this activity.

Links to the EYFS

This activity links to many aspects of the EYFS if you encourage the children to use Language for Thinking and Problem Solving, Reasoning and Numeracy. This activity will work best with small groups of children so that they can all talk about their ideas. You can count the items in the suitcase with children and also take photographs of it so that afterwards children can recount accurately what they have done.

Personal, Social and Emotional Development	Dispositions and Attitudes	Behaviour and Self-Control
	Self-confidence and Self-esteem	Sense of Community
Communication, Language and Literacy	Language for Communication	
	Language for Thinking	
Problem Solving, Reasoning and Numeracy	Numbers as Labels and for Counting	Shape, Space and Measures
	Calculating	
Knowledge and Understanding of the World	Exploration and Investigation	
	Time	
Physical Development	Movement and Space	
	Using Equipment and Materials	
Creative Development	Exploring Media and Materials	Developing Imagination and Imaginative Play

Postcards

Children love receiving items through the post. This activity encourages mark-making/writing as well as helping children to learn about posting.

Resources

- Digital camera
- Access to a printer
- Card
- Postcards
- Stamps
- Materials for marking

Health & Safety

- Parental permission is required for an outing to the post box and local features.

Activity

Bring in a selection of postcards. If you can, find some old ones so that the children can think about old and new. Find out what the children know about postcards. Ask them if they would like to make a postcard. Show them how to use a digital camera. Talk to them about what they would like to take a photograph of. You could take the children out of your setting to a park, memorial or other local feature.

Once the children have taken their picture, print it out onto a piece of card. Let the children see you write their address on one side of the postcard. The children can then put a stamp on their postcard and make their own marks or write on it. Once the postcards are finished, children can then post them. If you do not have a post box near to your setting, see if parents might take their children to a post box near to their house.

Next Steps

Observation points

- How engaged is the child in this activity?
- What does the child know about postcards?
- What language is generated by this activity?
- Can the child use the digital camera to take photographs?
- Does the child enjoy writing their postcard?

How can we take this outdoors?

Children will go outdoors to talk about where they wish to take their picture and when they post their postcard.

How can we vary/build on this activity?

There are plenty of ways in which this activity can be built upon.

- Ask a postal worker to come in and talk about the post.
- Visit a post office.
- Create a role play sorting office.
- Visit a tourist information centre.
- Collect postcards so that children can enjoy sorting them.

How can this become a child-initiated activity?

Many children will want to repeat this activity. Your role will then be to facilitate it rather than to direct it. Children may also enjoy role playing this activity.

Links to the EYFS

This activity links to many aspects of the EYFS provided you pick up on the learning opportunities provided by using ICT, going out to a post box and encouraging mark-making. Children can also look at old and new postcards, sort and count them, and spot the differences between them.

Personal, Social and Emotional Development	Dispositions and Attitudes	Behaviour and Self-Control
	Self-confidence and Self-esteem	Sense of Community
Communication, Language and Literacy	Language for Communication	Writing
	Language for Thinking	Handwriting
	Reading	
Problem Solving, Reasoning and Numeracy	Numbers as Labels and for Counting	
Knowledge and Understanding of the World	Exploration and Investigation	Time
	ICT	Place
Physical Development	Movement and Space	
	Using Equipment and Materials	
Creative Development	Being Creative – Responding to Experiences, Expressing and Communicating Ideas	

What's in the pot?

Learning about plants and the way that they grow can be fascinating for children. This activity gives children the opportunity to plant seeds and to use technology.

Resources

- Digital camera
- Large plant pots
- Books about plants
- Compost
- Selection of seeds including runner beans, cress, sunflowers, pansies, cornflowers
- Stickers and pens
- Magnifier
- Water bottles

Health & Safety

- Make sure that children wash their hands after handling compost.
- Be aware that some beans can be poisonous.

Activity

Ask the children if they would like to do some gardening. If possible, take them to buy some seeds or, if not, let them see the packets of seeds. Find out which of them have planted things before. Show the children how to use the digital camera. Open the packets and explore the seeds using a magnifier. Plant the seeds with the children. At each stage of the activity, a child can take a photograph. Mark some water bottles so that children know how much water to pour onto their pot. Afterwards, encourage the children to label their pots with a sticker. Over the next few days and weeks, return to the pots so that the children can see the progress of their seeds and take photographs. If necessary plant out some of the seedlings into main areas of your outdoor area. Use this activity to encourage children to look at books about plants.

Tip: If you are using pots choose large ones as they are less likely to dry out. Make sure that there is adequate drainage in case of over-watering.

Next Steps

Observation points

- How engaged is the child in this activity?
- Does the child understand that it takes time for plants to grow?
- What language is generated by this activity?
- Can the child use the digital camera to take photographs?
- Can the child fill their water bottle accurately?
- Can the child relate planting to their home life?
- What does the child notice when the plants begin to grow?

How can we take this outdoors?

This is a good outdoor activity, although it could be done indoors if you have limited access to the outdoor area.

How can we vary/build on this activity?

There are plenty of ways in which this activity can be built upon.

- Ask a gardener to come and talk to the children.
- Visit a garden, park or garden centre.
- Read stories such as Jack and the Giant Beanstalk.
- Plant other seeds and bulbs.

How can this become a child-initiated activity?

Many children will enjoy watering. Try to create opportunities for them to use the water bottles to water other areas in the setting. Consider setting up a 'plant stall' role play area.

Links to the EYFS

This activity links to many aspects of the EYFS if you take up the inherent learning opportunities: filling up the water bottles, looking through the magnifiers. You need to see if children can connect growing, gardening and plants to their home lives. It is also important that children keep looking back at the photographs that they have taken earlier so that they can gain a real sense of Time.

Personal, Social and Emotional Development	Dispositions and Attitudes	Behaviour and Self-Control
	Self-confidence and Self-esteem	Sense of Community
Communication, Language and Literacy	Language for Communication	Writing
	Language for Thinking	Handwriting
	Reading	
Problem Solving, Reasoning and Numeracy	Numbers as Labels and for Counting	Shape, Space and Measures
	Calculating	
Knowledge and Understanding of the World	Exploration and Investigation	Time
	ICT	
Physical Development	Using Equipment and Materials	
	Health and Bodily Awareness	
Creative Development	Exploring Media and Materials	

Piñatas

Piñatas, originally from Mexico, have become popular items at children's parties. Making and enjoying one can be a lovely small group activity.

Resources

- Balloon
- Strips of tissue paper or newspaper
- Paste
- Small items to put inside
- Paper and mark-making materials
- Thread
- Masking tape

Health & Safety

- Do not leave balloons unsupervised.
- Make sure that children are a safe distance from each other when hitting the piñata.
- Choose items that are safe to go inside the piñata.

Activity

Find out if any children have seen a *piñata* – if so, see if they can bring photographs in. Otherwise, show photographs of a *piñata* being used so that children know what this activity is about. Blow up a balloon and tie it. You may like to have some balloons spare so that children can just play with them separately. Tie the balloon up somewhere so that the children can paste strips of tissue or newspaper onto it. When the balloon is covered with three or four layers of paper, leave to dry.

Once dry, prick the balloon and remove it. Cut out a small hole and put the items inside. See if children would also like to put some messages or words there as well. Cover the hole with a piece of masking tape. Tie the balloon up and let the children take turns to hit the *piñata* with sticks or rolled up newspaper. Eventually, the *piñata* should break, releasing all the items inside. As this is an activity that is completed in several stages, it would be useful to take photographs at each stage.

Next Steps

Observation points

- How engaged is the child in this activity?
- Has the child seen a *piñata* before?
- What does the child say about parties?
- How easily does the child glue the tissue paper?
- Does the child take turns with other children?
- How interested is the child in mark-making a message?
- How co-ordinated are the child's arm movements?

How can we take this outdoors?

Use the *piñata* outdoors.

How can we vary/build on this activity?

There are plenty of ways in which this activity can be built upon.

- Look at other party traditions.
- Make other *papier mâché* products.
- Show children photographs of the activity.
- Create other opportunities for children to knock down things.

How can this become a child-initiated activity?

Many children will want to repeat this activity. Your role will then be to facilitate it rather than to direct it. Children may also enjoy role playing parties with dough and other games.

Links to the EYFS

This activity covers many aspects of the EYFS including physical movements, mark-making and learning about other traditions. Adults can increase learning opportunities by, for example, counting how many items go inside the *piñata* and how many times the *piñata* is hit before it breaks. There is also plenty of scope to develop children's language.

Personal, Social and Emotional Development	Dispositions and Attitudes	Behaviour and Self-control
	Self-confidence and Self-esteem	Sense of Community
Communication, Language and Literacy	Language for Communication	Writing
	Language for Thinking	Handwriting
Problem Solving, Reasoning and Numeracy	Numbers as Labels and for Counting	
Knowledge and Understanding of the World	Exploration and Investigation	Time
	ICT	Place
Physical Development	Movement and Space	
	Using Equipment and Materials	
Creative Development	Being Creative – Responding to Experiences, Expressing and Communicating Ideas	

My day here!

It can be hard for children to remember and talk about what they have been doing. This activity will create a personal resource for children, similar in some ways to a visual timetable.

Resources

- Digital camera
- Card for printing
- Small photograph album
- Pens (felt-tipped) or pencils

Health & Safety

- Supervise children as they are taking photographs.
- Check that parents of other children who may be photographed have no objection.

Activity

This activity will work best with pairs of children as the aim is that each child will create an album of photographs which show what they do and enjoy in your setting. Talk through with children what they enjoy doing when they are with you. You may use existing photographs to jog their memories. Show them how to use the camera and let them have a practice. During the session, children can capture various moments on the setting or they can go around taking photographs of places or people that they like being with. Once photographs have been taken, show all of the photographs to the children and encourage them to choose their favourites. You may use this as an opportunity to do some counting, saying for example, "we need 10". See if the children can order the photographs and talk about them. Bring out the photograph albums so that each child can make their own album. Encourage children to do a little mark-making using pencils, pens or felt tips about each photograph. You could also scribe for them. Children can then go on to share their album with other children and, of course, their parents.

Next Steps

Observation points

- How engaged is the child in this activity?
- Does the child know what they would like to photograph?
- How well does the child manage the camera?
- What does the child say about the photographs?
- Can the child count the number of photographs?
- Can the child sequence the order of the photographs?
- Does the child want to mark make?

How can we take this outdoors?

Children can take some photographs outdoors.

How can we vary/build on this activity?

There are plenty of ways in which this activity can be built upon.

- Create other photograph albums with children.
- Take a series of photographs so that children can sequence them.
- Talk to children about their likes and dislikes.
- Use this as a tool to support transition.
- Invite a photographer to talk to/work with children.

How can this become a child-initiated activity?

Look out for toy or old digital cameras so that children can pretend to take photographs. Some children may also ask to repeat this activity and so be ready to act more as facilitator.

Links to the EYFS

This activity can link to several aspects of the EYFS. There should be plenty of opportunities to promote children's language and for you to learn more about their interests, likes and dislikes. You need to avoid 'taking over' the activity as the choice of photographs needs to be the child's.

Personal, Social and Emotional Development	Dispositions and Attitudes	Behaviour and Self-control
	Self-confidence and Self-esteem	Sense of Community
Communication, Language and Literacy	Language for Communication	Writing
	Language for Thinking	Handwriting
Problem Solving, Reasoning and Numeracy	Numbers as Labels and for Counting	
Knowledge and Understanding of the World	Exploration and Investigation	Time
	ICT	Place
Physical Development	Movement and Space	
	Using Equipment and Materials	
Creative Development	Being creative – Responding to Experiences, Expressing and Communicating Ideas	Exploring Media and Materials

Useful references

Issues and Challenges

data.gov.uk/dataset/early-years-foundation-stage-profile-england-2009 – Early Years Foundation Stage Profile data for 2009

publications.education.gov.uk – provides a link to the Letters and Sounds pack nationalstrategies.

standards.dcsf.gov.uk/node/151379 –*Statutory Framework for the Early Years Foundation Stage*

Creative development

www.uk.freecycle.org – a website that matches people who have things they want to get rid of with people who can use them

Observation and planning

Carolyn Meggitt, *Child Development: An Illustrated Guide*, 2nd edn, Heinemann, 2006 ISBN 978 0 435420 48 2

Penny Tassoni's Practical EYFS Handbook, Heinemann, 2008
ISBN 978 0 435899 91 2

nationalstrategies.standards.dcsf.gov.uk/node/84490 – *Practice Guidance for the Early Years Foundation Stage*

www.ico.gov.uk – The Information Commissioner's Office website, which contains details of information rights, including the Data Protection Act

Outdoor play

www.sunsmart.org.uk – gives research-based advice on preventing skin cancer

www.uk.freecycle.org – a website that matches people who have things they want to get rid of with people who can use them

Activities

Penny Tassoni's Practical EYFS Handbook, Heinemann, 2008
ISBN 978 0 435899 91 2

Index

Your Continued Success with the **EYFS**

starts here...